THE LIFE STORY
OF THE FISH

His Morals and Manners

By

BRIAN CURTIS

DOVER PUBLICATIONS, INC.

NEW YORK

Published in Canada by General Publishing Company, Ltd., 30 Lesmill Road, Don Mills, Toronto, Ontario.
Published in the United Kingdom by Constable and Company, Ltd., 10 Orange Street, London WC 2.

This Dover edition, first published in 1961, is an unabridged and unaltered republication of the second revised edition, as published by Harcourt, Brace and Company in 1949.

Standard Book Number: 486-20929-6
Library of Congress Catalog Card Number: 65-23639

Manufactured in the United States of America
Dover Publications, Inc.
180 Varick Street
New York, N. Y. 10014

This Dover Edition

is dedicated to the memory of my beloved husband

BRIAN CURTIS

by M. R. C., to whom the original editions

were dedicated.

Author's Preface

WHEN *The Life Story of the Fish* was written some ten years ago, it endeavored to set forth all that was then known about fish which might be of interest to the angler, to the aquarist, and to the normal human being of inquiring mind. Since then, in spite of wars and world upheavals, piscatorial knowledge has continued to advance. New facts have come to light about the homing of salmon, about the spawning of tarpon, about the dynamics of fish populations, about the many ways in which man and fish affect each other. An event of great scientific importance has occurred in the discovery of a "living fossil": a huge fish, captured off the coast of South Africa, of a family which palaeontologists thought had become extinct a million centuries ago.

All of which made it evident, when the question of re-publication arose, that the book no longer fulfilled its original intent. It has therefore been re-written, with extensive revisions and additions, reference reading lists for those who wish to consult source material, and one entirely new chapter. The present volume is the result.

It is a great pleasure to set forth here again my gratitude to Dr. Willis H. Rich, Dr. Frank Weymouth, and Dr. George S. Myers, all of Stanford University, for their generous advice during the preparation of the earlier edition of this book. I am also indebted to Dr. W. K. Gregory, Dr. Charles M. Breder, Jr., Dr. Rolf Bolin, Mr. J. T. Nichols, and Mr. Leo Shapovalov, and to the late Dr. F. B. Sumner and Dr. G. K. Noble, for illuminating various dark places with the light of their special knowledge. Such freedom from error as this volume may enjoy is due in large measure to the wisdom and the friendly counsel of all these gentlemen.

The drawings were prepared by Jeanne Russell Janish.

BRIAN CURTIS

St. Helena, California
November, 1948

Contents

Illustrations

FIGURES

DIAGRAMS

PLATES
between pages 180-181

The Life Story of the Fish

CHAPTER I

Men and Fish

DO fish sleep? Can they distinguish color? Can they hear? Do they suffer pain?

These are questions which fishermen have been discussing since the days of Isaak Walton. They have sat under bridges on the Test while waiting for the rain to stop, and thought about them. They have lain beside camp-fires in the Maine woods and in the High Sierra, and argued them. They have dozed under the hot sun in small boats, trailing their lines in the Gulf Stream or across the waters of Catalina, and dreamed about them. Why is it that after all this time they are still uncertain about the answers? It is because they have had to learn by observation, helped only by trial-and-error experiments.

They have by these methods discovered a great many interesting and important things. They have discovered what waters different kinds of fish inhabit, what lure to use for each kind, and at what season or what state of the tide to fish for them. They have learned how to catch fish, and that is a prime requisite to knowing anything else about them.

Another group of people who ask questions are the aquarists. They keep brightly colored little fish from all parts of the world in glass tanks, and feed them and care for them and watch them fight and make love and have homes and wives and children. They lack the anglers' opportunities to see the animals in their native waters, but

3

they have the advantage of being able to watch them swim and eat and go about their affairs, whereas the angler rarely sees them except on the end of a line. They, too, have added to the general store of knowledge. They, too, have learned by observation.

But, after all, there are limits to what can be learned by observation and by trial-and-error experiment. Here is where science comes in. For centuries scientists have been studying fish. With their training and their facilities, they have been able to analyze the construction and the workings of their bodies, to carry out controlled experiments on their actions, to make systematic observations on their habits. They have not found out all there is to know. Some problems, such as where baby tarpon live, they are on the brink of solving; others they may never master. But to a great many questions they have, through years of painstaking and ingenious labor, of drudgery and endeavor and imaginative searching, found the answers. And these answers they have, after the incurable habit of scientists, scattered piecemeal through technical journals of different dates, or have entombed in large volumes with long titles. It is for this reason that, while the field naturalist who goes out and observes the habits of animals and writes about them from the popular point of view has added greatly to the knowledge and pleasure of sportsmen and others, the more orthodox biologist—the man who permits himself to be called a zoologist or, even worse, an ichthyologist—has been looked upon as a dull fellow, and his contributions often have remained unknown to the very people to whom they ought to be of the most interest and value.

On the one hand, then, we have the aquarists and anglers seeking for knowledge of fish; on the other hand, we have a great fund of knowledge about fish stored away in laboratories and scientific libraries. In one room, shelves full of excellent wine in tightly sealed bottles; in the next, a lot of thirsty people with no bottle-openers. To furnish the bottle-opener is the object of this book: to bring all that knowledge out of the musty atmosphere of the laboratory, where it now lies in a state of perfect but useless preservation, and to turn it over, in suitable form, to the seekers to consume; in short, to tell the anglers and aquarists what the scientists know about the things that they want to know.

If fish were all just alike, writing about them would be a great deal easier than it is. They differ, sometimes radically. It is impossible to make universal statements about fish; it is impossible to use the words "always," "all," "never," "none," when talking about them. Some of the differences are important, and will be discussed, but many are unimportant, at least to the reader. If we tried to treat them all, we should never end. Failure to point out exceptions to any rule does not mean that there are none. Let it be accepted therefore as our only rule that there is no statement in this book to which there are not some exceptions.

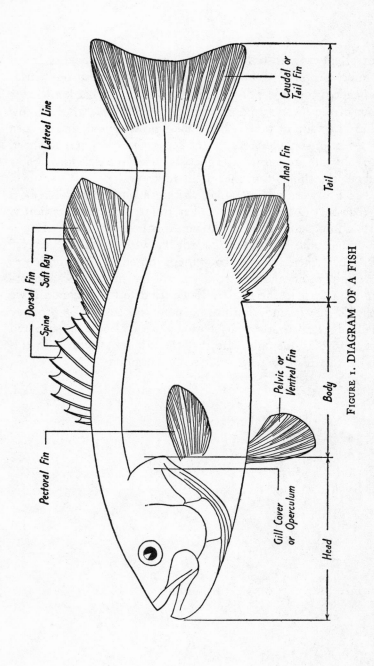

FIGURE 1. DIAGRAM OF A FISH

CHAPTER II

What Is a Fish?

THE fish is a vertebrate. This means that he belongs to that great group of creatures which have backbones. An animal with a backbone does not seem strange to us today. But at the time that the first fish appeared upon earth, which we know from geologic records to have been roughly five hundred million years ago, he must have seemed a miraculous thing. He was the very latest model in animal design, a radical, one might almost say a reckless, experiment of that force which we find it convenient to personify as Mother Nature.

For up to that time no creature had ever been made with the hard parts inside instead of outside. There had been animals with little or no hard parts at all, like the amoeba, the sea-anemone, and the jellyfish. And there had been animals with the hard parts outside, where they served as defensive armor and as framework for the muscles, like the starfish and the clam and the crab. We can trace the development of these lower forms, called invertebrates, and we can trace the development of the vertebrates from fish through amphibian through reptile to bird and mammal. But between invertebrate and vertebrate there is no connecting link. Nature might be said to have had a brainstorm, abandoned all the earlier methods, and turned out overnight something absolutely new and unheard of. Only one feature did she carry over from the old models. She didn't yet trust this new experiment of hers among her hard-shelled veterans, and so she gave it a certain amount of external armor, as well as the new inner hard parts, to protect it from the old-timers.

It will be argued by serious scientists that this is a very improper presentation of evolution. As a matter of fact, I much prefer not to present it at all, but since it has reared its head, it had better be dealt with at once. For whether you believe in evolution or not, it is impossible to talk about animals without using its terminology.

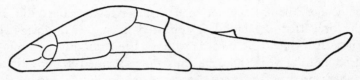

FIGURE 2. PTERICHTHYS

A fish of 350,000,000 years ago, with armor plates protecting his front end. (Appendages omitted.)

Scientists used to think that all the multifarious forms of animal life appeared full-blown upon the earth, each perfect in its present form, like Pallas emerging fully armed from the head of Zeus. They now reject this idea, and believe that all living animals developed from somewhat different animals which preceded them and which, in turn, developed from earlier and still different forms. This is the essence of the theory of evolution, the starting point, the foundation on which all evolutionists agree. It is practically the only point on which they all agree, for as soon as they begin to inquire into the ways in which one animal changed into another they divide into two schools of thought.

The first is the teleological. I would like to avoid this word, but there is no way around it, for zoologists have made it legal tender in their world. However, they should not be too severely blamed for using long words. In the first place, they lead a dull life, stuck away in their stuffy laboratories surrounded by dead animals, and the only way they can get any fun, or give their egos the occasional boost which all egos need, is to use a word which no one else understands. In the second place, some long words save a great deal of time and explanation. If they deal with things which we are never to meet again, we can pass them by, but if we are going to have to recur to their subject with some frequency, they are worth learning in order that we may say in one word what would otherwise take many. "Automobile," for instance, was once a long and unfamiliar word, but if we had to keep saying "a vehicle which is provided with machinery for propelling itself" each time we wanted to talk about an automobile, we should find it very awkward.

Teleology, then, means the assumption that there is a definite purpose, a definite goal, in the processes of cosmic evolution. The teleologist places the emphasis on adaptation to this purpose. He believes that animals develop new characteristics in response to the pressure of their environment, and that the characteristics so acquired can be inherited by succeeding generations. He believes that the primordial giraffe reached up into the trees, when grass became scarce, for leaves to eat, and thus elongated his neck, and that this long neck was inherited by his children.

On the opposing side is the "mutationist." He does not believe in the inheritance of such acquired characteristics. He holds that all the variations which brought about the differences in species were due to what he calls mutations— chance recombinations of the germ-cell material into what we would call lucky freaks. He believes that some of the primordial giraffes happened to have longer necks than others, and that when a grassless era came upon them the short-necked ones died, but the long-necked ones took to eating leaves and survived. The long neck being a constitutional, genetic characteristic, and not an acquired one, it passed on by inheritance to the next generation. And once the giraffe had become a tree-grazer the neck tended to become longer through selection. For the individual who happened to have a longer neck than the average obtained more food, grew stronger, had a better chance of securing mates, and produced more offspring than the others, and those of the offspring which inherited the parental neck flourished and produced in turn a disproportionate number of offspring, who inherited and passed on that neck. The shorter-necked individuals, being unable to compete for food, were weak, and died early and childless, and so the species continued to lengthen its neck until the point was reached where the feeding advantage of additional length was overbalanced by unwieldiness and weight, and there the process stopped. And the result is the present-day giraffe.

Or, to come back to our subject, the mutationist does not believe that the pickerel acquired his mottled coloration by hiding in the weeds until he came to resemble them. He believes that certain primordial pickerel chanced to have that mottling, and were therefore able to hide more successfully in the weeds than their fellows, and to snap up more primordial bass and trout fingerlings. These individuals grew larger and stronger than the rest, and were thus enabled to monopolize the food and the mates, and to have more children. And while not all of their children inherited this peculiarly successful coloration, those which did not failed to prosper, and from generation to generation grew fewer until eventually only the present-day pickerel survived.

While at first sight this theory of the mutationists seems far-fetched and the importance it places on the part played by chance distasteful, it has one great advantage: it does provide a mechanism which is capable of accounting for the whole history of organic evolution. And while the teleological point of view at first seems logical and pleasing, it has one great weakness: the inheritance of acquired characters, the corner-stone on which it rests, has never yet been proved possible. From time to time one scientist or another will almost persuade himself that he has found a clue which leads in that direction; but in spite of much research, not one undebatable case of such inheritance, either in the past or the present, has been brought to light. Human beings are occasionally born with extra vertebrae in their necks. If conditions of life were to become such that long necks were a distinct advantage to humans, those individuals would have a chance to dominate the scene, and might eventually produce a race of human giraffes; but no amount of effort in the line of mechanically stretching mothers' necks could add even one vertebral section to a baby's neck.

And yet in spite of all the evidence on their side—the fossil records, the experiments, the observation of natural processes —the mutationists themselves seem to have difficulty in believing that they are entirely right, for they frequently slip into a teleological way of speaking. The temptation to see a purpose in evolution is almost irresistible.

From the very first, anti-evolutionists have revolted at the suggestion that men were the descendants of monkeys. To a much more important aspect of the theory, that men are descended from fish, they have never objected. Perhaps to be called the great-great-great-etcetera-grandson of a sturgeon is so grotesque as to be beneath notice, whereas to be called the grandson of a gorilla is too close for comfort. The fact of the matter is that many experts believe, not that man descends from monkeys, but that both man and monkey descend from a remote, now extinct, common ancestor.

To emphasize this point for the benefit of the anti-simians, evolutionists have sometimes stated that no living animal descends from any other living animal; that, for instance, the fish from which the amphibians descend is extinct. The exponents of this theory received a shock when, in 1938, fishermen dredged up from the ocean off the South African coast a huge creature which was apparently a living fossil—a fish which should have been extinct geologic ages ago. For days after the news of this discovery ichthyologists went around with expressions of astonishment and doubt on their faces, asking each other if it were all a hoax. But when this specimen at last reached the hands of a qualified palaeontologist, he declared that not only was it undoubtedly a species of living fossil, but that it was so close to fossil remains and to the types which had been reconstructed therefrom that it could be positively identified as a member of the coelacanths. Now, the coelacanths are a group of fishes which had branched off from the main evolutionary stem before the amphibians appeared. *Latimeria,* as the new discovery was named, is therefore not a living ancestor of the amphibians, but a cousin of their ancestor's.

And so it can still be truthfully said that no living form descends from any other living form, at least insofar as the major groups are concerned. But within the groups, and above all within their narrower divisions, this is not true. The world is not a finished job. The processes of evolution are still going on, and nowhere is this more evident than in some of the families of fishes. The trouts and salmons [1] are an outstanding example: the great number of their species and subspecies which scientists are still struggling to sort out are the best possible indication that a single, formerly widespread animal is, under the influence of climatic changes and geographical differences, in the very act of

---

[1] The plural form of these words is used to denote several species. We say, "I caught four trout," but, "Among the trouts that spawn in the fall are the brook and the brown."

dividing itself up into separate forms. The rainbow trout has become the golden trout in the isolation of the high mountains. The salmon of the Atlantic has become the steelhead trout of the Pacific or vice versa, and if, as one authority states, there is no single external feature by which all members of these two species can at all times be told apart, then it is clear that the number of dead forms intervening between the two is just about zero.

Finally, it must be pointed out that, in spite of all that has been said, it is not compulsory to believe in evolution. Up to eighty years ago, most people had never heard of it, and they were just as happy as they are now. To be sure, three or four men, including the old Swedish naturalist Linnaeus back in the eighteenth century, had gone sniffing around the theory, picking at the wrappings that hid it, getting an intriguing but unrevealing glimpse of one part or another of it, but quite unable to understand what it was all about, to see it as a whole. That has often been the way when some new and universal principle was about to be revealed to the world. Then suddenly two Englishmen, one in Kent and one in Malaya, lifted the veil at the same time, one as a result of long and painstaking piecing together of fact and theory, the other as a result of a sudden brilliant inspiration; and it is because the younger man, with a generosity fortunately sometimes found among scientists, recognized that his lucky guess could not justifiably be placed on a par with the other man's far-reaching labor of synthesis, that the name of Charles Darwin, and not that of Alfred Russell Wallace, is taught to school children today as the founder of the theory of evolution.

Fish, then, are backboned animals which live in the water, breathe through gills, and have fins. As usual, there are exceptions. Some breathe with lungs, and some have no recognizable fins. Lung-fish and eels are fishes, but whales and porpoises are not, for they possess mammary glands for the suckling of their young. They therefore belong to the same class of vertebrates as humans. They are mammals gone to sea.

Fish are low in the vertebrate scale, but, to our way of thinking at least, they are high in the scale of animal life as a whole. Perhaps if they did not belong to this great

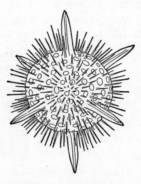

FIGURE 3. A RADIOLARIAN PROTOZOAN

vertebrate group which we honor with our presence, we would not place them above the more complicated of the insects or crustaceans, but no matter to what group we ourselves belonged—and here again we find ourselves speaking in terms of evolution, whether we believe in it or not—we would place them far above such creatures as the jellyfish, and still further above the *Protozoa*, the one-celled animals.

For in this last group, one single cell performs all the life functions: nourishment, movement, control, breathing, excretion, reproduction. A fish is to that simple, earnest unit what a great modern shoe factory, with its power-plant, its administrative offices, its purchasing department, its machine-tools, its sales forces, is to the old-fashioned cobbler who tanned his own leather, spun his own thread, and made his own hammer and awl. For the fish has many cells, and these cells are grouped together into what we may call organ-systems, and each of these systems takes care of one or more of the principal activities which are necessary to the fish's life. Like the modern factory, the fish has gone in for division of labor. Unlike the modern factory, he has not put his simple predecessor out of business, for protozoans still prosper mightily upon this earth. Although most of them are too small for us to see, their number is legion, and some have developed their single cell into most beautiful and even elaborate structures.

CHAPTER III

Body Covering

DIVISION of labor among the different organs in the body occurs in all animals except the very low forms. And since all animals have the same essential life processes, they all have organ systems designed for the same purposes. A crab, or even a snail, must have an integument to cover him, eyes to see food and danger with, muscles to move him toward or away from them, a skeleton for the muscles to work on, a stomach to digest his food, a circulating medium to carry the nourishing elements to various parts of the body, a disposal system to get rid of the waste products, a means of reproducing himself, a method for supplying himself with oxygen, and a brain to co-ordinate all these activities.

Quite an adequate equipment: as far as number of systems is concerned, we and the rest of the mammals have no more. But there is this difference, that the organs which compose the various systems of these invertebrates may be, and usually are, quite different from the organs which compose the same systems in mammals. The snail's brain consists of several groups of ganglia, located in his foot, near his mouth, and at the entrance to his stomach, whereas a monkey's brain is a great mass of nerve-tissue located in his head. A crab's circulatory system consists of a number of tubes leading out from his heart, but instead of joining themselves to returning tubes by a network of delicate capillaries so that the blood flows through a closed circuit, as in us, they open at their ends and let the blood escape into open spaces, to find its way back to the heart as best it can.

In the fish, the situation is different. The fish has the same systems which the invertebrate has, but the organs which make up these systems are different. They are for the most part remarkably similar to the corresponding organs in mammals. They are simpler, but they work on the same principles. They might be likened to earlier models of the same machine, accomplishing the result in the same way, but less adequately and less efficiently, just as the single-tube radio worked on the same principles as the most up-to-date multi-tube superheterodyne.

Like the owner of the primitive radio, the fish is limited in his range of interests by the imperfections of his machinery. He concentrates on food, shelter from danger, and a mate. He leads a simple, straightforward life, and his organs are adapted to the life he leads. Or, as the mutationists would say, the life he leads is adapted to the kind of organs he has.

SKIN

The first organ system to be met in an orderly examination is the body covering. This system is the most striking instance which we shall find of the fish doing things differently from the mammals, and for once in a more complicated way.

In the first place, the fish's skin is alive. The very outermost covering, the covering which comes in contact with the great world, is composed of living cells. This is not the case with us, for the living part of our skin is covered with several layers of hardened cells which, although transparent, are completely dead. They protect the living cells underneath. When you touch another human being, you do not come in contact with living flesh—unless you are a dentist, when, if you are a little clumsy, the dead skin of your finger may come in contact with the living cells which line the mouth of the patient—or unless you are engaged in amorous activities, which is practically the only occasion when the truly living parts of two separate human individuals come in contact with each other.

Why can the fish expose its living cells to the world while we cannot? The reason is very simple. Cells can live only in a liquid medium. This holds true of all cells, plant and animal, from bacteria to human. Any of our cells which are exposed permanently to the air will die. But the fish lives in water. The liquid medium which his cells need for existence surrounds him on all sides. He can wear them on his sleeve, so to speak, without danger. It was not until animals came out of the water that they had to protect their living cells with a dead covering—an accomplishment, incidentally, which poses the question squarely to the mutationists. Did this animal, fish, amphibian, or whatever he was, have to acquire, by a chance recombination of the germ material, a coating of dead cells for his skin before he came out on land? Or was it his emergence on land, with its necessity for protection, that brought about the creation of the protective coating? The latter hypothesis seems the easier one to accept. One can imagine the outer living layer dying when the animal became a land-dweller, and coming to form a protective coating for the cells underneath. To which the mutationists answer that no one has ever yet succeeded in training a goldfish to live out of the water, and that the fish which do successfully come out in the air and stay there for some time and even travel over dusty ground are those which have a special layer of dead material covering their skins, such as the armored catfish, and that several fish which remain permanently under the water, such as the trunk-fish, have coverings of dead material, proving that this requisite for land-life can be elaborated before coming out on land. It is not hard to see why the argument still boils.

However, even the fish does not expose his living skin entirely to contact with the world. He covers it with mucus, or slime, secreted by the living cells and exuded onto the surface. This is what makes a fish slippery. The quantity of slime varies with the species. Some, like the pickerel, have a large amount, as anglers can testify, while others, like the carp, have comparatively little.

The slime serves several purposes. In the first place, it acts as a lubricant, permitting the body of the fish to slide through the water without friction, thus increasing his speed while reducing his energy expenditure. In the second place, it protects him from attack by fungus, bacteria and other parasites, forming a coating through which it is difficult for these minute organisms to pass. In the third place, it helps to make the fish water-tight, and this is highly important for in most species the skin is in the nature of a semi-permeable membrane. As you will remember from the days when you studied physics, a semi-permeable membrane separating two solutions of unequal strength allows liquid to pass through it from the weaker solution toward the stronger. The fish's internal fluids are somewhat salty: less so than the ocean, but more so than fresh water. In the ocean, therefore, there is a tendency for water to pass out of the weaker internal solution into the stronger external solution; in fresh water the reverse is the case. In other words, the fresh water fish is in constant danger of becoming waterlogged, of absorbing so much water that his internal machinery is no longer able to function; and the ocean fish is in danger of losing water until his insides dry up. The slime helps to save them from these fates.

It is because of the importance of the slime as a protection against external parasites and against internal liquid unbalances that the angler has been so often told that he should handle a fish only with wet hands if he wants to return it to the water alive: dry hands would remove so much of the mucus coating as to expose the fish to fatal attacks. This theory has recently been undermined by an experiment in which trout, caught on flies, were removed from the hook in equal numbers with wet and dry hands, and retained alive in ponds for observation. There was no significant difference in the mortality of the two groups. The explanation seems to be that dry hands need to squeeze a fish less than wet ones, and that the slight amount of mucus removed by dry hands during the short time needed to free a lightly hooked fish is no more damaging than the greater pressure of wet hands. In the case of a deeply embedded hook the physical injury to the internal anatomy caused by its removal would be more apt to bring about death than the application of hands, whether wet or dry, to its external surface.

Let it be hastily added, however, that the removal of *large* amounts of slime by extensive use of dry hands could not be other than injurious. It is for this reason that moistened woolen or cotton gloves, which give a firm grip without undue squeezing or drying, are worn by fisheries workers when taking spawn or scales from live fish. These spawn-taking operations, when eggs and milt are stripped from fish which are then returned to the water, offer excellent opportunities for procuring the large numbers of scale samples needed by the biologists in life-history studies. The accusation has at times been made by fishermen that such scale-taking injures the fish, but it has been proved again and again that, if properly done, it causes no harm. I have taken scales from trout, and then penned the specimens in a cage for several weeks afterward, until the skin had grown back into place. No harm was done. And I know a small stream on the Pacific Coast where the steelhead are stripped of their eggs. Each powerful, struggling female is firmly held by one man while another squeezes from her the gushing stream of pink eggs. A third man then removes with forceps half a dozen of her scales, and fastens on her back, just under the dorsal fin, a wire with red and white celluloid tags, numbered for identification. And yet in spite of all this handling, the fish go out to sea, and return in perfect health to the same place the following year to go through the same process again.

But it must be remembered that these fish are handled by men who have had long practice. It must be remembered that the scales are removed from only a very small spot, which it would be easy for mucus from the surrounding skin to cover. It must be remembered that, at the time that scales are most commonly taken, the water temperatures happen to be low, a condition in itself unfavorable to bacterial growth, as we recognize when we put our food in ice-chests to preserve it. And it must be remembered also that different species vary greatly in their ability to withstand handling. The small "green fry," which most visitors to Bermuda have seen swimming in vast schools in shallow bays, have scales so loose that when one of them is gobbled up by a snapper the surrounding water sparkles with tiny green points of reflected light. They will die from little more than a touch. At the other extreme is the Alaska blackfish, the staple diet of the Eskimos and their dogs. This fish, about six inches long, has a leathery skin in which degenerate scales are embedded at intervals, like polka-dots. Maltreatment cannot shake its hold on life. In its natural haunts, according to reports, it can remain frozen in solid ice for weeks on end, thawing out again, as the spring approaches, in active condition. But the crowning story, quoted by no less respectable a source than the late David Starr Jordan, narrates that one blackfish, fed to a Husky dog from a pile of frozen fish, and being as usual swallowed whole, was, a few minutes later, coughed up alive by the startled animal, and was last seen flopping back into the water through a hole in the ice, having been revived by the heat of the dog's stomach, which it probably found uncomfortably warm.

As for aquarium fish, I have seen guppies removed from the water in an experimental laboratory, and thoroughly dried with blotting paper, live to tell about it to their sons and grandsons, but this practice is certainly not to be recommended. The cichlid known as the "jewel," *Hemichromis bimaculatus* Gill, will stand a great amount of handling, as was proved in this same laboratory, although with this species care was taken to hold it only with wet hands or a wet cloth. But it is obvious just the same that handling never does a fish any good, and that, although a certain amount of it is unavoidable, the less of it aquarium inhabitants get the better off they will be.

SCALES

Beneath the living skin of the fish is dead material. For the scales are as dead as our fingernails, and, like them, are created by living cells which secrete or excrete the material of which they are formed. In the great majority of fishes there is a layer of skin over the scales. In some it is so thin as to be almost invisible. In others, such as the eastern brook trout, it is fairly heavy and makes the scales hard to see. In still others, like the eel, it is so thick that the scales are entirely hidden.

The principal function of the scales is protection. They are the remnants of the heavy armor-plate which the earliest-known fossil fishes wore. As the fish became more active this armor-plate had to become more flexible, and this was accomplished by breaking it up into small sections. Also, as the fish acquired powerful teeth and jaws, it became less dependent on protective armor. Mother Nature evidently was aware of the theory so successfully applied in modern football that a good offense is the best defense. The infant swordfish starts life equipped with defensive spines and rudimentary scales, and with not a sign of a sword. As it grows up and produces on its face the most impressive piece of offensive armament in the whole world of fishes, it completely abandons its defensive armor: not a scale nor a

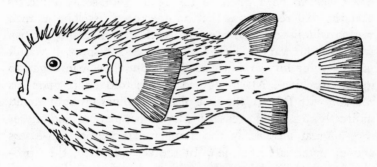

FIGURE 4. PORCUPINE-FISH

From Jordan and Evermann, *Fishes of North and Middle America,* by permission of the United States National Museum.

spine is to be found on the body of the adult (see Figure 26). And another fish, the surgeon-fish, has gone so far as to change some of its defensive into offensive weapons, for it has modified two of the scales at the base of its tail into sharp knives, carried most of the time in sheaths in the skin, but ready to swing out into action when it wishes to attack. On the other hand, some fish have tended to revert to the old method, and have concentrated on protection. The porcupine-fish bristles like its namesake with spiny points, while the trunk-fish's body is so stiff with horny plates that it cannot bend at all, and has to depend on its tail and its fins for locomotion.

For thousands of centuries fish have had scales and men

have known it, but it is only within the last fifty years that they have known how much the scale might reveal about its owner. This was partly because until Leeuwenhoek, the early lens-maker, began his painstaking grinding of glass in Holland in the late seventeenth century, there was no way to see what the scale had to tell. But the fact that it was not until two hundred years after Leeuwenhoek that his discovery began to be applied to the reading of scales indicates that the real reason was that no one cared. As long as man was so widely scattered over the earth that he could get fish whenever he wanted, either for food or for sport, it wasn't necessary for him to cultivate them. But then man began to invent machines. Machines had a threefold effect upon his relation with fish. In the first place, machines brought about, indirectly, a great increase in human population, and therefore a great increase in the number of potential fish-eaters and of potential fishermen. In the second place, they provided means whereby fish could be brought to fish-eaters far from the home of the fish without becoming unappetizing. And in the third place, they made it possible for sportsmen to transport themselves with the greatest of ease from cities, inland prairies, and other places where fish do not live to streams and oceans where they do live.

When the resulting demand began to outrun the supply, man realized that he was in danger of destroying one of his most valuable resources. He began to study fish from the practical point of view as well as the scientific. In other words, he began to study the animal as a crop to be harvested, as well as a specimen to be classified and dissected. He brought the microscope to bear on the subject, and found that, at least in certain of the species in which he was particularly interested, the scales contained a record of the fish's life.

When the fish first comes out of its egg, it has no scales.

As ichthyologists put it, it is "naked." Some, like the common catfish, remain naked throughout life, but the great majority decide to give up nakedness before they are very old. The size at which they first clothe themselves varies. The striped bass, for instance, is only half an inch long when he succumbs to modesty, whereas the various salmons and trouts range between one and two inches. In any case, at the appointed length, the scales begin to appear, and the so-called *nuclei* are formed under the skin, of such a size

FIGURE 5. DIAGRAMMATIC CROSS-SECTION OF SCALES AND SKIN

that, just touching each other, they just about cover the fish. The forward end of each scale is embedded in the dermis (Figure 5), and the free after-end comes eventually to cover the forward end of the scale next behind it, like the shingles on a roof. This free end, which is the only part which we see when we look at a fish, is very much smaller than the covered part, so that by far the larger portion of each scale is hidden from view. In the black-bass and its relatives, the scale has radial furrows, and the exposed after-end is covered with tiny teeth, which is what makes the fish feel rough to the touch. This type of scale is called *ctenoid* (meaning comblike). In the trouts and salmons, the whole scale, including the exposed after portion, is smooth, and is called *cycloid* (Plate I).

As the fish grows, he must continue to be covered by overlapping scales. This effect he does not achieve, as might be expected, by adding to the number of his scales. The number never varies. It remains that which he fixed for himself when he first put on scales. It is the same, within close limits, as is worn by all his species. The number does not change, but each individual scale does. Each scale grows to keep up with that fraction of the fish's body which it covered in the beginning. And this growth is accomplished by adding rings of new material around the edge, in somewhat the way in which a tree adds to its girth. The new material being furnished by the dermis, the after-end of the scale, covered only by the epidermis, shows irregular and poorly marked accretions, but the larger portion which is surrounded by the dermis carries clearly defined rings throughout the life of the fish.

The tree, as we have all been taught, adds only one ring each year, and it is by counting the total number of rings that the tree's age can be told. Each fish-scale adds many rings each year; and yet the character of this ring-growth varies with the seasons to such an extent that it is possible for a practiced person to look at a salmon scale under a microscope and tell not only how old the fish is, but also how many years it spent in the sea, and how many times it has spawned—even, if it has not spawned, to calculate how long it was at the end of each year of its life. No other animal known to man carries about with it such a complete autobiography.

The method by which this autobiography can be read was originated by Johnston and Dahl, working separately in England and in Norway, at the turn of the century, and in the light of their findings, the whole thing seems as simple as Columbus' egg. In summer, when the water is warm and food is plentiful, the fish feeds actively and grows fast. The scale, during this period, must also grow fast in order to keep on covering its portion of the fish, and the growth-rings of the scales are therefore far apart. In winter, on the other hand, food is scarce, and temperatures are so low that the fish has not much appetite. He feeds little, and grows slowly, if at all. The scale grows slowly, if at all, the growth-rings are close together, and a dark band is formed, called the annual check. Count the number of annual checks, and you have the fish's age (Plate I).

Furthermore, when a fish such as a salmon migrates from fresh water, where food is comparatively scarce, to salt water, where food is enormously abundant, he grows much faster. The spacing between the .summer bands increases greatly, and the salt-water years stand out in conspicuous contrast to the preceding fresh-water years (Plate II).

Still further, when a fish like the trout is preparing to spawn, it gives up eating for a while. It ceases to grow, and lives upon its accumulated fat. During that period the edge of the scale is slightly resorbed, leaving an unmistakable wavy line to mark the experience forever. And in the salmon, which fights its way upstream from the ocean to the spawning-bed, covering hundreds of miles and going for weeks or months without eating, the drain on the reserves causes deep resorption of the scales, and the heavy "spawning-mark" which cuts across the old rings and divides them from the new stands out like a black eye. This refers, needless to say, to the salmon of the Atlantic Coast. Pacific salmon die on spawning.

As for determining the length of the fish at various times in its life from its scales, while the methods actually used are complicated by subsidiary factors, the underlying principle is simplicity itself. It is merely a matter of the ratio between the present length of the scale and its length at any previous annual check, in proportion to the ratio between the present length of the fish and *its* length at the time of that same annual check. Suppose we have a trout which measures twelve inches. We take a few scales, examine them under the microscope, and find that it is now in its third year and has never spawned. This is an essential condition; the method cannot be applied to fish which have spawned because in them the scale-resorption which we have already mentioned destroys the relation between scale-length and fish-length. We want to know how long this trout was at the end of its first year.

We measure, with a microscope micrometer or some other device, the distance from the center of the scale to its front edge. Let us suppose that this is 0.9 millimeter. Similarly, we measure the distance from the center of the scale to the front of the first annual check, which we will suppose in this case to be 0.3 millimeter. Since the scale grows at the same rate as the fish, the length which the fish had reached at the end of its first year must be the same fraction of its present length that the size which the scale had reached at the end of the first year is of its present size. Now, the first annual check we have just found to be 0.3/0.9, or ⅓, of the present scale-size. The fish at the same time had reached the same fraction, ⅓, of its present length, 12 inches. The fish was therefore 4 inches long at the end of its first year.

The only remaining question is, why does anyone want to know these things? In general, to satisfy the curiosity of that enormously inquisitive animal, the human being. More particularly, because age and growth-rate are two of the most important tools of the fisheries workers—and this not very enlightening reply may be best elucidated by an example.

The main object of fisheries work, whether in the field of commercial or of sport fishing, is to maintain the supply of fish at a level sufficiently high to provide good fishing. One of the methods employed is to determine at what size the fish spawns, and to forbid the capture of fish under this size, thus giving each individual a chance to reproduce itself at least once before it goes to market or into the angler's creel.

Now, consider the California golden trout. This fish was originally found in two small streams near Mount Whitney, and nowhere else in the world. These two streams were fantastically full of extremely beautiful and very hungry little trout most of which matured before they were six inches long, which is to say that they had spawned at least once before that time. A regulation fixing a minimum size of six inches for golden trout seemed to serve the purpose.

Later, the species was transplanted. It reached a high barren lake not many miles away, and there, as is often the case when trout are introduced into suitable waters unoccupied by competing forms of life, it flourished mightily. It grew to much greater size, reaching the not ignoble length of fifteen inches. An examination of scales revealed two things: that no fish in this lake laid eggs before it reached the end of its third year of life, and that at the end of the third year the fish averaged ten inches in length. A six-inch-minimum regulation was, therefore, of not the slightest avail in preventing the destruction of fish in this lake before they had spawned once, but it was only by a study of scales that this fact could be brought to light.

It must not be thought that the fisheries worker pretends that he can take any scale from any fish and recite its past history therefrom. In some species the scales are inscrutable, and reveal nothing even to the most careful searcher. And in the species in which the scales are readable, individual scales are often ambiguous in their indications. Some are blurred, some are scarred, and still others are regenerated— that is to say, they are replacements of the scales which first occupied those positions on the fish and which have in some way been lost. The number of regenerated scales varies with the species, but in all cases such scales have a blank center, seeming to indicate that they grew in one jump to the size of the scale which they replaced, and that only after they had reached the size of the other scales did they begin to trace the record with growth-rings.

What the fisheries worker needs is large numbers of specimens, to enable him to discard uncertain cases, and to average out inaccuracies, errors, and exceptional cases. It is for this reason that the method of calculating past lengths of fish from their scales is especially valuable to him. From a hundred three-year-old specimens he can get not only the lengths of a hundred three-year fish, but the lengths of a hundred two-year fish, and of a hundred one-year fish, as well. Using scale-readings, he can construct the life-history of a species with far fewer specimens than he could in any other way.

It would seem obvious that the fish-fancier's aquarium-dwellers would show no records on their scales. Conditions of temperature and food remain practically constant, and in most of the favorite species spawning is either continuous, once maturity is reached, or very irregular. None of the scales which I have examined, although showing the usual growth-increment rings, are readable. It is possible that the same species in their natural haunts would produce annual checks, for some of the marine tropical fishes in their native waters seem to show them, although there are no well-known seasonal differences in their feeding or other conditions to account for such checks.

COLOR

Most people admit that fish are beautiful, but with a note of reservation in their voices—an unexpressed "but." This reservation, it may be hazarded, has to do with the fact that the beauty of fish is purely one of esthetic design, and is lacking in the emotional quality which plays an important part in our appreciation of such beauty as that of dogs, horses, ships, cathedrals, and women. Dogs are beautiful, in part at least, because we see in them creatures of undying and often undeserved devotion to ourselves. Horses are associated in man's mind with his moments of reckless gallantry—the Charge of the Light Brigade, the pink-coated huntsman bouncing over fences behind the hounds, the cowboy on his bucking bronco. Ships are the tall vessels which man created to carry him through storm and violence in his search for new lands beyond the seas. Cathedrals represent his aspirations toward God and toward immortality. Women—well, the reactions of *man* toward women have been too often told to need repeating here, and the reactions of other women to them will never, in spite of all our researches, be known to us if we are men.

To the beauty of each of these the beholder contributes by adding the beauty of his own emotions which the prophets and the artists and the poets have taught him to associate with them. The poor fish has no such advantages. No pity or gratitude or love or excitement is stirred in us by the sight of a fish. If a fish wants to be admired, it must forego these enhancements, and produce for our contemplation something out of the ordinary in the line of pure, intrinsic beauty: beauty of form, beauty of movement, beauty of color. And this at last brings us back to the body covering, for on it depends the fish's greatest claim to beauty, its coloring. Fish can boast a brilliance, an iridescence, a variety of pattern, and an ability to change color, unequaled by any other group in the animal world, and in producing these results nature makes use of a couple of devices which she has abandoned in the animals higher up the ladder.

The fish's iridescent hues are caused by crystals of a substance called guanin. These appear in their undisguised silvery whiteness under the transparent skin of the animal's belly, but on its back they are overshadowed by the thick black pigment which forms in that portion of the skin. It is a temptation to say that this shading is a beautiful example of protective coloration, the dark back being almost invisible to an enemy like a fish-hunting bird looking down from above into the dark water, while to an enemy looking up from below the light belly would be inconspicuous against the light coming from above. However, there is a school of thought which claims that protective coloration is a myth, and that what seem to be examples of it can all be explained on purely mechanical grounds. They believe that the fish's back is dark solely because the light shining on it from above turns it dark, and the under side is pale only because it receives no light. One worker, to prove this, carried out an experiment on the flounder. The flounder habitually rests on bottom, and its under side is completely without coloring matter, whereas the upper side is well supplied with it. It being impossible to persuade the flounder to reverse its position, this man resorted to trickery. He put it in a glass tank through which by means of mirrors a constant stream of light was brought to play on it from beneath. The flounder did eventually succeed in producing colored pigment on its theretofore immaculate under side, but the fact that it took over a year to do it leaves one uncertain whether this scientist proved his theory, or merely showed what changes can be made in nature's arrangements when they are forcibly submitted to unnatural conditions. In any case, that light plays at least some part in the distribution of pigment is shown by a species of African catfish which, swimming habitually wrong side up, has reversed the conventional color scheme: its belly is dark, its back almost white.

To return to our guanin crystals, the interesting point about them is that they are by-products. They were not put there to give the fish iridescence. They are there because, at the time she designed the fish, Nature had not yet got around to working out a really good waste-disposal system. Those guanin crystals are waste products of the blood, carried out to the skin and deposited there where they can do no harm; and the same thing may be true of scales. As soon as a good excretory system came on the market, guanin crystals went out of use.

Against this theoretically interesting but visually unexciting background, the color pattern of the fish is traced by

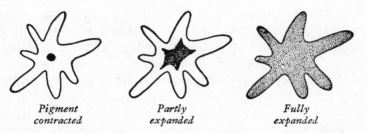

Pigment contracted   *Partly expanded*   *Fully expanded*

FIGURE 6. CHROMATOPHORE, GREATLY MAGNIFIED

pigments in the skin. Some fish never vary, but the majority have the ability to change color to a greater or less extent. To accomplish this they make use principally of a simple but ingenious set of mechanisms known as chromatophores. Chromatophores are little sac-like cells, shaped like many-armed stars, which are scattered through the skin in great numbers. They contain pigment. The pigment can become practically invisible by withdrawing into the center of the cell, or it can expose its color in varying degrees by the extent to which it spreads out into the arms of the star.

Each chromatophore contains only one color—red, orange, yellow, or black—and it is the amount of this color exposed to view, in combination with the amount of each other color exposed to view by the other chromatophores, and also in combination with a certain amount of permanent, invariable pigmentation existing in most fishes, which determines the color pattern at any moment.[1]

It was for many years taken for granted that these color changes were for the most part concerned with the business of protective coloring. Then there appeared upon the scene the aforementioned gentlemen who refuse to believe in protective coloration. Exemplifying the fact that all people, even scientists, go to extremes, they are in revulsion against the generation of naturalists who talked about "our little feathered friends" and "the finny denizens of the deep," who saw in everything from the shell of the oyster to the skull of man the workings of an all-wise and all-foreseeing providence. These upholders of the opposite extreme not only snort with rage at anything savoring of the teleological, but they object to applying in any way man's standards of values or his sense of relationships to any of the workings of nature. They seem to lean over backward, and, in fear of being contaminated by human ideas in the interpretation of nature, to deny what appear, in the light of common sense, to be the most obvious explanations.

These people denied the existence of protective coloration. They refused to believe that the fish's color changes had any connection with its background, and some of them even refused to believe that color changes took place in fish at all, arguing that what appeared to be such were optical illusions on the part of the observer. It was not long before first one laboratory, and then another, was working to refute them, and each, because of the facility with which these animals change color, chose members of the flounder family for experimentation. Flounders were transferred back and forth from one kind of background to another until they must

---

[1] The blue and green colors seen in fish are generally due to the reflections and interferences of light by the colorless surfaces of the guanin crystals and the scales, acting in conjunction with the different pigment combinations.

have been dizzy. They were put on pale backgrounds and on dark backgrounds, on sand and on mud, on fine gravel and on coarse gravel, on black-and-white checker-boards, and on black polka-dots on a white field. One poor fish was even kept in a glass-bottomed tank under which a checker-board slowly but continually revolved.

To eliminate all question of the optical illusions of the observers, careful photographs of each experiment were taken. And when the evidence was all in, there was no room left for argument. The resemblances between the patterns of the fishes' skin and the backgrounds on which they lay were unquestionable, even in the case of the merry-go-round. Not that the animals had been able to reproduce polka-dots and squares on their skin; these actual shapes were beyond them. But in every case, the general effect of the skin-pattern was remarkably close to the general effect of the background. If it was white, the skin was almost colorless; if it was black, the skin was very dark. If it was made up of very small black-and-white squares, or polka-dots, the skin had a fine-grained light-and-dark pattern; if it was made up of large checker-boards or polka-dots, the skin had a correspondingly coarse light-and-dark pattern. Some of the photographs which were taken are reproduced here (Plate III), and give a better idea of what happened than any amount of description.

It was also found that, in addition to being able to adapt their skins to various shades of light and dark and to various degrees of coarseness of pattern such as might be found in their own habitats, some of these fishes were able to simulate different colors, blues, greens and purples, which they would never meet under natural conditions. Other points were brought out in the course of the experiments which add significance to the whole picture.

In the first place, it was found that individual fish varied greatly in their color-changing abilities. Some fish changed only very slowly, and never succeeded in making a good match with the background, while others changed quickly into a very close imitation of whatever bottom they were placed on. Here we have a perfect piece of machinery for the working of selective evolution. Those individuals very expert at color adaptations might be expected to live long and successful lives, and produce a great host of offspring, whereas those that clung obstinately to one color regardless of background might be expected to perish miserably at an early age, leaving no descendants behind them. And so color adaptability, once it had occurred by mutation, might be expected to be handed on until it included the whole race, while those unhappy individuals in which it failed to reach its full efficacy would be eliminated by nature before they could spread their misfortune.

In passing, it is of interest to note that the fish definitely improved with practice, that is, the more often they were shifted from one pattern to another, the more quickly they learned to make the necessary change. One individual even became so adept that, when placed in a tank with one part of the bottom black and the other part white, it could be observed to change from dark to light as it swam slowly across the dividing line between the two sections. This, remember, is not a fish story, but a scientist's report.

It was also found that the eyes played an indispensable part in making color adaptations. Fish which had been excellent performers lost their ability entirely when they were prevented from seeing. If, in normal condition, they were placed on a black background until they had adapted themselves to it, and were then blindfolded in one way or another and moved to a white bottom, they remained dark in color, and the reverse was in principle true if they started on white and went to black.

To the reader this may not seem a particularly startling

discovery, and he might well permit himself to say, "Naturally the fish's eyes play an important part in his color adaptation. What else would you expect?" But to those scientists who believe that things are never what they seem it was a blow, for they had maintained that the color changes were caused by the action of light on the pigment cells in the skin, and that the eyes had little or nothing to do with it.

It was also found that with either eye alone, color adaptation took place just as well as with both; in other words, *each* eye acted on *all* the chromatophores of the body, and this was confirmed by the finding that if a fish were held right on the dividing line between white and black, so that one eye was on the black side and one on the white, it assumed a uniform gray color. The chromatophores, acted on equally by each eye, were held in a state of balance. However, not all species are like these flat-fishes. Trout with one eye put out of action will show color changes only on one side.

There still remained one refuge for the die-hards. What proof is there, they asked, that the eyes of other animals see the same things that ours do? What right have we to assume that just because a certain animal pattern is invisible against a certain background to us, it is also invisible to that animal's enemies? Does protective coloration protect?

This point is not as far-fetched as it may seem, because the difference between the machinery of our eyes and that of the lower animals is considerable, as will appear in a later chapter. Moreover, it is a difficult point to controvert, for how is anyone ever to find out what the world looks like to any other person, especially when that other person is a bird or a fish?

Theoretical arguments went back and forth for years without breaking the stalemate, until one of the leading exponents in the earlier flounder work hit upon a series of experiments of a simplicity nothing short of beautiful. In experimental biology, the principal problem is how to put a question to an animal in such a way that it can answer it. There is no use in asking an animal what it sees, because it cannot tell you, but you can ask what it is going to do about what it sees, and it can answer you by its actions.

Employing this well-known method, this scientist made use of the fact, learned in his previous work, that in many fish the color change takes a long time to complete. There is a first, immediate change of small extent in the direction of the new color, and then the rest of the adaptation proceeds quite slowly. The explanation appears to be that some of the chromatophore machinery is less sensitive and therefore slower-acting than the rest, and also that there is a change in the amount of permanent, or semipermanent, pigmentation. A fish kept for a long time on a white background loses much of this pigmentation, and when it is moved to a black background it takes some time to produce anew enough of this semipermanent pigment to bring it back to its darkest possible shade.

A certain small killifish called *Gambusia affinis,* better know as the "mosquito fish," a common and easily handled species, was found to operate its color-changing machinery along the desired lines. Fish kept in a black tank became dark, fish kept in a white tank became pale. If now the pale fish were placed in the black tank, they at once became appreciably darker than they had been, but they remained for some time very much lighter than the old-time residents of that tank.

The prey having been found, the next step was to find the predator. Predator means in general a bird or beast of prey, but it is used more specifically to refer to the particular animal which preys on a particular species. The first predator tried was a little Galápagos penguin which happened to be living in a near-by zoo. Quantities of mosquito fish were kept in black tanks and in white until they had reached, respectively, the maximum shade of darkness or of pallor. Then, into a large, *light-colored* tank, fifty of each kind of fish were placed at the same time as two of the penguins. The dark fish grew somewhat lighter than they had been, but remained very much darker than the pale ones. To the human eye they were conspicuous against the light background, whereas the pale ones were not. The penguins plunged happily about, scooping up little fish at a great rate. The experimenter stood by, watch in hand, hopeful, but quite unable to see how it was all turning out. At the end of two minutes the penguins were removed and the fish counted. Fourteen of the dark fish had been eaten, but only six of the pale ones. A four-hour test was next made, and this time twenty-nine dark fish were eaten to only fourteen pale ones. In a light-colored tank, twice as many dark fish had been eaten as light-colored fish! Protective coloration had actually protected. Four more tests gave the same answer, although not quite so strikingly. And when the reverse of this experiment was tried, putting both kinds of fish into a black tank, the results, perhaps because the dark residents were here even less visible than the pale ones had been in the light tank, were still more convincing: 217 pale victims in all were eaten, against only 78 dark ones—74 per cent pale to 26 per cent dark, almost three to one.

Not content with this, the experimenter went on to try his system on other predators. He used a heron, which sees its prey only from above, and got approximately the same results. And then, inasmuch as the majority of predators of fish are other fish, he used a species of sunfish which happened to be available, and got even more definite results. After years of futile theoretical argument, one man had solved the old problem by the simplest and most straightforward of methods. To the satisfaction of most people, he definitely established that protective coloration exists, and that protective coloration does protect.

Not all fishes have this ability to adapt their coloring. In the tuna and the swordfish it is, so far as we can tell, very little developed. These are fishes which spend most of their time in the upper waters of the open sea. Here conditions change very little, and there is therefore little need for color change. The basic scheme of dark back and light belly is the suitable dress for all occasions.

The trouts live in a different kind of world. Sometimes they are on a dark bottom, sometimes on light. Sometimes they are in the sunshine, sometimes in the shadow. In color and pattern adaptation they are far behind the flounder, but their shade they can alter to meet conditions. With them, too, the eye is the principal instrument in bringing the adjustment about, and this fact I learned before I ever looked into a microscope. It was when I first fished the Test in England many years ago. Catching trout in the Test is a different problem from catching them in our American streams. In the Test, the fish lie in plain sight, and the ability to cast a dry fly with sufficient skill to make them want it is the principal requirement. In our American streams, such as the Broadhead or the Gunnison, to take widely separated examples, the fish are almost never visible, and the knowledge of where to fish for them is the first requirement. The most skillful caster gets nothing more than an occasional chance rise unless he knows where to cast.

The Test is an exciting stream because there are always lots of fish to be seen. One- and two- and three-pounders float in the slow, clear water, fins just moving to hold them against the current, sometimes as many as seven or eight all in sight at once. You may see a thousand fish in the course of a day, and yet, if you are no more expert than I was, have difficulty getting as many as six. For only about one in six of the fish you see is feeding, and of those that are feeding, only about one in six will look at your fly, and of those that rise only one in six will actually take it, and of those that take it, so small are the flies and so slender the leaders that must be used in this transparent water, only about one in six reach the net.

The bottom is generally sandy, and most of the fish are a sandy color to match it, but a few are dark and stand out conspicuously against the background. Naturally they are the easiest ones to see, and on the first day they were the ones which attracted my attention. I must have cast over three or four of them without getting a sign of a rise, when the keeper came along. He watched me for a minute in silence. Then he touched my arm. "See that pale one over there?" He pointed to a two-pounder, just the color of the bottom, near the far shore, which I had not noticed. "Give him a try. You'll have a better chance with him. This black fellow will never rise for you. He's blind."

In streams like the Test, where the fresh-water shrimp and other forms of food are immensely abundant, the blind trout can keep himself well fed by the use of his other senses; but he cannot match the bottom.

Contrasting with this confident self-exposure in which the Test trout felt free to indulge was the shyness of the fish in a certain small high-Sierra stream which I had a chance to watch one summer. Inhabitants of other waters in that region are far from wary, but this particular stretch of stream ran beside a major trail. Into it, from a near-by lake, a great number of trout had crowded during the spawning season. At the end of the season, and before all the spawners had returned to the lake, the stream was barred in two places for experimental reasons. I knew, or thought I knew, that three fish had been penned in between the barriers. Two of these I caught with hook and line and replaced in the lake, but the third, a specimen about ten inches long, I was, in spite of all my efforts, unable to catch. I knew the rock under which he lived, and I saw him several times. I pricked him once, and after that he never came near the hook. Finally, much against my will, I placed a trap in the stream for him. The next morning there were six ten-inch trout in the trap. In spite of the fact that I had watched that short stretch of stream, not over thirty feet long, and nowhere more than two feet deep and eight feet broad, steadily throughout a whole month, I had never seen more than one fish in it, and him only rarely.

No protective motivation has been discovered for the spectacular changes in color and pattern which some of the coral reef fishes go through. Species are known which have at least seven distinct costumes which they change with almost unbelievable rapidity. The transformations appear to be connected with emotional or physiological disturbances. Why this should be so, or its value, is not known; but that chromatophores furnish the mechanism is recognized.

Aside from color-change by means of chromatophores, at least two other general types occur in fish. One is the intensification of coloring and the addition of brighter colors which accompany spawning—the so-called "nuptial coloring." This occurs most frequently in fresh-water species, and is rarely found in salt water. It is conspicuous in the primitive "bowfin" of our Middle West and in some of the trouts. It occurs to a certain extent among the sunfishes and black basses. Very little attempt has been made to find out the machinery of these changes, but it may be deduced from what is already known that chromatophores play no large part, and that the effect is due to the general excitement of the fish—for even human beings are brighter colored when in love—and to an addition of bright pigment to the permanent pattern, brought about in some way by hormones generated by the ripening sex-products.

But there is one group of fish well-known to the aquarist whose nuptial brilliance *does* depend on chromatophores. These are the cichlids—the scalares, the orange chromides, the acaras, and, most striking of all, the already-mentioned "jewel." This little fish from tropical Africa spawns with great frequency, sometimes oftener than once a week, and it might be supposed that the flaming color which it puts on for each occasion, and which fades to a dull gray in the interludes, is again an effect of generative hormones. There is this difference, however, between it and such a fish as the trout, that the latter retains its nuptial colors in unvarying brilliance until the sex-products are disposed of, whereas the jewel, male or female, will lose its color and revert to the pale gray of the unripe fish if it is caught by a human hand or cowed by a more powerful rival, to reacquire its brilliance as soon as it is undisturbed. The courting dress is therefore due not to a direct secretion of the ripe ovaries or testes acting upon the coloring agents, but to an excitement brought about by the ripeness of the sex organs, which excitement stimulates the nerves which control the chromatophores. That this is the case is further illustrated by the fact that the administration of a drug called yohimbine to the male or female jewel in its neuter, or unripe, stage will produce the courting costume, without any of the courting behavior, and this is because yohimbine acts upon the controlling nerves and disperses the pigment throughout the chromatophores. The artificial blushes will remain for three or four days, gradually disappearing as the effects of the drug wear off.

"How" and "why" are the two questions which man is always asking. Long before the "how" of nuptial coloring had been considered, the "why" was being asked, and Charles Darwin himself gave one of the first answers in his "sexual-selection" theory. This theory applies especially to those animals in which the male only displays the bright colors. Influenced, perhaps, by the inability of women to resist soldiers, a worldly fact so well known that even a scientist could not escape it, Darwin pronounced the theory that the female animal, throughout the ages, has been attracted by bright colors. The most brilliant males, according to him, have always had the best chance of getting mates and offspring and of passing on their brilliance, and the result is that it eventually spreads throughout the species. Experiments have shown that in some animals at least Darwin's psychology was wrong, and that the bright male coloring is used not to seduce the female, but to frighten off rival males. It is a warning rather than a promise, but the evolutionary result is the same: the most brilliant male has the best chance of getting a mate.

In those species in which both sexes display the bright colors, and especially in the jewel-fish, Darwin may have been right. Recent experiments show that, given her choice between a gentleman in bright courting red and one in the drab neutral gray, the lady chooses the flashy clothes. The bright coloring, in either sex, we may suppose, is a signal. It attracts the attention. It announces to members of the other sex that the wearer is ready and looking for trouble.

A third kind of color-change sometimes occurs as part of the normal growth of fish. In many species there is very little color difference between the infant and the parent, but in a few this difference is marked. In Bermuda, the male of the "blue-head," a common reef-wrasse about six inches long, goes through so many color-changes during growth that for years it was classified as several different species. A less striking, but more widespread and better-known, example is the "parr-mark" of the salmon family. Rainbows, cutthroats, browns, Atlantic salmon, Pacific salmon, brook trout, all have, at some period of their infancy, a series of not very clearly defined, oval, bluish-gray patches along their sides. In the California golden trout and a similar Canadian form, both inhabitants of small streams in high mountain regions, these parr-marks often remain visible throughout life, but in other species they vanish before maturity is reached. The theory is that these markings were permanent features of the extinct ancestors of the salmon family, and that in the course of evolution they were pushed out of the picture until now the only chance they get to appear is during the early life of each individual. This is called the recapitulation theory, or the *biogenetic law*, and we shall meet it again in the course of this book. It is a theory devised by biologists for their own edification and enlightenment. It holds that the developmental history of the individual recapitulates the evolutionary history of the species. In more but shorter words, each individual is supposed to go through, during its growth and more especially during its early embryonic period, stages which resemble various features characteristic of the species which were its evolutionary ancestors. For instance, the gill slits which are present for a short while in the early human embryo are supposed to represent the fish-stage of our evolutionary history. It is an hypothesis rather than a law, and in spite of much evidence in its favor it is incapable of conclusive proof, but biologists delight in hauling it out, whenever opportunity offers, to see how it matches up with the facts. As for the developmental color-changes which led us off on this side-track, it may be assumed that they are due to slow alterations in the permanent pigment pattern, and not to chromatophores.

What happened to chromatophores in the course of evolution? Why can't we change our color? To be sure, we get red when angry, pale when frightened, but that is due only to the change in the amount of blood in our surface capillaries just under our skin. Would it be of any advantage to a human being to be able to resemble his background? Hardly, in the present state of civilization. Therefore, if by an unexpected mutation a human were born with chromatophores, he would not have any advantage in the acquisition of mates and the production of offspring. More likely the contrary.

If, on the other hand, a field-mouse could rapidly change its coloring to resemble its background, it might conceivably be of advantage to it. However, a field-mouse has a coat of hair, which is dead matter, and which would hide chromatophores in the living skin underneath. And there we have a clue to the absence of chromatophores in the higher vertebrates: they have to be in living skin to function, and the higher vertebrates—including man up to the comparatively recent time when he took to skinning other animals for his covering—have hidden the living skin under feathers or fur.

There remains to be discussed a major exception to this whole chapter—a group of fishes so different from all the rest that they absolutely insist on some attention from time to time. I refer to the sharks and rays, known technically as the *elasmobranch* or cartilaginous fishes because they have skeletons of cartilage, whereas the composite fish which we agreed to make the subject of this book has a skeleton of bone and is known as a *teleost*, or bony fish. In the eyes of zoologists there are almost as many differences between the cartilaginous and the bony fishes as there are between the birds and the reptiles.

The sharks and rays have no fingernail-like scales embedded in a delicate skin. Instead, they have a tough, thick hide of which the "scales," which are more like our teeth in origin and growth, are a part. These harden into little "denticles," and project from the surface. The result is the roughness of the familiar "shark-skin" which in some cases has such rasp-like qualities that it is used in industrial processes.

CHAPTER IV

Framework

THAT the trout and the tarpon are considered by the ich-thyologist low forms of fish is a shock to the sportsman, who looks upon them as among God's fairest creations. It must hastily be added that the ichthyologist's opinion is in no way derogatory. He bases his judgment on the structure of the animal, not on its mode of life nor its fighting ability nor its food value. He uses the words "low" and "primitive" to denote similarity to a generalized ancestral type. The trout and the tarpon, with their symmetrical bodies and their widely spaced paired fins, have diverged less than most living fish from the creatures which are thought to have been the common ancestors of most present-day fish and of all the higher land animals.

SKELETON

The essential elements of the fish framework are a skull, a backbone made up of a series of vertebrae, and two pairs of fins: the pectorals, and the pelvics or ventrals. Allow for the transformation of these paired fins into limbs, and they are the same elements which are found throughout the verte-brates. In addition, the fish skeleton has some features which are either omitted or modified in the higher animals. It has, along the mid-line of the body, one or more dorsal fins on the back and one or more anal fins on the under side, made up of bony or cartilaginous elements unattached to the rest of the skeleton. It has a caudal, or tail, fin, firmly attached

to the end of the backbone. It has a series of gill arches which
support the breathing apparatus. In the higher animals these
have come to form part of the voice-box. Further, and this is
one of the fish's most noticeable features, it has no neck. It
has a tail, extending from the caudal fin forward to the vent,
which is just in front of the anal fin. It has a body, extending
from the vent to the gill opening. And it has a head, extending from the gill opening to the front end. It even has
shoulder-blades, strange as that may seem, supporting the
pectoral fins, but in most fish these attach to the top of the
head. It was not until, in the land animals, the shoulder-
blades moved back and relinquished their hold on the skull
that room was made for a neck—a visible separation between
head and body.

What makes the trout a low fish, in so far as the skeleton
is concerned, is that the pelvic fins are located far behind the
pectorals and have no connection with the rest of the bony
structure, that all of the fins are made up of soft rays with
no spines, and that the bones of the head are primitive in
number and position.[1]

If we compare the skeleton of the trout with that of such
a fish as the perch—to pick one low in the scale of the sportsman but high in the scale of the ichthyologist—we find differences. Most of the fins have stiff spines in them as well as
soft rays, and there is a general tendency to an unfriendly
spininess all over, from the spikes on the side of the head
to the microscopic teeth on the after-end of each ctenoid
scale. Ichthyologists consider this a specialization and, therefore, an advance. More conspicuous, though, is the propin-

[1] The bones of the fish's head are highly significant, and their persistence
and evolution through the amphibians and the reptiles to the birds and
mammals are extremely interesting, but too many erudite men have written
too many large books on the subject to make it possible to treat it superficially, and it is too involved to treat seriously here. Therefore, we shall
say no more about it.

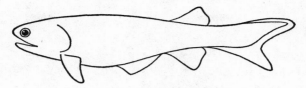

Cheirolepis, *a Palaeozoic fish*

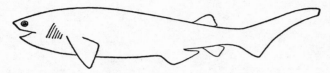

Cow shark, *a "primitive" modern cartilaginous fish*

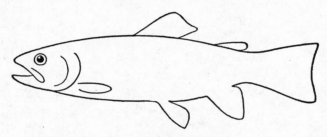

Rainbow trout, *a "primitive" modern bony fish*

Yellow perch, *an "advanced" modern bony fish*

FIGURE 7. PRIMITIVE AND ADVANCED FISHES

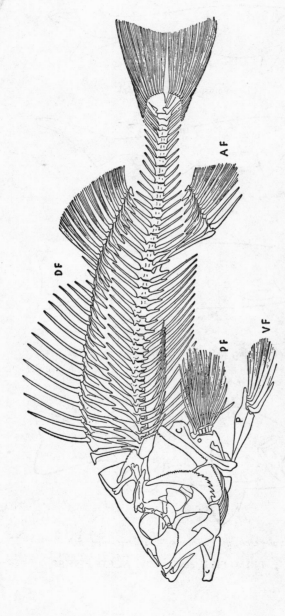

FIGURE 8. SKELETON OF THE YELLOW PERCH

After Cuvier. Note that the pectoral fin (PF) is attached to the skull by the shoulder bone (C), and the ventral fin (VF) fastened to the shoulder through the medium of the pelvic bone (P). The dorsal fin (DF) and the anal fin (AF) can be seen to have no bony connection with the rest of the skeleton. The sunfish, bass, and other "advanced" fishes have skeletons very similar to this.

quity of the two pairs of fins. The pelvics have moved forward until they are under the pectorals, and the pelvis, which corresponds to our hip, fastens them to the cleithrum, which corresponds to our shoulder. To have your shoulders resting on your hips, and the attachment of your legs almost under your ears, is an ichthyologist's idea of the way to change from a lower to a higher form.

To be fair to the ichthyologist, it must be repeated that when he says low he means primitive, and when he says primitive he means unspecialized. The trout is so unspecialized that it could conceivably be transformed into a land animal; in fact, the earliest fossil animal which walked on land had its hind legs where the trout's pelvic fins are, its hips did not fasten to its backbone, any more than the trout's do, and its shoulder-blades were fastened to the top of its skull, just as the trout's are. Further, the trout's air-bladder, which we shall consider more in detail later on, opens into its throat, even as lungs do.

The perch, on the other hand, with all its potential limbs huddled against its head, and with the opening from the air-bladder to the throat lost, is in a blind alley of the evolutionary highway. It is so specialized that it can never be anything but a fish, so advanced that it can never advance to anything but a more advanced fish. And this holds true of the bass and the tuna and the other advanced fishes, up to and including those which, like the frogfish with its pelvic fins up in front of its pectorals, are so advanced that even the ichthyologist considers them degenerate (Figure 9).

And it is of interest to note that while some of the fish-fancier's favorites are in the advanced category, like the bettas, the gouramis, the scalares, and the rest of the cichlids, the majority rank lower in the scale: for characins, danios, barbs, guppies, swordtails, and platies are all among the more primitive fish.

✦

How is it that we can catch a twenty-pound salmon on a leader of only five pounds' breaking strength? We all know that it is because, as long as our fish is in the water, practically all of that twenty pounds is supported by the water. If he tries to use his muscular energy to bring a greater

FIGURE 9. FROGFISH

From David Starr Jordan, *Fishes,* by permission of D. Appleton-Century Company.

strain on the tackle, we let him run, and when he is finally brought to the shore, we do not try to lift him out of the water by means of that leader, but use a gaff or a net.

Most of us never stop to think what this means to the fish in terms of efficiency, of economy of effort. We ourselves are engaged in a constant struggle with the force of gravity. When we go upstairs or climb a hill, we have to lift our whole weight. Even when we walk along the level, every step we take means lifting that weight a fraction of a foot and letting it down again. And when we fall, we come down with a teeth-rattling crash that seems totally out of proportion with the short distance involved. Whoever thought up the force of gravity was a pretty clever fellow, but he went too far. It looks as if half, or even a quarter, of its present power would have been sufficient to keep us from flying off the earth into space, without being a constant nuisance to us.

The fish is more fortunate than we. The element in which he lives, water, has a specific gravity almost the same as that of his own body. This means that his weight is held up by the water, and that it requires no effort on his part to support himself. To be definite, a twenty-pound fish, even if he is all lean and no fat—and most fish do have a certain amount of fat and other buoyant auxiliaries—weighs only about one pound in salt water. If he wants to go up, all he has to lift is one pound. All the rest of his energy is free to use in other ways. It is as if a 150-pound man were to find his weight suddenly reduced to 7½ pounds. If you can imagine how fast this man could run or how high he could jump, you get some idea of how easy it is for the fish to move about. To go straight upwards, as you do when you pull yourself up a rope hand over hand, is no harder for our fish than it is for you to lift a 7½-pound brief-case. And if we abandon our lean fish in favor of the many kinds, of which the salmon is one, whose specific gravity is just about equal to water's, no energy at all is devoted to weight-lifting. All he has to overcome is the resistance of the water, and in this he has the help of the original, and still the best, stream-lined body.

Now, while this is all very nice for the fish, it has, in the long run, been a bad thing for us. The fish's body being supported on all sides by the medium in which it lived, all it needed in the way of a skeleton was something to keep it stiff while it cleaved the water, and something for its muscles to pull against. The fins had no work to do in the way of holding the body up, and it was not necessary for them to be attached to the principal element of the skeleton, the backbone. As we have seen, the pectoral fins did come to be fastened to the skull, but that was perhaps as much due to the requirements of the gill apparatus, of which their supporting bones formed the rear end, as to anything else. The ventral fins in all the primitive fishes, including those still alive today like the tarpon and the salmon family, had no connection with the backbone. They were attached to pieces of cartilage or bone, and these pieces reposed without support in the flesh of the body.

When the fish came up out of the water and turned itself into a land animal, the paired fins, which had been of no great importance to it, turned into limbs, and became extremely important. Some method had to be found by which they could be made to support the body, and to do this it was obviously necessary to attach them to the main element of the skeleton. At the front end this was accomplished very cleverly. In quadrupeds the front end, with its weighty, overhanging head and its ribs for the protection of the lungs and heart, is the heavier and needs the most support. Using the old bones which had braced the pectoral fins, a kind of cradle was devised, itself resting on good solid bearings on the front legs, from which the heavy weight was slung by means of more or less elastic connections. The shoulder-blade and its dependent muscles and ligaments are the principal elements in this arrangement, and the whole thing is flexible, so that the shocks received on the front feet when running or jumping do not jar the whole body.

The rear end was a tougher problem. Here there was no existing connection, and in the very earliest land animal, an amphibian known only through fossils, the fish system still prevailed, and the hind limbs were not attached to the backbone at all. It soon became obvious that that was not going to be satisfactory, and a new system was designed. A number of the vertebrae, the joints of the backbone, were fused or consolidated into a single piece. This is called the *sacrum*. Against that, on each side, was placed a bone called the *ilium*, and each ilium had on its under side a nicely made bearing surface for the upper end of the hind leg. The whole thing was, theoretically at least, rigid, and the system of having the animal take off from a rigid hind end in which no power was lost, and land on a flexible front end which took up the shocks, was mechanically excellent.

The weak spot in it was the articulation between the sacrum and the ilium, the now notorious sacro-iliac joint. The sacrum does not rest *on* the two ilia, it merely rests *between* them, and the principal factor in holding the whole business together is friction. Now, an animal that walks on four feet, with most of the weight on the two front ones, can get along this way all right, but when he tries to stand up on the two hind ones, all the weight comes on that joint, and all the shocks are received by it. The supposedly rigid mechanism, being after all a "hand-me-down," sometimes shifts under the strain. And when you or your friend turns up in the doctor's office with a sacro-iliac sprain, you can blame the fish, for it was his failure to provide a proper connection between his pelvic fins and his backbone which is at the bottom of the trouble.

MUSCLES

The fish's face is one of its notoriously weak features. Even allowing for the fact that it was the first real face ever attempted, little more can be said for it than that the mouth, nose, eyes, and forehead—if such it can be called—are in the proper order. It is of no use for frowning or smiling; if the fish could do these things, it would receive a great deal more sympathy than it does.

The reason that it cannot is that it has no facial muscles.

It can open and shut its gill covers. It can open and shut its jaws, and some fishes can protrude the upper lip in a startling but not particularly endearing fashion. There are muscles to perform these operations. There are also muscles to move the various fins. All of these muscles, however, are comparatively insignificant. Both in bulk and in strength, they are as nothing compared to the great mass which forms the

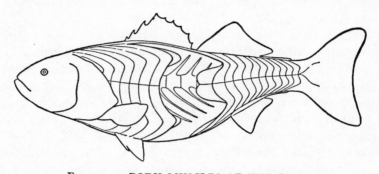

FIGURE 10. BODY MUSCLES OF THE FISH
Drawn from a model by Dr. W. K. Gregory in the American Museum of Natural History.

main part of the fish's muscular system. This is the series of W-shaped segments adjoining and fitting into one another along the whole length of each side of the body, which form the part of the fish which you eat. You can verify this structure the next time a whole fish is served to you by stripping off the skin and examining the meat.

The fish's principal motive force is concentrated in this compact mass in the body wall, and each muscle is limited in its action to the region immediately surrounding it. In the higher animals, including ourselves, the situation is very different. The body wall plays practically no part in movement. The principal motive force is decentralized. It is broken up into separate units, the long muscles of the limbs.

And these muscles, instead of being limited in their action to their immediate surroundings, have developed a system of long, non-muscular tendons by means of which their force can be brought into play at points remote from their own location. When you lift your heels off the ground and stand on the balls of your feet, it is the muscles well up in the calves of your legs which are doing the work, as you can determine by feeling them. Nothing like this takes place in the fish.

Furthermore, in us, every muscle is different from every other muscle, except for its counterpart on the other side of the body. Efficiency and power have been achieved by a high degree of specialization. At the time that the fish was being designed, this idea had no currency, and the only way to achieve greater power was to keep on adding more of the same thing. The fish is confined to a few elements, used over and over again—the muscle segment, the fin-ray or spine, the vertebra—whereas we have many elements, each designed for a special purpose, and each used only once. Some units are, it is true, repeated, like the fingers and the ribs, but they differ from each other, and even our vertebrae change their shape from one part of the backbone to another. Progress has consisted in reduction of numbers and in specialization.

The great mass of potential motive force being located in the body, and not in the fins, how does the fish move? Mainly by body strokes, alternately to the right and left. The muscle segments contract in succession, first along one side and then along the other, and the fish pushes against the water first on one side and then on the other, somewhat in the way a skater pushes against the ice. No one who has ever watched a fish move at full speed will forget that violent side-to-side swinging of the body, culminating in the wide sweep of the tail fin. It is in contrast to the apparent effortlessness with which a porpoise coasts along in front of a ship. The reason for this is that, while the porpoise swims on much the same principle, his movements are in the up-and-down, instead of in the side-to-side, plane, and therefore cannot be seen as we look down on him from the bow of a steamer. They become apparent only when an extra wide move brings him up out of the water entirely. The porpoise being a mammal which has readapted itself to the water and having different body musculature from the fish, it has found the vertical motion preferable to the horizontal and more useful in giving it access to the air which it has to breathe.

The amazing part of the whole phenomenon of readaptation is that this land animal, which has had to learn to swim, is a better swimmer than most fish. It slips through, and in and out of, the waves like a shadow, and it has been estimated to make over thirty miles an hour. The salmon's speed has been variously estimated at from seven to fourteen miles per hour, and the top for fish at about thirty, in the tunas.[1] This "typical" fish with the "ideal" shape has grooves in its body surface into which the fins can be retracted while swimming so that they will offer less resistance to the water, and its form is the last word in stream-lining, while its wide, deeply forked tail fin fastened to the body by the narrow "caudal peduncle" is another indication of speed. Man himself, in the person of a champion athlete running one hundred yards, can make only about twenty miles per hour. The horse can double this, the antelope triple it, and some birds have been estimated to do better than a hundred miles an hour; but in view of the heavy

[1] It is difficult to measure the speed of wild animals with any degree of accuracy. Sixty miles an hour has been attributed, although without substantiating evidence, to that distant relative of the tunas, the sailfish. To place the maximum for fish at thirty is therefore conservative.

medium through which he has to push himself, and of the fact that amphibians and reptiles, which are looked on as higher animals, cannot go as fast, thirty miles an hour is not so bad for the poor fish after all.

It was formerly held that the caudal fin, at the end of the fish's tail, was its most important instrument in swimming. The idea seemed plausible, and was for a long time accepted by many people. Then there came a man who wondered. He took two identical fish. From one he amputated the caudal fin. This may sound like a serious operation, but it is in reality very simple, for fishes' fins do not bleed, and all that is necessary is to take a pair of scissors and trim off the undesired part, just as you trim excess material off a piece of cloth. He placed them both, the fish with and the fish without a tail fin, at one end of a tank, and slapped the tank sharply with his hand to frighten them. Both scurried off for all they were worth, and they reached the other end of the tank at precisely the same instant. The caudal fin may make it *easier* for the fish to swim, but it is the muscular action of the body which really accomplishes the result.

To determine the importance of the other fins, he carried out similar experiments. It had been stated that the dorsal and anal act as keels, to keep the fish straight up. He cut off both of these, and found that while the fish rolled a little at first, it soon learned to get on without them. He then cut *all* the fins off, and found that even in that denuded state the fish could navigate. He did find, though, that the pectorals and ventrals play a part in maneuvering. In straight swimming they are folded back; when the fish wants to make a quick stop, it opens them out, and they act as brakes. When it wants to turn, it uses them on one side or the other as rudders or pivots. The primitive fish, like the salmons and the tarpon, have not much control over the brakes. They are apt to swerve aside to avoid an object, instead of coming to a stop, and they cannot back water very successfully. The advanced fishes, like the black bass and the striped bass, have more flexible fins, and the position of the ventrals up forward under the pectorals makes them of more use in maneuvering. It is easy to see that by thrusting one ventral straight down and giving a flip of its tail, the bass can spin around as if it were on a pivot. Trout spend a great deal of their time heading in one direction, upstream, and most things come at them from the direction in which they are headed, whereas bass live in quieter water, swim in all directions, and have to be ready to spin around to any point of the compass to confront enemies or food. However, this line of thought should not be carried too far. The trout, fishermen will agree, can turn around quickly enough if it has to, whereas the shark, with no directional influences in its life, is a pretty lumbering maneuverer.

And in the delicate movements whose precision fascinates us, the fins play the major rôle. No one who has ever watched fishes can help being aware of the fact that they have a control of their own bodies in their own element unequaled by any other animal. Birds are the nearest approach, with their ability to fly and to soar, but the fish is their master. He can move imperceptibly forward a fraction of an inch, or shoot forward from a standing start with lightning speed. He can go straight up and straight down. He can go backward. He can even remain suspended absolutely motionless in the water for an indefinite length of time, and while this stationary position depends upon the equilibrium between the fish and the water which we spoke of earlier, it also calls the fins into play. For the fish must breathe, and his method of breathing is to pass water backward over the gills and out through the gill openings. This backwardly directed current tends to move him forward, and must in most cases be counteracted by backing water with the fins.

It is obvious that if this gill-current is an obstacle when the fish wants to stand still, it can be an advantage when he wants to move. The flounders and the other flatfishes spend much time lying on the bottom on one side, which brings one gill underneath. One might think that this would be a drawback in breathing, but they turn it to advantage. If they breathed through the upper gill, its movement might betray their presence, thus nullifying all the hard work of the chromatophores to conceal them with protective coloration. They get around this by breathing through the hidden lower gill only. They arch the body slightly along the midline, and the outgoing current of water passes along this tunnel between the body and the ground, and so out past the tail. Further, and this is the part which has to do with locomotion, when they want to move in a hurry, they shoot a quick jet of water out through the under gill with such force that it lifts them right off the bottom and starts them on their way. This jet propulsion is probably used by many fishes in making a quick start. There is also a theory that in their normal swimming fishes make use of this current from the gills, not so much for its propulsive force as for the effect which a stream of water along the sides has in reducing friction and cavitation. Interesting arguments are advanced to support it, but insufficient experimental evidence. It still remains a theory.

All that we have said so far about locomotion is true of the great majority of fishes, but there are some exceptions which make little or no use of the body movement for locomotion. The brilliant parrot-fish of tropical waters, with its large, thick scales, rows itself along with its pectoral fins. The trunk-fish, with its body encased in immovable armor, has to depend on the sculling movement of its free caudal fin, with some help from its pectorals. And the little sea-horse progresses through the water standing on its tail, propelled mainly by its dorsal fin, which waves so fast that it looks like a whirling propeller.

The conclusion which we cannot escape as the result of all this discussion is the one which we touched on earlier, that fins are not indispensable to most fish. The ventrals give the secret away; the manner in which they shift about from one part of the body to another, and vanish entirely in some species, is clear proof that the fish does not know what to do with them. Here is where those who believe in a wise and far-seeing and all-providing directing Force have an opportunity for propaganda. The fish can get along without fins, but the mammal cannot get along without limbs. Why, then, was the fish given fins, unless it was prearranged in the master plan that he should some day come out on land and use them to walk with?

It is a good argument. Its supporters may be right, and certainly no one is in a position to go so far as to state flatly that they are wrong. However, anyone wishing to give consideration to the other side might point out that not much foresight was shown in making preparations for that sacro-iliac joint. He might suggest that perhaps it was because the fish had fins that it was able to become a quadruped, rather than that it was given fins in order to become a quadruped. He might ask what part, if fins were given fish in preparation for quadruped use, the dorsal and anal played in the plan. And this would bring him to the fin-fold theory, which holds that fins came into being solely through the action of the environment on the material. It holds that the earliest fishlike creatures had no fins, but that, as they moved about, the flow of the water against their soft bodies pressed out ridges or keels along their upper and lower surfaces. One ingenious experimenter has taken a penholder, coated it with soft wax, and by moving it back and forth in the water produced just such "fin-folds." According to the theory, the

fold would run without interruption along the back to the
end of the tail, and on the under side would extend forward
as long as the cross-section of the body remained an elongated oval, like this.

But at the point where the cross-section changed, as it is
supposed to have done in some of the earlier fishes and still
does in the sharks, to triangular in the forward part of the
body, the lower fin-fold split up into parts and followed
along the angles, like this.

Once these hypotheses are accepted, the rest is easy. The
fin-fold, originally continuous, disappeared in spots, and the
fragments of it which remained became the dorsal, caudal,
anal, ventral, and pectoral 'fins.

Anyone who objects that it is preposterous to build a
theory on the evidence of a penholder coated with wax will
be referred to two of science's favorite sources of information about the past: fossils and the biogenetic law. For the
remains of the very early fishes do suggest that something
like this happened. And our infant trout, and other fishes of
today, do come into the world bearing along their back a
continuous fin-fold, which extends around their tail and
along their under side as far as the vent; and parts of this
fin-fold do disappear, and the remaining fragments do become the dorsal, caudal, and anal fins. Interpreted by the
biogenetic law, this corroborates the fossil evidence that the
remote ancestors of the trout did once wear a continuous
fin-fold throughout life, and that only through the processes

of evolution did it break up into separate fins. On the other hand—and there is always an "other hand"—some palaeontologists point to the fact that the fossil spiny "sharks" had paired lateral spines, acting apparently as stabilizers, and maintain that these were the forerunners of paired fins.

There remain for consideration the sharks and rays. They cannot be passed over, especially in any discussion of frame-

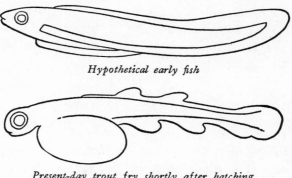

Hypothetical early fish

Present-day trout fry shortly after hatching

FIGURE 11. THE FIN-FOLD THEORY

works, for it is in this very feature that they reveal themselves at their most primitive. A mere glance at a shark (Figure 7) ought to be enough to indicate this to anyone who has read this far: the ventral fins, back near the middle of the body, are enough to give him away. In addition, the shape of the tail, drawn out to a high point, with a big fin-lobe on the under side, is a very primitive feature. It is called a *heterocercal* tail, in case you would like to know, whereas the symmetrical-looking tail of the trout and the bass and the characin and the danio is called *homocercal*.

But the supreme difference between the sharks and rays, and the other fish, can only be told by going into them with a knife. Take a shark's skull, and you can whittle it like a piece of wood, for it is just one big block of cartilage. Take a tuna's skull, and the most you can do is to knock chips off it with a chisel, for it is composed of bones, with visible joints or sutures between them. The sharks and rays haven't a bone in their bodies—nothing but cartilage all the way through. Whether this is a truly primitive condition in the sense that they were that way originally and never made any improvements, or whether it is a degenerate condition to which they have come after once having had bone, is still undecided by scientists, although at present the verdict favors the latter theory.

There are minor differences in the structure, such as in the gill slits and the fin construction, but the general arrangements of the skeleton and the muscular system are so close to those of the bony fishes that nothing more need be said about them here.

CHAPTER V

The Senses and the Nervous System

ALL animals except the very lowest have nervous systems. In all, the principal elements are the same. There are sense-organs, which receive impressions from the outside world. There are nerves, over which the sense-organs send reports. There is a center, or group of centers—brain, spinal cord, ganglia—which receive these reports. And there are other nerves over which the centers send instructions to the muscles as to what action to take.

THE SENSES

It is the popular conception that man has five senses. This, like many other popular conceptions, is not true. It is based on the fact that man has only five clearly visible sense-organs: eyes, ears, skin, mouth, and nose. But in addition to the popular five senses of sight, hearing, touch, taste, and smell, he has at least four others: a sense of equilibrium, which keeps him right side up and going straight; of "kinesthesia," which tells him whether his hand is at his side or above his head; of heat and cold; and of pain. These four senses are not generally recognized, partly because they seem to act through the organs provided for the other senses instead of through organs of their own, and partly because they act so automatically that we are unaware of them.

If fish had reached the same level of mental development

that we have, it would be their popular conception that they have six senses. For in addition to our five traditional sense-organs, which we inherit from them, they have a sixth, the lateral line. What appears to us to be just a pleasantly ornamental stripe running along the side of the fish from gills to tail, and carrying out the stream-lining in much the same way that the body-stripe does on a modern automobile, is in reality a distinct and extremely important sense-organ.

How many of the four additional senses mentioned above are possessed by the fish is one of those questions which science will probably never be able to answer fully, for it is obviously impossible to know fully what the fish's sensations are. And this applies to all his senses, even to those whose workings we understand best, such as sight. What another human being sees we can tell with some assurance from what he says. What a dog sees we can imagine from his reactions, which, from his closeness to us, we assume to have the same significance as our own. But what a fish sees, in a different medium, with different reactions, and with an optical apparatus differently constructed from our own, is not an easy problem. It is regrettable that no one, even with the best intentions, has ever succeeded in turning himself into a fish.

SIGHT

The fish has two eyes, even as you and I. From this we permit ourselves to conclude, without further argument, that the fish sees. From an analysis of his actions and an examination of his brain, we conclude that eyes are to him, or at least to such of him as we are most interested in, the most important of the sense-organs, even as they are to us. But when we come to trying to find out what his eyes see we cannot go so fast.

We find ourselves confronted with two difficulties. The first is of an objective nature. It has to do, not with what the fish is capable of seeing, but with what there is to be seen. To put it in one sentence, what is visible to the fish?

As long as we remain under water there is no difficulty. Under water, visibility is not as good as in the air, but similar

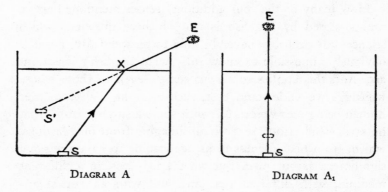

DIAGRAM A   DIAGRAM A₁

in its workings. Things cannot be seen at so great a distance, and darkness increases with depth, but there is no distortion. Light does not travel as fast or as far as in the air, but, as long as it remains under water, it does travel in a straight line.

It is when it comes out of the water into the air, or when it goes from air into water, that light gets into trouble, for then it meets with the phenomenon known as refraction, and gets bent. This is the old trick of the soap not being where it appeared to be through the water in the bathtub, which used to fascinate us in our childhood days before both bathtubs and the mysteries of nature became commonplaces.

It is to be noted that it is the light passing *from* the soap *to* our eye, and not *from* our eye *to* the soap, by which we see the soap (Diagram A). If S is the soap on the bottom of the tub, the ray of light from S is bent as it comes out of the water at X and goes in the direction XE to reach our eye at E. Now, as we are accustomed to objects being in line with the path over which the light from them reaches us, the soap seems to us to be along the prolongation of the line EX, and as the effect of the water is also to make it slightly nearer to us, our eye sees the soap at S′, on the line EXS′, instead of at S. The only exception is that if we look directly down, as in Diagram A_1, the soap is actually on the line of sight that it appears to be, for what is called the "normal" ray of light, that is, the ray whose path is at right angles to the surface, is not bent at all.

It is this principle of refraction which serves as the basis of operation of all lenses, whether for magnifying-glass or spectacles or telescope or microscope or eye. It is a matter which we shall not try to penetrate for fear of becoming bogged in the laws and mathematics of optics, but over whose surface we shall skim in order to get an understanding of what the fish is up against.

If the fish never tries to see outside its own element, its life is simple. The swordfish passes its life in the open sea, finds its food beneath the waters, and probably takes no interest in what goes on outside. On the contrary, the basses and the trouts and the salmons spend a large part of their time near the shore, in shallow water, and have to look beyond the surface for both food and enemies. And when they do that, the lines of vision get bent, and things are no longer what they seem. Fish can see a man on the bank when, if man and fish were both in the air, the man would be hidden by the corner of the bank. For, if we replace our soap in a tub by a fish in a stream, we have the diagram on the following page.

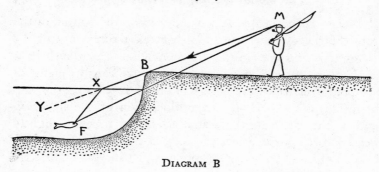

DIAGRAM B

Remember that it is now the light traveling from man toward fish which we wish to consider, for we are investigating what the fish sees, not what the man sees. The light travels along the path MX, just missing the top of the bank at B. If it were not for the refractive power of the water, it would continue on in the direction XY, passing over fish's back, and fish would not see man. But actually it gets bent at X, takes the new direction XF, and reaches fish's eye at F. Fish sees man, although the straight line from man to fish, MF, is cut off by the bank of the stream at B. The fish sees around a corner.

This is one basis for the argument which has sometimes been advanced that a fish can see a man before the man can see the fish. This overlooks the fact that the principle of refraction is reversible. The line of sight is equally bent going in both directions, and man sees around the same corner that fish does.

But that is not the end of the matter. Consider the diagram on the opposite page.

Here we again have both fish and man able to see each other around the corner of the bank B, because the line of sight is bent at X. But note the result. To man, fish appears to be along the prolongation of the line MX, at F'. To fish, man appears to be poised precariously at M', peering down

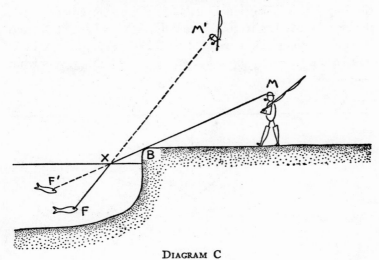

DIAGRAM C

at him along the line M'XF. Neither one is in reality where he appears to be to the other, and this makes it seem a real achievement on the part of both fisherman and fish when they succeed in connecting with one another. However, it is to be noted that when the fisherman's fly is on the water it is at one of those surface points X, which really are where they appear to be to both man and fish; and if the bait is an underwater lure, the fish sees it where it really is and it does not matter whether the fisherman does or not.

We now come to the heart of the whole matter, which is that, to the fish peering upward, the surface of the water is opaque except within a circle directly over its head. This circle alone is transparent. In other words, the surface of the water is to the fish an impenetrable ceiling with a circular transparent window in it. This is because of the phenomenon known as total refraction. For it is a characteristic of the refractive processes that the sharper the angle at which light approaches the surface, the greater the angle through which it is bent. Light going from water to air along the line FX in Diagram D is bent at X and proceeds in the direction XM. Light going from F to X′ is bent at X′ and continues along the horizontal X′H. The angle FX′H is more acute than the angle FXM. If, now, light travels from

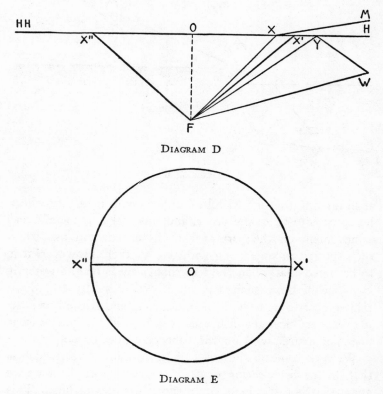

DIAGRAM D

DIAGRAM E

F to Y, the angle at which it approaches the surface is even sharper than that made by FX′, and the angle through which it is bent must be even sharper than the angle FX′H. The result is that it is bent back beneath the surface, and never gets out at all. This is total refraction. It is the same thing as reflection, for if we reverse our directions and consider the light traveling from an object at W toward Y, we find that it is bent back and goes toward F. In other words, the fish at F sees not only the object at W along the line FW, but it also sees the reflection of W, upside down, along the line FY. The surface outside the point X′, in addition to being an impenetrable ceiling, is a mirror.

The line FX′, then, marks the limit on one side, and the line FX″ on the other side, of light from above which can reach the fish. If we now place ourselves above the water and look down on it, we transfer ourselves from Diagram D to Diagram E. X′ and X″ become points on the rim of the circle, on the surface, through which the fish can see out into the air. The line X′X″ becomes a diameter of this circle, and the center is at O, directly above the fish. Outside the limits of that circle the surface is to the fish an impenetrable ceiling-mirror. The circle itself is the transparent window through which he sees. And the final effect of refraction is that the whole visible above-water world outside the circle becomes a border on the inner edge of that window.

To understand this, consider Diagram F. The horizontal lines, HX′ and HHX″ will become to the fish the lines FX′ and FX″ and will bound the visible world. Anything on the horizon, at H and HH, will appear to be in the prolongation of those lines. Anything above the horizon, like the bank B or the man M or the tree T, will appear to project inward from those lines. It is as if the surface of the water were a moving-picture screen with a circular picture thrown on it. If Diagram F is a cross-section of a round pool with the banks the same height all around, then what the fish sees as he looks up is roughly represented by the circle X′X″ sketched in Diagram G.

If you understand all this from reading it over once, well and good. You are fortunate in having that kind of a mind. If you do not understand, go and lie flat on your back, hold the book over your head, and look steadily at Diagram G. Forget all the rest, and just make believe that you are a

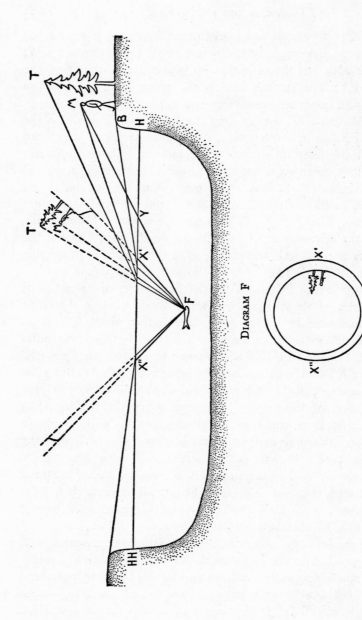

DIAGRAM F

DIAGRAM G

fish and that that is what is visible to you as you float effort-
lessly beneath the waters and cock an eye at the surface. If
this makes you dizzy, close your eyes for five minutes, then
skip to the next section. Or take a nice long walk.

However, if you feel capable of resuming the struggle,
consider Diagram H. The slope of the lines FX' and FX"
can never change. They mark the angle at which horizontal
light would be bent if it entered the water, and are im-

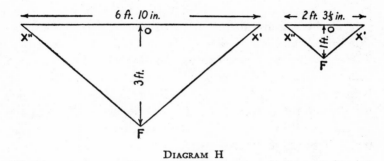

DIAGRAM H

mutably fixed by the laws of refraction. This means that the
angle X'FX" is unalterably fixed. It is slightly greater than
90 degrees. And *this* means that the size of the fish's circular
window will vary with his distance from the surface.

For, by all the laws of God and man, if the angle X'FX"
remains constant at a little over 90 degrees, the relation between OF and X'X" must remain constant, and X'X" must
always be a little more than twice as long as OF. If the fish
is three feet below the surface, his circular window is over
six feet in diameter; if he comes up to within one foot of
the surface his window shrinks to little more than two feet
in diameter (Diagram H). But, although the window actually shrinks, it appears to the fish to remain the same size,
for the apparent size of any object is governed by the angle
it subtends, which is why a pencil looks larger to you when
held just in front of your nose than at arm's length. We have

just said that the angle X'FX" of the fish's window is unalterably fixed; therefore the *apparent* size of his window is
unalterably fixed, no matter what his depth.

However, other things change as he changes his level.
Anything floating on the surface subtends a larger angle as
he approaches it and therefore appears to grow larger, even
as it would to us. A piece of wood two feet long and directly
overhead will be only about one-third the diameter of his
window when he is three feet down (Diagram H), but when
he rises to a one-foot depth, it will reach almost from one
side of the window to the other. Anything floating just inside the edge of his window—such as a boat with a man in it
—when he is, let us say, twelve feet down and his window is
about 26 feet in diameter, will be seen as one image: the
bottom of the boat clear and undistorted under water, and
the side of the boat and the man somewhat distorted above
water, but all in one continuous piece. When the fish rises to
a depth of three feet, his window will be only six feet in
diameter. The boat will no longer be within the circle of the
window. Its bottom will be clearly visible off to one side,
protruding through the ceiling-mirror, but the man will
appear in an entirely different spot, as part of the border of
his window somewhat as in Diagram G. The bottom of the
boat and the man will be completely dissociated.

Any object in the air directly overhead, such as a dragon-
fly hanging over the surface of the water, will appear to
grow larger as the fish rises, for the subtended angle will
increase, but a man standing on the bank will, so long as his
location is such that he is not included in the angle X'FX",
appear to shrink. He forms part of the border of the window,
as in Diagram G. As the fish comes closer to the surface, the
window will actually become smaller as we have seen, although retaining the same apparent size to the fish. The
man will remain part of the border of the window, but the
angle subtended by his image will, because of the workings

of the laws of refraction, become slightly less. He will, therefore, occupy a slightly smaller portion of the window, and
will appear to the fish to grow smaller.

And so we see that as the fish rises in the water objects
may appear to shrink or expand or remain the same size,
depending upon their location. To us, accustomed to having
all things grow larger as we approach them, smaller as we
withdraw from them, it seems as if the fish must have a
pretty cock-eyed idea of what the world is like; but as he is
used to it, it doubtless seems perfectly normal to him. Which
leads us to speculate as to what distortions there may be in
our own view of the universe, and how far it is from being
the "normal" which it appears to our eyes.

Theoretically the whole world above water, right out to
the horizon, is visible to the fish as a border on the inner
edge of his window, but under natural conditions this is not

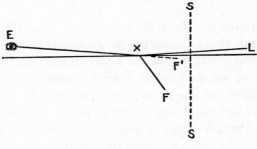

DIAGRAM J

entirely true. In the laboratory, an eye just above the surface at E clearly sees the object F, at a new position F′, if
there is a screen SS to cut off any light which might otherwise be coming from the direction L (Diagram J). You can
demonstrate this by sinking the cap of a toothpaste tube at
one end of the bathtub and placing your eye at the surface at
the other end, with the light behind you. On the other hand,
if light is coming from the direction L, so much of it is

reflected by the surface of the water toward your eye at
E that the object at F (or F′, its apparent position) is obliterated. This is what often happens in nature, and under these
circumstances a fish at F *might* be invisible to you on account of the light on the water while at the same time you
were visible to the fish. The compensating factor is that
when a ray of light approaches the water in a direction almost
parallel to the surface, as for instance the light traveling

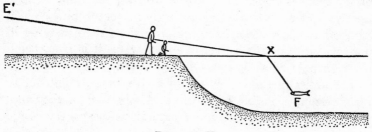

DIAGRAM K

from you to the fish along the line EX, most of it is reflected
back into the air by the surface at X, and only a very small
amount reaches the fish at F. To all intents and purposes,
you at E are invisible to the fish. It is only when light approaches the water at a steeper angle, as from E′ in Diagram
K, that enough of it enters the water to be visible at F.
There is, then, a limiting angle E′XF which constitutes
under natural conditions a kind of "blind spot" for the fish.
Anything below the line E′X is invisible, and that is why
you try to keep as low as possible when fishing. In the diagram, the whole upper half of the standing man is conspicuous, while only the top of the head of the kneeling man
is visible to the fish, although in neither case is there any
obstacle between man and fish.

The state of the water has also a very important bearing
on the situation. If the surface is smooth and flat, you seem
when you come out on the bank, to loom suddenly over

the fish, and every move you make is clearly visible in the round motion-picture on the screen above him. He naturally eyes you and your movements with distrust, and when the still, opaque, overhead mirror outside the circle is abruptly cut by your line reaching out toward him it is the last straw which sends him off to hide until normalcy is restored.

If there are waves, everything is changed. The surface is no longer a single refracting unit with a single round, unified picture of the world above, set in a mirror-ceiling. It becomes a great number of refracting units, all at different angles, and all changing all the time. Any particular part of the surface is at one moment horizontal, and refracting light as we have described; at the next it is tipped to one side by a wave, and the refraction is exaggerated; at the next it is tipped in the opposite direction, and the rays of light become normal to it, and suffer no refraction at all. Every object in the picture wobbles around in dizzy fashion. The opaque mirror-surface surrounding the circular window being also in motion, the things in it are bobbing around too. Further, parts of it are frequently being tipped by waves at angles normal to the light from the bank, and the fish gets a momentary glimpse of you as you really are—but entirely outside the circular frame in which he sees you when the water is calm. The result is that the whole ring of objects around the fish's circular window, the window itself, and the surrounding mirror-screen, are in an unceasing, wavering, shifting dance beyond the imagination of even the most extreme alcoholic among humans. The man and the tree on the bank are at M and T one second, at M' and T' the next (Diagram F); or they may be at both at the same instant, if there happen to be simultaneously a horizontal surface at X' and just the right kind of a wave at Y. And the same thing holds true in any stream with enough flow so that the surface angles are constantly being changed by the currents of water.

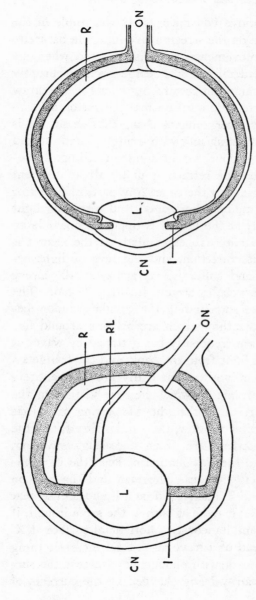

FIGURE 12. EYES, FISH AND HUMAN

On the left, a diagrammatic representation of the cross-section of the eye of the fish; on the right, that of the human. The lens (L), almost globular in the fish, is much flattened in the human. The cornea (CN), the iris (I), the optic nerve (ON), and the retina (R) occupy the same relative positions in each, but the retractor lentis (RL), which serves to move the lens of the fish toward or away from the retina to focus for varying distances is lacking in the human. This is because the human lens can be adjusted as to curvature, becoming flatter for faraway sight, more curved for near; whereas the lens of the fish is rigid and its curvature cannot be changed.

So, when the stream is flowing or there is a ripple on the pool, not only does your line cease to be conspicuous as it cuts the water, but you yourself, instead of being the active protagonist in a single, steady picture, become merely another moving object in a kaleidoscope of pictures, all of which are in constant motion.

So much for what is visible under water. The next question is, how much of what is visible is the fish capable of seeing?

The fish's eye is fundamentally very like our own (see Figure 12). It consists in essence of a curved lens inside a transparent covering called a cornea, both of which bend the incoming light rays so as to form an image on a screen composed of sensitive rods and cones called a retina. From the retina this image is carried to the brain by the optic nerve. Every word said so far would apply equally well to the human eye, and yet there are between the fish's visual machinery and ours two minor differences, two major differences, and one surprising resemblance.

Starting from the outside, the first difference is that the fish has no true eyelids. This seems to us like a very uncomfortable state of affairs, for we are not able to go for more than a few seconds without bringing our lids down across our eyes. If we did not do this, the surface of the eye would become dry, dirt would collect on it, and we should not be able to see. This constant moistening and cleaning of the cornea is a more essential function of our lids than the one we are likely to think of first, the closing of our eyes in sleep. Our lids are more important to see with than to sleep with.

But the fish lives under water. Water is in constant contact with the surface of its eye, and keeps it constantly moist and clean. It therefore has no need of a lid. And the truth of all this is demonstrated by the Central American four-eyed fish *Anableps*. This creature has eyes divided into two sections, one for seeing in the air and one for seeing in water. Lying habitually at the surface so that the upper half of each eye is in the air, it has to duck its head under water every few moments to freshen up that exposed portion of the eye.

One of the features of the lid in our eyes is the lachrymal gland. This furnishes the moisture for the proper working of the eye, and also furnishes tears for us when we wish to weep. The fish has no lachrymal gland, and it therefore cannot weep. It is of interest that the human infant cannot weep until it is several weeks old. It can bawl, but not produce tears. No, I am not calling your baby a fish; I am merely pointing out another of the reasons why the biogenetic law fascinates biologists.

The second difference in the fish's eye is that there is little or no provision for altering the amount of light that enters the pupil. The iris, the colored ring, in our eyes can widen or shrink, leaving only a pin-point in the center when the light is bright, or exposing practically the whole lens when the light is very dim. The fish also has an iris, the metallic-looking ring around the dark circular center, but this iris is practically incapable of movement. Teleologically speaking, we might say that that is because the light under water never attains such brilliance as to make protection against it necessary.

The next thing which we meet on our way into the fish's eye is the lens, and here we encounter a major difference. Our lens is comparatively flat. It is in shape not unlike the common hand magnifying-glass or "reading-glass." The fish's lens is spherical (see Figure 12). Where our lens is a disk, the fish's lens is a globe. It is, in fact, that unappetizing little white ball which you sometimes find rolling around on your plate when a whole fish is served to you. The lens has come

out of the eye, and in the processes of death and cooking has
lost its transparency.

The eye, in both man and fish, is filled with transparent
substances. The light, passing from air into these substances,
is refracted and forms an image on our retina, just as it forms
an image after passing through the lens of a camera. But in
the case of the fish, the light passes not from air into the
lens, but from water into the lens. It is obvious that light
passing from water into water will not be refracted. The
substance inside the eye is of almost the same density as
water. Therefore, in passing from water into the eye light
undergoes much less refraction than in passing from air into
the eye. This is why our vision is blurred when we open our
eyes under water. Our lens mechanisms, adequate for forming an image from light-rays passing into the dense substance of the eye from air, are not sufficiently curved to bend
the rays into a sharp image when they pass into the dense
substance of the eye from the scarcely less dense water. To
overcome the difficulty, the fish curves the lens more. He
goes the limit in degree of curvature, and uses a spherical
lens, but even at that some authorities doubt whether he
succeeds in bringing the light to a proper focus and in producing a really clear picture on his retina. And for the same
reason that our vision is blurred when our eyes are under
water, we are justified in assuming that the fish cannot see
clearly when his eyes are in the air. His lens mechanism is
designed to handle light coming through water, not light
coming through air.

To accommodate our eyes to varying distances—in other
words, to bring the rays of light from any object to a focus
on the retina, no matter how far away the object—we are
able to change the curvature of our lens. For long range we
make it flatter, for short range more curved. But the fish
needs all the curvature possible, all the time. If he flattened

the lens he would not get enough refraction. Further, perhaps because of this fact, his lens is not elastic like ours. It is rigid and its curvature cannot be changed. The only means left to the fish to accommodate for varying distances is to move his lens toward or away from the retina, just as a camera lens is moved toward or away from the plate. To do this, he has a special muscle, the retractor lentis. By means of this muscle the distance between the lens and the retina can be varied. For long-range vision the lens is brought nearer to the retina than for short range.

Now, all muscles expect to be allowed to rest when not in use. It is customary for them to spend their time off in a relaxed condition. In the human eye, the apparatus is so designed that when the small muscles which control the curvature of the lens are relaxed, the lens is at its flattest, and is, therefore, set for distant vision. In the fish, when the retractor lentis relaxes, the lens remains in the forward position, and is thus set for near-by vision. And all this is very proper and fitting. For air is a medium through which light travels a long way, and man is expected to have his eyes on the horizon, whereas water permits light to travel only a short way, and the fish is expected to concentrate on near-by details. The fish goes poking around in the immediate foreground with his little round lenses way out at the front ends of his eyes, as far from the retina as he can get them, and when he wants to look into the distance he has to haul them in by means of the retractor lentis, like toy balloons on a string. A German observer goes so far as to claim that he has actually been able to see this back-and-forth movement of the lens in the large eyes of trigger-fish in aquaria.

The surprising resemblance which we spoke of between the fish's visual machinery and the human's is that in each the eyeball is moved by the same set of six muscles. For the fish does move its eyes, although very much less than we do. The reader's surprise is expected to be caused by three facts. First, that each eye needs as many as six muscles to bring about such slight movements as it makes; second, that the fish, with its otherwise elementary muscular system, could develop such complicated musculature; and third, that the same six muscles, controlled by the same nerves, act in just the same way to move the eye of the human as to move the eye of the fish, in spite of the fact that in every other way the human muscular system is so much more advanced than that of the fish.

So far we have found no basic difference between the eyes of fish and human. The human has made additions and improvements. He has added the eyelid. He has perfected the iris-diaphragm for governing the amount of light. He has adapted the lens to his environment, and altered the mechanism whereby it accommodates for distance. But he has not changed the basic principle of a lens focusing light so as to form an image on a sensitive screen. We are, therefore, up to this point, able to form a pretty clear conception of how the fish's apparatus works. It is merely an earlier model of the same machine we are using.

We now come to a difference so fundamental that it will probably never be possible for science fully to explain its significance. It has to do with the placing of the eyes, and their connection with the brain. Our eyes face in the same direction, the fish's eyes face in almost diametrically opposite directions. Each of our eyes is connected with both right and left sides of the brain; each of the fish's eyes is connected with only one side of the brain. So little experimental work and so many essays in pure theory have been produced on this question that it is permissible for us to do a little theorizing of our own, provided we keep firmly in mind that much of what follows is hypothesis.

In the first place, it is necessary for us to understand that one of the striking features of the vertebrates is that many nerves cross from one side of the body to the other. The nerves from the organs of touch in your left hand, for instance, go to the right side of your brain. The fish applies this principle faithfully to his eyes: the right eye connects with the left side of the brain, and vice versa. All the fibers of the right optic nerve cross those of the left on the way from the eye to the brain and this is called *complete* decussation (complete crossing).

In the human, this has been changed. The nerve tract from the left eye starts out toward the right side of the

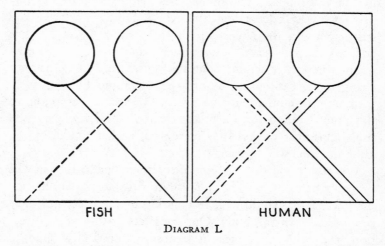

FISH   HUMAN

DIAGRAM L

brain in orthodox fashion, but when it gets to the point where it should cross the tract from the right eye, some of its fibers turn aside from their course, join the other tract, and end in the left side of the brain. The remaining fibers continue in the original direction and end in the right side of the brain (see Diagram L). This is called *incomplete* decussation of the optic nerves.

Complete decussation is found in those animals in which

the eyes typically face in different directions—in which, to be technical, the optic axes are not parallel. This includes the fish, the amphibians, the reptiles, and the birds. In the mammals, the nerve-fibers begin to stray even in those forms where the eyes look in opposite directions, and as the lines of sight become more nearly parallel, more and more of them are affected. In the horse a small fraction fail to decussate, in the cat the number is larger, and by the time we reach the higher apes we find half of them leaving the path on which they started and joining the tract from the other eye. These being animals which left the ground some aeons ago to seek safety in the trees, this arrangement of the nerves and the placing of the eyes so that both face in the same direction are thought to provide the unerring judgment of distance needed in swinging from limb to limb, and are termed an "arboreal adaptation." The phrase is suggestively descriptive, but does not tell us how the machinery works.

It is not difficult to cook up a theory which explains everything. In animals whose eyes face in diametrically opposite directions, each eye has a separate field of vision. Anything on the animal's left side is seen by the left eye only, and its presence is therefore signaled to the right side of the brain. In man, the two eyes face in the same direction. Anything to the left, unless very far to the left, is seen by both eyes. If decussation were complete, it would be signaled to both sides of the brain, which might cause confusion. If, however, fibers from that part of each retina which registers objects on the left go only to the right side of the brain, the original system is restored. Objects to the left register on the right half of each retina. Nerve-fibers from the right half of the right retina, as well as from the right half of the left retina, must therefore go to the right side of the brain in order to register in that side of the brain objects seen to the left—in other words, objects affecting the side of the body which is under

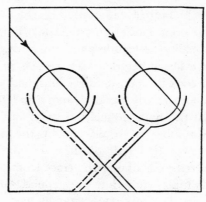

DIAGRAM M

its jurisdiction. By this system the images are allocated to the two halves of our brain in the same way in which they would be if our eyes were placed so that each saw only one side, and if decussation were complete. The incomplete decussation is a compensation for the fact that the two eyes now see the same thing.

Having concocted this theory, we are at liberty to shoot holes in it. The first hole comes of the fact that, although the fish's two eyes face in different directions, those directions, in many fish, are not diametrically opposite, and there is a small section of the world which both of them see at the same time. This statement is based on theoretical deduction, for obviously no one knows just what a fish's eyes see. But the placing of most fishes' eyes and the extent to which they protrude permit us to argue as follows.

As we look down on the fish (Diagram N), the field of vision of the right eye, E', is bounded by its side and by its nose. The limiting lines of sight are E'B and E'C, and the whole field between those two lines, comprising a little more than a half circle, is visible to the right eye. Similarly, the

field of vision of the left eye is limited by the lines E"D and
E"A. But these two fields overlap. Anything within the
limits AOC is visible to both eyes. In other words, AOC is
a common field of vision for the two eyes. It is a very much
smaller common field than we have. Ours varies around 90
degrees, depending on our features. If our eyes are far apart
and our nose is flat, it is larger; if our eyes are close together
and our nose high, it is smaller. A dish-faced person can see

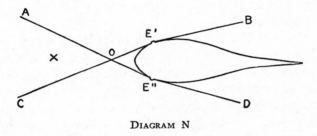

DIAGRAM N

more than a hawk-nosed one. In the fish, the nose is very
large, and the position of the eyes gives him no help in seeing around it. His common field of vision is small. In the
trout it is probably somewhere in the neighborhood of 30
degrees. In some species it is much less. But whatever it is,
anything within that field of vision is visible to both eyes.
And it seems probable, using the same line of reasoning, that
this field extends upward as well as forward, and that the fish
sees with both eyes whatever is directly over his head.

While all this is theoretical, observation bears it out. If a
piece of food is at the point X in Diagram N, the fish approaches it directly. He does not turn his head to one side to
look at it. This means that he must be able to see what is
directly in front of him. If he can see what is in front of him
with one eye, he can obviously see it with the other eye also,
and there must be a common field of vision.

Having proved this to our own satisfaction, what of it? Just this. Any object to the fish's right, outside the lines AOE'B, is seen by the right eye only, and its image is sent to the left side of the brain. Any object to the fish's left, outside the lines COE''D, is seen by the left eye only, and its image is sent to the right side of the brain. But any object within the angle AOC is seen by both eyes, and its image is sent to both sides of the brain. The fish's visual sensations are divided into two distinct classes: one occurring in one side of the brain *or* the other, and one occurring in both sides of the brain simultaneously.

We are now in a position to ask ourselves a lot of questions many of which we cannot answer. In the first place, do the two classes of sensations make different final impressions on the fish's consciousness? Is an object on one side of him, producing an image in only one eye and stimulating only one half of his brain, seen less clearly than the same object when it is directly in front, seen by both eyes and stimulating both halves of the brain? We are all familiar with the way in which a fish whirls, when something appears to one side or the other, and brings itself head on. Does not this mean that the single image so produced is inadequate, merely a signal that there is something which needs more thorough examination, and that it is necessary to bring both eyes to bear on it to see it really well? And if this is so, of what use are the large portions of each eye through which come the single images produced by objects to the right and left of the common field?

You can obtain some of the answers by an experiment performed without getting out of your chair, and with apparatus no more complex than your own finger. Close your left eye and hold your finger, at a comfortable distance away and on a level with your eyes, at a point as far to the left as you can see it distinctly. Then without moving the finger, open the left and close the right eye. You still see the finger (in fact, even more distinctly, since it is nearer to the center of your visual field). This proves that the finger in that position is in the common field of vision, and that when both eyes are open both see it and send messages to both sides of your brain. But when the left eye is closed, and the right eye alone sees it, it is registering only on the right side of the right retina, and the message is being sent only to the right side of your brain (see Diagram M). Is the final impression on your consciousness when the image is being registered on only one side of your brain different from when it is being registered on both? Essentially, no; but there is one difference which is important, and that is that when both eyes see the object you are able to make a much quicker and more accurate estimate of its distance, especially if there is no light and shade, and no other object in view, to guide your judgment. And here we have the answer to why the fish turns head on to an object it wishes to examine: in order to estimate its distance. The large portions of each eye through which come the single images produced by things to the right and left of the common field serve to keep the fish informed of what is going on over a wide area—perhaps to warn of approaching danger; but he must bring an object into the common field if he wants to obtain his best estimate of its distance—as would be the case with something he wanted to pounce on and eat.

The next question is, if seeing a thing with both eyes improves judgment of distance, why have not the rays and the flatfishes taken advantage of the opportunity offered by their peculiar bodily shape to locate their eyes in such a position as to have a large common field? (See Figure 29.) Instead of this, each eye, in many of them at least, is surrounded by a socket or mounted on a stalk in such a way as to be cut off from what the other eye can see. And, as if to emphasize their indifference to a common field of vision, the flounder's eyes move independently. They swivel around without any regard for each other, whereas most fishes' eyes move in unison, as ours do, swinging to the right or the left at the same time. This means that, in a fish like the trout, the left eye moves toward the front and center at the same time that the right eye moves toward the rear and out. If it is directly in front of him, in the common field, that the trout sees best, as we proved to ourselves a little further back, why are not his eyes arranged so that both move toward the front and center at the same time? Just another one of those questions which no one can answer. It is no wonder that people end in a daze when they try to puzzle out the fish's optical apparatus, and find themselves setting forth as their conclusion the very fact which started them on their investigation, namely: that the fish's eyes are different from ours, and very hard to understand.

We have, however, gained one thing. We are now in a position to appreciate the point of view of those who claim that fish do not see very well, and to appraise the validity of their arguments. Such people think that the unvarying amount of light admitted by the unvarying iris must be unfavorable to distinctness of vision. They maintain that the globular lens, with its back-and-forth system of adjustment, cannot be capable of bringing light to a proper focus and of producing a clear image on the retina. And they question whether fish can judge distance with anything like our speed and accuracy. For it is now believed by leading authorities that our partial decussation is a device for putting our oculomotor apparatus in control of the pair of images and making it responsible for the co-ordination of eye movements which is essential for precise and rapid estimation of distances. The fish's eyes, as we have seen, do not work in that way.

These arguments are not without logic, but they are theoretical. They are based on differences in the structure of fish and human visual machinery, and such a base is not always a safe one. Rather than reply theoretically, with the same lack of safety, let us see what factual evidence we can find on the other side. Controlled experiments being few in number and limited in scope, we shall fall back on observation. What can we tell about how much fish see from what they do in the course of their daily lives?

Star witness for the defense is *Toxotes jaculator*. This is a little fish which lives in Siam. It earns its living by knocking insects off twigs above the surface with a drop of water which it shoots from its mouth. How it does this is an interesting matter for speculation, but we are trying to shun theory now. The fact is that it does succeed in shooting down insects as much as three feet above the surface. This, it seems to me, is good proof of three things: that *Toxotes* sees objects in the air with considerable distinctness, or he could not tell the insect from the twig; that he has an excellent sense of direction; and that his judgment of distance is not at all bad.

So much for what the fish can see in the air. Now for some light on what he can see under water. The witness with which I happen to be best acquainted is the jewel-fish already mentioned in Chapter III. This fish is unpopular with tropical-fish fanciers on account of his bad temper, but popular with seekers after information because he lives and breeds unconcernedly in an aquarium and can thus be easily observed. He is among the few fishes which feel some responsibility about their children. He has several hundred at a time, each less than one-quarter of an inch long when they begin to swim, and he and his mate ride herd over their flock, driving off intruders, and picking up any stragglers in their mouths and spitting them out unharmed into the middle of the band. If you take a few of these young ones, anesthetize them until they are absolutely motionless, and lay them on the bottom of the tank, they are indistinguishable to the human eye from the sand and debris collected there, but not to the jewel. He picks them up and carries them back to where they belong. Further, there is another species of cichlid whose habits are the same, and whose young are so much like the jewel in shape, size, and marking, that they are difficult to tell apart without a microscope. If you take ten of the jewel's children away from the flock, and a moment later return to a different part of the tank five baby jewels and five of the other species, he will take them, one by one, into his mouth to carry them back to where they belong. Then, if you watch closely, you will see that each jewel is spat out into the bosom of the family, but the little strangers go into his mouth never to emerge. Instead of joining the little jewels, they become part of a big jewel. And what is more, even if both sets of young are rendered motionless by anesthesia, to eliminate any telltale responses, he can still tell them apart. That sight is the sense which operates here, and not smell, has been demonstrated by experiments which we do not need to go into. It is hard to believe that there are any blurred lines in the picture on the jewel's retina.

Let us now consider the trout. The trout unquestionably sees the fly before it hits the water. One method of attracting his attention, in dry-fly fishing, is to make false casts just over him, without allowing the fly to come down. He has been known to leap out of the water after the fly, and, although it is always dangerous to apply what is known of one species to another, this indicates that he has at least some of the abilities of *Toxotes* when it comes to seeing things above the surface. As for flies *on* the surface, we all know that he has not only extremely keen perception in telling one from another, but also extremely good judgment of distance. To be sure, we have all seen a trout miss a fly that it rose for, but it must be remembered that the fish is moving, the water is moving, and the fly is sometimes moving also. The preponderant number of times that the trout does take the fly seems to me proof of its ability to judge distance. Its eye may have technical faults, but it does the work.

To sum up, we find that the testimony of these three species refutes the charges against the fish. The acuteness of its vision is considerable, at least at close range, and it seems probable that distinctness of vision at long range is not important, for even in the clearest water light travels but a comparatively short way, and far objects are hidden from sight. Of what use is the ability to distinguish things a quarter of a mile away if there is such a haze that they become invisible at a distance of one hundred feet? It may well be that the fish cannot focus properly for long range, and that distant objects are blurs which become evident to it only by their movement. Certainly movement plays a very important part in attracting its attention—as is true of all animals, including ourselves. In any case, once it has become aware of a distant object, it approaches it; and once it has come close to it, it is able to see it very distinctly. For extremely close work its vision is apparently better than ours, for it seems to see clearly an object within an inch of its nose, which we do not. And this is important to it, for it must bring its eyes very close to whatever it eats.

As to judgment of distance the testimony is not so clear, but it is still favorable. And, after all, consider a bird like the phoebe. The location of its eyes and their connections with the brain are very much the same as the fish's, and yet no one doubts its distance judgment because its eyes are not arranged the way ours are. Birds are easier to observe than fish, and everyone knows that when a phoebe darts after a moving insect in the air, its beak comes together with a snap not behind its prey or in front of its prey, but on it.

We have not yet said a word about a very important point. Can fish tell color? There have been more experiments on this than on any other phase of the fish's vision, and hotter debate, and the answer is, Yes, at least in so far as the fisherman is concerned.

Color experimentation can be very simple. Aquarium fish have been taught to take food when offered on blue forceps, avoid it when offered on red. Native fish at the Tortugas have been taught to come to a certain place for feeding, and to take food when dyed one color, but not another color. The method in each case is to make the food associated with the undesired color in some way unpalatable, and the assumption is that it is the fish's discrimination between the two colors which enables him to leave the unpalatable food alone.

One of the prettiest demonstrations of color discrimination was offered by the aforementioned jewel. The young of this species, while still in the herding stage, will assemble around the parent if the latter gives a sharp, quick movement of the fins. The parent at this stage is bright red. In a closely related species, *Cichlasoma bimaculatum*, the young will obey the same signal, but the outstanding color of the parent at this stage is an intense, very dark blue. A small tank was rigged up with two metal disks, one just outside the glass at each end. One was red, the other dark blue. By means of a mechanism, the disks were made to give periodic sharp jerks. If young jewels were put in the tank they soon assembled at the end where the red disk was in operation. If cichlasomas were put in the tank, they assembled at the blue end. If both were in the tank at the same time, they separated out at the blue and red ends very nicely according to species.

And if the disks were reversed, the blue being moved to where the red had been and *vice versa,* two mass migrations took place. The little jewels swam across the tank to their red foster-parent, and the cichlasomas took the place where the jewels had been, now in front of the blue disk.

Why, in the face of such evidence, is there any question that fish can tell color? Because of the possibility that it is brightness, rather than color, which is distinguished. If a certain red gives off more light than a certain blue, then it may be difference in brightness which enables the fish to tell one from the other, rather than difference in color. And even if apparatus is used to provide colors of equal brightness-value, the die-hards are not satisfied, maintaining that there is no justification for believing that two colors have the same brightness-value to the fish eye just because they have to the human eye.

However, recent experiments have offered convincing proof that actual color rather than brightness is the determining value for at least one species—the large-mouth black bass. These experiments were of the conditioned response type, the fish being trained to associate one color with reward —food—and another color with punishment—in this case a mild electric shock. Young black bass one to two inches long lived for weeks in white enameled basins six inches across, one to each basin. They were fed on daphnia ("water fleas") and mosquito larvae, which were presented to them in what scientists call pipettes and normal people call eye-droppers. Opaque pipettes were used of different colors: the red pipette, let us say, always contained daphnia, the yellow one did not; if the fish approached the red he got food, if he approached the yellow he got a warning shock. The question was: could the fish distinguish between the two colors, and learn to keep away when the yellow pipette entered the water? Of course, other colors were used also; and to take care of the brightness factor, each color was finally tested against a whole range of grays, from pure white to absolute black—probably a more conclusive method than trying to measure the brightness values of different colors and equate them.

One of the first findings was that the untrained black bass, before conditioning had started, had a strong preference for red over all other colors, with yellow in second place. To the bass angler this means that a red lure has the best chance of attracting his prey, with yellow a second choice. As the experiments proceeded, it developed that the fish learned quickly, from five to ten trials being enough for them to get the idea; and furthermore that they learned more quickly to avoid the color which brought the electric shock than to approach the one that brought food. In the words of the report, they "learn more quickly to avoid an unpleasant stimulus than to react positively to a pleasant one." In terms of survival value in the wild, this is understandable: one single failure to avoid death (presumably unpleasant) is fatal, whereas failure to approach food (presumably pleasant) may be repeated quite often without bringing the end.

Memory played a part in the experiments. The fish showed almost perfect retention of what they had learned from one day to the next, and some were able to go for a week without a lesson and still make the proper response when tested. Vision through the surface film was demonstrated: as soon as the "food color" appeared above the basin, the well tutored little fish made a dash for the place where it customarily entered the water.

In the end, the experiments proved that the bass could tell red from any other color with the exception of violet, and was almost equally sure on yellow. Greens and blues were the hardest for him to distinguish from each other and from black. Brightness was proved to play no part, for not only was he able to tell the training red from any of the shades of gray, but if he were offered some other shade of red, he would choose that rather than any of the grays. Without any indoctrination, he was aware that there was a relationship between red and pink which did not exist for red and gray! And the final conclusion was that the black bass responds in color vision about like a normal human being looking through a pair of yellowish glasses.

At this point we must remember that species differ, and that other fish may not be able to do what the black bass can. Black bass and trout are as far apart in the taxonomic scale as, for instance, man and dog. Dog can smell odors that man cannot, and man can see colors that dog cannot. Black bass may be able to see colors that trout cannot; and while we know from experience that trout do have what *appears* to be color discrimination, we have no experimental proof that in this case it is not actually a matter of *brightness* discrimination.

However, to the fisherman this brightness question is academic. To him, it does not matter how the fish tells two colors apart. The main point is that two colors which look different to him look different to the fish also. The fish can tell a blue fly from a red fly. That being the case, it is important for him to have both a blue fly and a red fly, and flies of various other colors and combinations of colors in his book. He has an excellent excuse for stocking up with the various patterns which the tackle store offers, for the fish can tell them apart, and what the fish like one day, or in one stream, they may not like another day, or in another stream. But it is possible that none of this applies to dry flies, or to wet flies fished dry. For when a fly is *on* the surface, with the strong light behind it, it is doubtful if the fish can see its color. Even man cannot tell the color of a small object held directly against a strong light. It becomes just a black silhouette. It is probable that it is only when a lure is *beneath* the surface that its color can be told.

Finally we come to a question which has little to do with the eyes except that, in man's mind and through man's habit, it is associated with them. Do fish sleep? The answer is, Yes —at least certain species—if the opinions of the majority of scientific observers are to be accepted. After all, why should the mere fact that a fish has no lids with which to close its eyes make us question that it sleeps? We have no way of closing our ears, and yet we sleep. Sleep is a state in which, among other things, our conscious minds are temporarily disconnected from the outside world. If we can sleep in spite of the messages which our ears are continually sending in to headquarters—and which, in a large city, are neither few nor faint—why cannot a fish sleep in spite of the messages which its eyes send in? It is all a question of what you are accustomed to. Fish do sleep. Some sleep suspended in the water, some rest erect on the bottom, some lie on their sides on the bottom. The "Slippery Dick" (*Iridio bivittata*), a small Bermuda wrasse, literally goes to bed and pulls the covers over its head. Put one into a tank with a sand bottom, and go back at night and switch on a light, and there is no fish to be seen. You have to look very closely to find the small crater in the tiny volcanic peak of sand, quietly rising and falling as your fish breathes, which marks the gill opening. And if you watch this disappearing act, you find that it is almost like a magician's trick: the fish dives slantingly into the sand, gives a couple of strong wiggles with its tail, and is lost to sight.

As usual, the sharks require a separate paragraph. In three particulars, their eyes differ from those of the bony fishes. The lens is set for distant rather than near-by vision, and in some species cannot be moved. The amount of light entering the eye can to a certain extent be controlled. And there exists a kind of eyelid, called a nictitating membrane, which contracts into the forward angle of the eye when not in use. The little red triangle in the inner corner of the human eye is a vestige of the same apparatus. Just what the shark does with it is something no one seems to know.

HEARING

For a long, long time, people looked at fish, saw no ears, nodded their heads, and repeated, "Fish cannot hear." Then a Benedictine monk at a place called Krems, in Austria, started keeping trout in a pond. Being of a romantic nature, he rang a dinner-bell when he fed them. Before very long he found out that, whenever he stood at the edge of the pond and swung his bell, the fish gathered for their meal. Experimental evidence of the simplest and seemingly most conclusive sort that fish could hear. Then came a skeptic. He stood on the bank, swung his arm in the air, but left the dinner-bell in the house. The hungry fish gathered for their meal just the same. Experimental evidence of the simplest and seemingly most conclusive sort that it was the sight of a man on the bank swinging his arm, and not the sound of the bell, which attracted the fish. And ever since, people have been debating whether fish hear.

The differences of opinion have been due to differences in structure. Man indisputably has an ear, a visible feature on the side of his head which acts as a funnel to collect sound-waves coming through the air. This is called the outer ear. From it a passage leads to the middle ear. Here are located the ear-drum, which is set in vibration by the sound-waves, and the ossicles, the three little bones poetically named anvil, hammer, and stirrup, which transmit those vibrations to the inner ear. The inner ear is the indispensable part of the machine. It is a capsule filled with fluid and surrounded by bone. It contains two very different mechanisms. One is the beautiful and delicate spiral cochlea, in which takes place the actual transformation of sound-waves into nervous impulses. It is attached to a sac-like region

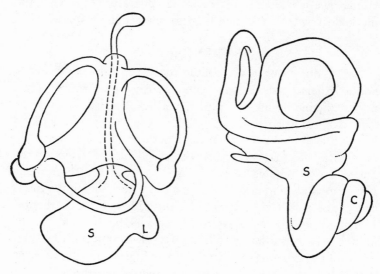

FIGURE 13. EARS, FISH AND HUMAN

On the left is the inner ear of the fish, on the right that of the human. Both possess the three semicircular canals, but the cochlea (C), the organ in which sounds are actually transformed into nerve impulses for the human, is missing in the ear of the fish, being represented only by a process of the sacculus (S) called the lagena (L). This is one of the reasons why many people have doubted that fish hear in the same sense that humans do. (Fish ear from Wiedersheim, *Comparative Anatomy of the Vertebrates*, by permission of the Macmillan Company, publishers. Human ear redrawn from Martin, *The Human Body*, Henry Holt and Company.)

called the sacculus. The other is composed of the three semi-circular canals, connected to another sac called the utriculus, which serves to keep us standing upright and going straight ahead. Our ear, therefore, has two functions, hearing and equilibration (Figure 13).

The fish has no outer ear. It has no middle ear. It does have an inner ear, embedded in the bones of the skull. That inner ear has the three semicircular canals, and the utriculus and sacculus, but it has no spiral cochlea. The nearest thing to it is a small projection of the sacculus called the lagena, which has approximately the same location as the cochlea, but none of its delicate machinery.

Water is a much more positive conductor of sound-waves than air. Therefore, the absence of an outer ear and a middle ear would not in themselves preclude the possibility of the fish hearing, for the sound-waves might impinge directly on the skull with enough power to be sensed. Our ear-drum and its ossicles are only mechanisms to transmute the sound-waves in air into sound-waves in the liquid of the inner ear, and the fish does not need them because its ear is already in a liquid, the water.

But the absence of the spiral cochlea is another matter. It is this which furnished ammunition for those who did not believe that fish hear. The cochlea, they pointed out, is in us the ultimate instrument for hearing. The fish has no cochlea, therefore it does not hear. Because two things are not alike, they cannot produce the same result. This is doubtful logic, and experimental results fail to support it.

Complete proof of hearing came from a series of experiments on goldfish in which great care was taken to meet the objections which had been raised against previous demonstrations. For instance, it had been argued that such noises as are made by tapping on a tank, or by placing a tuning-fork against the side of the tank, are not heard by the fish, but sensed by him through the skin in the same way we feel the sound when we place our hand on a piano. It is probably true that some sounds, especially of a sharp or explosive nature, do reach the fish in this way. To circumvent this possibility, the experimenter took a small balloon, placed a telephone instrument in it, and submerged the whole thing in water. Next he defined hearing in fish. "Any disturbance," he said, "that produces hearing through the human ear . . . calls forth hearing in fish if it acts through the ear and not simply through the skin or some other organ." Having cleared the atmosphere of quibbling, he was ready to go ahead with his experiment.

He produced on his instrument a series of tones beginning with 43 double vibrations per second, and going up through 86, 172, and so on, doubling the number each time. He found that *normal* goldfish responded to all vibrations from 43 to 2,752—a much smaller range than that of our hearing, which extends from 30 to 30,000, with middle C at 256. He then performed some operations—and this, incidentally, is a simple matter in fish. All that is necessary is to place a little of some anesthetic, like urethane, in the water, and when the fish go to sleep, cut them up. No sterilization of instruments or other complicated antisepsis is necessary because their insides are very resistant to infection. He first removed the sacculus, with its lagena—which, you recall, is the nearest approach in fish to a spiral cochlea. This destroyed response to 1,376 and 2,752 double vibrations per second. He next removed the utriculus, and found that this destroyed response to 344 and 688. Conclusion: vibrations from 344 to 2,752 are sensed by the ear and, therefore, heard. But with both of these organs gone, the fish still responded to 43, 86, and 172, and he concluded that these lower frequencies came through the skin or the lateral line, and were thus by definition excluded from hearing. Tests on the catfish showed that it received vibrations only up to 688, and that below 172 the skin played a part. In the weakfish, it was found that removal of the utriculus and its three semicircular canals made practically no difference in hearing, but that elimination of the sacculus did.

And from a noted German physiologist there came in 1938 reports of experiments along the same lines as those just described. Working with a European minnow (*Phoxinus laevis*) and with one of the common catfishes (*Ameiurus nebulosus*), he corroborated in general the earlier findings and, with improved techniques and more sensitive methods, proved that the range of hearing was even greater than had been thought. The upper limit of his minnow's ear was at 7,000 vibrations per second (A^5), while his catfish reached 13,000—almost as high as in human beings. Furthermore, in conditioned response experiments, the minnows showed tone-discriminating ability, intervals as small as. one-half tone being distinguished by the most musically gifted of the subjects! If, without the cochlea, such fine distinctions are possible, what purpose does our beautiful spiral serve? Possibly the quality or timbre of the sound, regardless of its position in the diatonic scale, is what this organ registers; possibly without it the high C in the most gifted soprano's aria would sound no better to us than the same note in a donkey's bray.

The German investigators also found out that hearing was more acute in those fishes in which the ear is connected in one way or another to the air-bladder, but this matter will be treated in the chapter to be devoted to that organ. Suffice it to say at this point that we have incontrovertible proof that at least certain species of fish, including the catfish, minnow, eel, goldfish, and weakfish, do hear. The sacculus with its lagena plays the important part, and this is borne out by analogy with the amphibians. And a conclusion that we may permit ourselves is that if these species can hear without a spiral cochlea, it is perfectly possible that trout, bass, tarpon, and tuna hear without a spiral cochlea also.

The question which inevitably arises at this point is, why

do fish hear? The concept is general that, except in the shallows, sounds are rare beneath the surface. Sounds made in the air do enter the water to some extent, but only with difficulty. They tend to bounce back off its surface, and the only fish which seem to pay much attention to them are the group just mentioned in which hearing is reinforced by the air-bladder—a group made up largely of shallow-water dwellers. In the shallows, hearing can understandably be useful to fish. But what about the fishes of the open sea, those whose lives are passed in what we had been led to believe was the all-pervading hush of the subsurface ocean, untroubled by the rush of winds, undisturbed by the roar of waves, and beyond the reach of man-made noises? The truth is that the all-pervading hush turns out to be a myth, and that the subsurface ocean is a pretty noisy place.

An emphatic and practical demonstration of this fact occurred during the war. Our Navy developed a highly sensitive instrument for detecting the noise of submarines under water, and was about to put it triumphantly into service when they found that it picked up so many other sounds that the submarines could not be identified. Most of these noises were made by submarine animals, and it was not until they had learned to screen out these sounds that they were able to use the instrument against submarine vessels. But that there are plenty of noises for the oceanic fish to hear can no longer be doubted.

Our constant exceptions, the sharks and rays, have auditory apparatus as complete as the other fish, but hear poorly. This is to be expected, for their skulls are cartilage, not bone. Bone is a good conductor of sound, cartilage is not. It would be only with difficulty that sound-waves could make their way through it to the inner ear.

The sharks and rays have a spiracle, inherited from the common Palaeozoic ancestor, but absent in most other present-day fishes. This is a hole in the top of their heads which leads by a passage to the mouth. It is an accessory of their breathing-system, and has nothing to do with their hearing. In the course of evolution, however, it has become part of the auditory apparatus, for the higher animals have made from it the cavity of the middle ear, and the passage called the Eustachian tube which leads from the inside of the ear-drum to an opening in the throat. The business of this tube is to keep the pressure on the two sides of the ear-drum the same. Its lower end, in the throat, is closed except during the act of swallowing. When your ear-drums feel funny going through the Holland Tunnel, it is because atmospheric pressure under the Hudson River is greater than the atmospheric pressure on New York streets. The former is on the outside of your ear-drum; the latter, brought in by you, is on the inside; and the ear-drum has to keep the two apart. When you swallow, the Hudson River atmosphere enters the Eustachian tube, the pressure on the two sides of the drum is equalized, and you are a happier and healthier man than if the shark had no spiracle.

And while we are on this trend of thought, it is of note that the little bones called the hammer, anvil, and stirrup which transmit the vibrations from our ear-drums to our inner ears are modifications of three bones at the rear end of the fish's jaw. This is one of the more recent discoveries of science, and it explains why the fish has no hammer, anvil, and stirrup. He is still using them to eat with.

EQUILIBRIUM

In the equilibrium of the fish, the sacculus and lagena play no part. The German investigators mentioned in the preceding section found that removal of these destroyed true hearing but left equilibrium unimpaired; whereas hearing remained, but equilibrium was lost, if the utriculus and the three semi-circular canals were excised.

These parts, then, compose the true equilibrating mechanism. Like the sacculus and lagena, they contain a fluid called endolymph, and are surrounded by the fluid of the auditory capsule. The three canals being at right angles to each other, a turn in any direction brings about a movement of the endolymph in at least one of them through force of inertia, which is registered for the brain by appropriate nerves. Further, there are tiny bulbs made of bone, which are free to move in the endolymph, and are surrounded by nerve endings. They indicate by the particular nerve endings on which they rest at any moment whether the body is upright, upside down, or on its side.

The utriculus and its connecting canals are also involved in maintaining the muscular tonus of the fish. The muscles in all normal living creatures are never completely relaxed; they are always, even when at rest, alert and ready for action. But if the nerves coming from the upper inner ear are cut, the fish's muscles become flabby—the tonus is lost.

The whole equilibrating machinery is identical with ours. What was good enough for the fish is good enough for us. It may even be too good for us, for our problem is easier than theirs. What we see helps to keep us going straight and right side up. A tuna or a swordfish, in mid-ocean and far enough down to be out of sight of the surface, sees nothing but uniform water. It has no landmarks to steer by. It must have the automatic control. To the fresh-water fishes, which are usually in sight of bottom or shore, this is not so essential. Remove the machinery from such a fish, and it at first wobbles, but soon learns to handle itself. Blindfold, now, that same fish, and it is again out of control—proof that the eyes alone are capable of doing the work, provided they have something to guide on. This suggests the thought that it is just possible that the automatic equilibrating system is not indispensable to us, who live on land and have a strong force of gravity to tell us what is up and down and things to look at to tell us which is right and left. Perhaps we should never have developed such a system by ourselves. Perhaps it is only because the animals from which we are descended lived in the unmarked waters that we have it. And yet, if we did not have it, we might have more difficulties flying our airplanes than we do. Perhaps it is only because we come from fish that we are able to learn to fly.

LATERAL LINE

In close connection with the ear is that mysterious organ, the lateral-line canal. It is an organ found only in animals

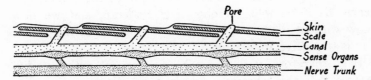

FIGURE 14. DIAGRAMMATIC REPRESENTATION OF THE LATERAL-LINE SYSTEM

dwelling in the water. It is visible on most fish—with the exception of the gobies, and with the more notable exception of the guppies, sword-tails, platies, and other killifishes —as a line extending along the side from the gill opening to the tail. It consists of a tube beneath the skin, filled with mucus, and opening to the exterior at intervals through pores which may pass either through the scales or between them. In most fish it continues on to the head, where it breaks up into several branches, but these are generally buried in the surface bones of the skull and therefore invisible. Beneath the canal runs a nerve which at frequent intervals sends out branches to it, each branch having a sensory ending. In some fish there are several canals on each side, and in some the line is broken rather than continuous.

The purpose of this organ was for long a mystery, and many guesses were made about it, until an American scientist settled the question by a simple but ingenious and logical set of experiments. He operated on certain fish, cutting the nerve which connected the lateral line with the brain, and he left intact other fish of the same species. After the operated fish had recovered he put them all through a series of tests to find out what the normal fish could do that the operated fish could not do. He found that they were alike in every way, except that the normal fish would respond to vibrations of low frequency in the water whereas the operated fish would not. Later experiments in England, using an oscillograph to measure the electric discharges in the lateral-line nerve, have brought corroborating evidence, and we now know without doubt that at least one function of the lateral line is to receive low-frequency vibrations.

It is, therefore, very like a hearing organ, with the difference that the vibrations which it receives are of a frequency so low that they would reach our ears only as a series of intermittent noises, or more likely would not be heard at all. These vibrations are such as might be caused by the straining of an oar against an oarlock in an angler's boat, or by his footfall as he moves along the bank of a stream. Or, to use a simile more in keeping with the normal life under water, they might be caused by the passing of another fish, or by nearness to an obstacle which would send back through the water the vibrations caused by an approaching fish. In the detection of such disturbances the lateral line would serve almost as a long-distance touch organ—a method of touching an object without being actually in contact with it, which might be especially useful in avoiding obstacles in the dark corners of pools and streams, or in finding mates or prey in parts of the sea where light does not reach. The lateral-line canal, therefore, operates on the principle of a hearing organ, but functions more as an accessory organ of touch. Lacking the ability to imagine just what its messages mean to the fish's brain, we are probably explaining its nature to ourselves as well as we can if we say that it is an organ which combines the senses of hearing and touch.

Very recently another activity of the lateral line has been discovered. It helps the fish to recognize heat and cold. The fish's situation in this regard is difficult for us to imagine, for it is normally at the same temperature as the water in which it lives, whereas we are normally at 98 degrees while the air may be at 110 degrees or below zero. We are designed to operate at a constant temperature, and when we suffer from cold or heat it is a warning that the temperature outside our bodies is attempting to invade the inside, and that we had better make efforts either to get warm or to cool off. The fish's sufferings from cold or heat, if any, are obviously different, since he makes no such efforts. When the water is warm, he is warm, and when the water is cold, he is cold. Such discomfort as he feels, if any, is caused by whatever difficulty his insides may have in carrying on their work at high or low temperatures. However, occasion sometimes offers for the fish to go abruptly from colder into warmer water or *vice versa*. If he does this, he is in the condition to which we are accustomed, with his insides at a different temperature from the outside. Lacking our control mechanism, his insides then change temperature rapidly, and this is bad for him. The hormonal machinery which helps to adjust his metabolic rate to temperature conditions takes time to get into action. This is why many fish which can stand considerable extremes of temperature when the change is gradual die when the change is sudden. To prevent unwitting suicide by warning him when the water which he is entering is colder or warmer than the water he has left is a duty of the lateral line.

And only recently, one of the long-standing misconceptions about the lateral line has been cleared up. Scientists of old looked at the lateral line, scratched their heads, and tried to imagine what uses it might be put to. Someone suggested that the fish ought to have some way of sensing currents, and that seemed like a happy thought. Contentedly the scientists wrote down in their books, "Lateral line: current detector," and put the matter out of their minds. This was not even theorizing; it was plain guesswork.

The fact is that the fish detects currents in the same way you do. If you are swimming in the middle of the Gulf Stream out of sight of land, the whole body of water surrounding you, on account of the uniformity of its motion and the fact that you can see nothing else, appears to be standing still, and you do not realize that you are being carried along at anywhere from two to four miles an hour. If, now, the water were suddenly to grow so shoal that you could touch bottom, or if the shore-line were suddenly brought out to where you could see it, you would know that the water was not stationary, for the speed at which you dragged over the bottom or at which things on shore moved by you would be quite at variance with the exertions you were putting forth in swimming. In the same way, the fish recognizes that it is in a current by the fact that it has to swim in order to keep up with things on shore, or to keep from being dragged over things on the bottom. Differential currents, coming into still water or striking at an angle to or a different speed from the main current, may conceivably have an effect on the lateral line, but the principal "current detectors" are the eyes and the skin.

TOUCH

Touch is the most fundamental sense in the animal kingdom. It exists in the lowest forms, and it is probable that many of the other sense-organs of the higher animals were derived from organs of touch. In the fish, the touch papillae are spread over the surface of the skin, as they are in man. The whole system is so similar to our own that we do not need to go into it here.

SMELL AND TASTE

The senses which have been discussed so far are all alike in that they may be called physical senses: they all receive physical phenomena—sound-waves, light-waves, heat, pressure, contact—and transform them into nervous energy. The two remaining popular senses, smell and taste, are, in contrast, chemical senses: they transform chemical phenomena into nervous energy.

That the sense of smell is present in fish has long been believed by dam-tenders and small boys from their experiences with lampreys. Lampreys are primitive, jawless, finless, eel-shaped, fish-like animals which make a living in the ocean by attaching themselves with their suctorial oral disks to decent fish and gouging out flesh and blood with their rasp-like "tongues." Like the salmon, they come into fresh-water streams to spawn, and are often found in great numbers at dams, being able to surmount low ones by attaching to the surface with their oral disks and hitching upward like "inch-worms." If you spit in the water above such an aggregation of lampreys, they loosen their hold and dash off in all directions, presumably because of the repulsive or fear-inspiring odor of human saliva. On a different level, palaeontologists have long believed that the sense of smell exists in fish because they have found in fossil fishes hollows in the inside of the skull which they are sure harbored the cranial elements of what must have been an olfactory apparatus.

In the present-day fishes the receptors of smell are located, like ours, in the nostrils, but the nostrils are not like ours. They are little holes in the top of the snout, but instead of connecting with the throat by a passage, they open into small blind sacs just under the skin, and go no further. The sacs are lined with the organs of smell. There are two such sacs, one on each side of the snout, and in most fishes there are two external openings, two nostrils, one behind the other, connecting with each sac. To bring the water carrying the odors into the sac where the organs are, there are either muscles, or little moving hairs called cilia, which keep a current flowing in the front opening and out the rear.

The fish's tongue is a flat cartilaginous and gristly projection from the floor of the mouth. It has no muscles, and it cannot move, but it does have taste-buds which experiment has proved do distinguish between at least some of the flavors which our taste-buds sense. Many fish are insensitive to sweet flavors, perhaps because, as our experience indicates, few things from under the water taste sweet; but many species have an acute sense of sour, salt, and bitter.

We are all aware of the fact that taste and smell are closely related. The principal difference is that we can smell things at a distance, while we can taste things only when we are in contact with them. The explanation of this is that the tongue must have a much stronger stimulus than the nostrils. The very small amount of material that reaches us through the air from a distant body will form a solution on the moist surfaces of both, but it is too dilute to have any effect on the tongue, and only the nostrils register it. The sense of taste appears to have been designed to tell animals whether what they have taken into their mouths is edible or not. What tastes good is, in general, good to eat. The sense of smell is like a sense of taste operating at a distance. It helps the animal to find what is good for it to take into its mouth.

The catfish is an excellent example of this. The catfish often feeds on detritus lying in the muddy bottom. It seems to have given up using its eyes to locate food, but it wears on its chin some projections called barbels, which are provided with taste-buds. They are auxiliary tongues. As soon as food is put into the animal's tank, it shows excitement, and begins to swim about over the bottom. This is due to smell. But it is not until a barbel touches a fragment of food that it is seized and eaten. This is taste. And some catfish even go so far as to have taste-buds all over their bodies. The remarkable creatures can actually taste with their tails —doubtless a useful adjunct when searching for food in dark waters.

The sharks have a very keen sense of smell, on which they depend entirely for locating food. Put a broken-up crab into a dogfish's tank (a dogfish is a small species of shark), and it starts swimming in a rough figure eight. Gradually it draws near, but it is not until it is right on top of the bait that it seems to see it and grasp it. Its eyes, as you recall, have little if any ability to focus for distance, and its vision is probably poor. If the animal's nostrils are put out of commission by stuffing them with cotton soaked in vaseline, it shows no consciousness of the food at all. If only one nostril is so treated, it finds the crab, but instead of making figure eights, it circles in one direction only, with the unobstructed nostril on the inside of the circle. This complete dependence on smell may be the explanation of why sharks are apt to leave potential prey alone unless it is wounded. Their eyes are incapable of telling them that food is at hand, and they must wait until the odor of flesh reaches their nostrils.

Few fish have as keen a sense of smell as this. Some, like the cichlids, with only one opening to each nasal sac, appear to have none at all, and many others use sight much more than smell in feeding. Certainly the trout rising for surface food depends solely on its eyes. But trout and salmon, and the other game fish so far as is known, do smell, and in some this sense is very acute.

OTHER SENSES

The existence of the kinesthetic sense in fish is one thing which it might be expected that we should never be able to demonstrate. If you close your eyes, and I take hold of your arm and lift it until it sticks straight out in front, and ask you where your arm is, and you answer correctly, and if I then move it so that it sticks out at the side, and you again give the correct answer, I know that you have the kinesthetic sense. From this it would be only natural to assume that until fish learned to talk there would be no way of testing them for this sensibility. However, scientists are impatient, inquisitive, and inventive. By delicate measurements they have recently shown that the electrical discharge from the lateral-line nerve varies with the amount of tension in the body muscles. No one has yet followed this lead far enough for certain proof, but the indication is that the lateral line, in addition to its other functions, keeps the fish advised of the disposition of its body, and that the kinesthetic sense does exist.

Of the sense of pain we can speak with more definiteness, but as we shall be in a better position to do so after we have considered the fish's brain, we shall leave it until then.

THE BRAIN

It is the intention of this book to give the reader not a detailed knowledge of the physiology of fish, but a general understanding of why fish behave as they do. It would be out of place, therefore, to go into a particularized description of the brain, the cranial nerves, the nerve areas in the spinal cord, the spinal nerves, and the sympathetic nerves.

All we need to know is that basically the nervous system

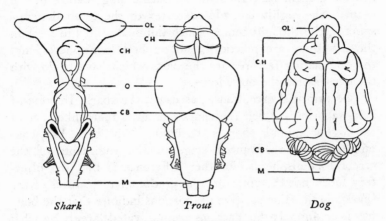

Shark   *Trout*   *Dog*

FIGURE 15. BRAINS

In the three brains shown above, that of the dog is on a different scale from the other two, which are in reality very much smaller. It is to be noted that the cerebral hemispheres (CH), the parts of the brain used for reasoning and imagination, are large and highly folded in the dog, rudimentary in the shark and the trout. The olfactory regions (OL) are very highly developed in the shark—in proportion even more than in the dog —and are small in the trout. On the other hand, the optic lobes (O) are comparatively tremendous in the trout; in the dog they are hidden beneath the cerebral hemispheres. The medulla (M), the part of the brain where simple responses originate, is largest in the shark and smallest in the dog. The cerebellum (CB) is more important in the fish brains than in that of the dog. It is obvious that the brain of the shark is dominated by the olfactory area, that of the trout by the optic area, and that of the dog by the reasoning area. (From Wiedersheim, *Comparative Anatomy of the Vertebrates*, by permission of the Macmillan Company, publishers.)

is the same as in higher animals, with one set of nerve-fibers to carry sense-impressions from the sense-organs to the spinal cord and the brain, another set of nerves to carry orders from these centers out to the muscles, and a sympathetic system to control the "automatic" workings of the internal organs.

At the same time, the brain is a very much smaller and simpler structure than it is in the higher animals. In man the weight of the brain in proportion to the body is much greater than in fish. In man the outstanding feature of the brain is the highly convoluted cortex of the cerebral hemispheres, the thought center which dominates all the rest; in the fish there are practically no cerebral hemispheres, and the dominating features are the parts which have to do with the eyes, called the optic lobes.

The principal exception is, as usual, the shark. In spite of being a primitive fish the shark's brain is more like that of the higher animals than is the brain of the bony fish, containing a more advanced stage of the rudiments of the cerebral hemispheres. Another difference is that the olfactory lobes, not the optic, are the predominant features of the shark's brain. The relative proportions indicate that the bony fish is an animal whose actions are motivated largely by what it sees, whereas the shark depends to a great extent on what it smells; and the differences in behavior in the two groups show that this is in general true.

Having surveyed the fish's sense-organs and nervous system, we are now in a position to consider that much discussed question, "Do fish feel pain?" How the answer can be any other than an unqualified yes is hard to see. But if the question is changed to "Do fish suffer?"—or, better still, "Do fish suffer as human beings do?"—then there is room for argument. One of the earlier psychologists, William James, maintained that our feelings are the result rather than the cause of our expressions of emotion. His theory that, "We are sad because we weep, not we weep because we are sad," and, "We are happy because we laugh, not we laugh because we are happy," was well known to an earlier generation of college students. If there is any truth in this—and certainly there is to the extent that we can make ourselves happier by laughing, sadder by weeping—then the poor fish has no emotions comparable to ours, for he can neither laugh nor weep. However, there are some feelings which he can express. He can express hunger by searching for food. He can express anger by expanding his fins and gill covers and attacking his enemy. He can express love by pursuing the female of the species. He may also have other ways of expressing his feelings, and one, at least, we can understand, because we sometimes use it ourselves: flight from what he fears.

Pain seems to be an instrument which nature has devised for the preservation of the individual. What tends to destroy hurts, and is avoided. If putting your hand on a hot stove brought no pain, but only a sizzling sound, a little smoke, and a faintly appetizing odor, you would not be nearly so expert in avoiding burns as you are. By the same token, if it did not hurt a fish when another fish ate it, that fish would not be nearly so desirous of avoiding the experience as it actually is. Why does a Siamese fighting fish dart aside each time it is bitten by its opponent in a fight, if the bite does not give it pain?

All of the foregoing is obvious, and yet many people, of whom I am one, shrink from killing a deer, but have no scruples about the often more lingering death which they inflict on a trout. They like to tell themselves that it is because the fish cannot feel pain, while the real reason is that the fish, regardless of what it feels, cannot express pain. If every trout were to scream unceasingly as long as it had a hook in its mouth, trout-fishing would be a nerve-shattering experience which few of its present devotees could undergo more than once.

However, in defense of the fisherman, I find two reasons for believing that the fish's suffering is, comparatively speaking, slight. One is that the actual sensation of pain is apparently not so keen in fish as in some of the higher animals. The other is that the brain of the fish, lacking the cerebral cortex of which we spoke, fails to provide a home for the conscious association of ideas, and therefore robs pain of an imagination to work on. The well-known and authentic tale of the fish which was caught with its own eye illustrates both my points. This poor fish was foul-hooked, and the only way to remove the hook was to remove one of the eyes. The fisherman decided he did not want his catch, and replaced it in the water. It then occurred to this man, who must have been of an experimental turn of mind, to see how good a bait the eye might be, so he placed it on the hook and dropped it in the water, to pull out a few minutes later the very fish from which the eye had been taken. Now, disregarding its failure to recognize its own eye, which is hardly surprising in view of the fact that it had never seen it before, the points to bear in mind are these: first, that a very short time after the removal of the eye its pain from that operation was so unimportant that it was out and about prospecting for food; and second, that the pain which had resulted from taking into its mouth a bait on a hook on a line made so little impression on its mind that it did the same thing again a very few moments afterward. Number one, physical sensation of pain not very keen; number two, mental impression of pain not very keen or else very quickly forgotten. And pain that is forgotten is no longer pain.

Naturally fishes vary, not only as between individuals but also as between species. Some are more sensitive than others, some learn more than others. But at best fishes are reflex animals. There are no inhibitions, no moments of hesitation to think about the desirability of doing or not doing a given thing. The sight of food means open the mouth and snatch, the sight of a larger enemy means run and hide, each without stopping to consider whether the food is really beneficial or the enemy really dangerous. To be sure, fish can learn. We all know trout that have learned to avoid flies with visible lines attached to them. But here again we may permit ourselves to guess that it is probably not so much a case of the trout saying to itself, "There is what looks like a nice morsel, but it has a line tied to it, and flies with lines tied to them hurt, and trout that eat them go away and do not come back," as it is a case of, "Line on water . . . run and hide"—just as pure a primary reflex action as when you pull your hand away from a hot stove.

Trying to imagine what goes on in the fish's brain is a dangerous proceeding, and one wholly unbecoming to a scientist, but it is permissible to a layman, and any layman who did try it might not be far wrong if he concluded that a fish on the end of a line had a dull sensation of physical pain at the point where the hook held it; that it felt fear and discomfort from the restriction of its movements; and that it learned that a line was a thing to avoid, to the point that in future, provided it succeeded in having a future, it ran for cover each time it saw one. But that this fish henceforth went about in fear of lines, or that it bore in its mind a memory of the pain caused by a hook, or even that the sight of a line brought back to its mind the pain caused by a hook, would be an unjustifiable conclusion.

And in this connection the question of how much fish actually learn is worth taking a look at. We speak of "educated trout" in certain streams, and we say that the larger fish are harder to catch because they are older and have had a chance to learn more. Obviously fish do have a capacity for learning—that has been proved by laboratory experiment as well as by field observation—but just as obviously, all the fish that are hard to catch have not had personal experience with the hook which has taught them to avoid it. Do we mean, then, that fish learn from each other? Or are we perhaps trying to put our explanations on too high a plane?

I am inclined to think that this is the case, and that hereditary, or environmentally produced, caution plays a larger part than learning. In streams which are continually disturbed, the fish are in a constant state of fright. Anything the least bit out of the ordinary will make them hide, and it is only when conditions are, so to speak, "supernormal," that they will come out and feed. They are "educated" only in that they are in a state of chronic wariness.

As for the big fish, they are harder to catch than the little ones because they are wary, and they are big because they are wary, and they are wary partly because of what they have learned, but largely because they were born that way. If they had not been born that way they would not have lived to grow big. The fish that are easy to catch all get caught when they are small, for life is a struggle, and the rash little fish which goes around poking its nose into everything which arouses its curiosity soon becomes a victim of one enemy or another, beast or human. But the fish which at birth is constitutionally supplied with more than the usual share of caution lives to grow old and large, and to become the anguish and the delight of the angler.

CHAPTER VI

The Air-Bladder

ONCE upon a time, all the bony fishes breathed air. This was many, many million years ago, long before there were any human beings. The bony fishes were then living in streams, lakes, pools, and swamps, where they at first breathed only water. When, in the Devonian era, the climate changed, the inland waters began to dry up and stagnate. They no longer contained enough oxygen to sustain animal life. By processes which we still do not entirely understand but which we name evolution, the fish acquired a pouch, opening out of the throat, into which air could be taken to provide the oxygen which the water no longer held.

By the time the climate changed again and the waters increased once more, some of the fishes, armed with the new pouch which made them free of water, had gone out on land and become amphibians and reptiles. A few remained in the water but kept on breathing air, like the present African lung-fish. The majority ceased to breathe air and went back to complete water-dwelling, but they retained, and still carry, the remains of that pouch without which they would have perished. It is now called the air-bladder. And so both the human lungs and the fish's air-bladder derive from the same primitive respiratory sac.

The sharks and rays lack all trace of an air-bladder. All the bony fishes alive today either have an air-bladder, or show that they once had it. The sharks and rays must have left the fresh water and gone out to sea before the great

Devonian drought set in. They must have branched off from the other fishes before the fish which gave rise to both humans and present fishes developed. We do not descend from sharks.

And this is a scientific fairy story which many scientists believe.

The air-bladder is, as its name indicates, a bladder. It lies between the stomach and the backbone. In the trouts it is a fragile organ, noticeable only in the inflated condition it assumes when the fish has been dwelling in deep water. In shallow-living individuals, it appears to be nothing more than a space inclosed at the top and sides by the inner body wall, at the bottom by a thin shining membrane which the angler's thumb-nail punctures when it pokes in to remove the blood from under the backbone in cleaning the fish. In other species, like the Lower California "sea-bass" (*Totuava*) whose air-bladder the Chinese esteem highly as a soup-base, it is a conspicuous sac with thick walls which shut it off from the other organs. In all the soft-rayed fishes—the salmon, trout, tarpon, herring, pike, pickerel—a tube leads from the air-bladder to the gullet. This is the tube through which their ancestors breathed air, and because they still retain it they are called primitive—near to the first fishes. In the other fishes the tube no longer exists, and they are called advanced.

What the air-bladder used to do is pretty well known. It saved the fish from perishing by acting as an auxiliary air-breathing organ. What it does now is not altogether certain. In some fish it serves as an auxiliary sense-organ, in others it is purely part of the internal workings. This is why we have given it a chapter to itself between the two.

The scientists of the old guesswork school had a theory which seemed to solve the problem. They believed that the purpose of the air-bladder was to act as a hydrostatic stabilizer—an organ which would permit the fish to change depth without trouble, and to remain at any level without exertion. If the fish is to be at rest in the water, its weight must be the same as that of the volume of water it occupies. Technically speaking, it must have the same specific gravity, the same weight-to-volume ratio, as the surrounding water. It will then neither rise nor sink. Suppose that a fish is so adjusted that this condition is met at a depth of, let us say, twenty feet. If the fish rises ten feet, the pressure of water on its exterior will decrease, and its body will, according to their theory, expand. It will take up more space. The volume of water it occupies increases. Since its weight is unchanged, it will now weigh less than that water, and it will be unable to stop rising until it floats at the surface. To avert this danger, the fish decreases the size of its air-bladder as it rises, and thus keeps its volume constant in spite of the diminishing pressure. The ratio of its weight to its volume remains unchanged, and it is still stable at ten feet depth.

When it descends to thirty feet, the reverse takes place. The pressure of the water on its exterior increases as it goes down, crushes it into a smaller space, diminishes its volume. It takes up less space, but its weight is unchanged. It therefore weighs more than the volume of water it occupies, and it would sink down and down with ever-increasing speed until it struck bottom, if it did not inflate its air-bladder sufficiently to keep its volume constant and thus maintain itself in equilibrium with the water. Some scientists even went further, and asserted that the fish could make active use of the air-bladder to raise or lower itself. If it wanted to rise, it pumped up its air-bladder, and up it popped. If it wanted to sink, it deflated its air-bladder, and down it went.

This theory is engaging, and has the merit of harboring some truth. Certainly in fish in which there is an air-bladder it must have a hydrostatic effect. In some this effect is far from beneficent. Most widely publicized is the "explosion" of fish from abyssal depths when brought to the surface by scientists. This is, of course, caused by the expansion of the air-bladder when released from pressure. Its occurrence is much rarer than is popularly supposed because many deep-sea fish do not have air-bladders, and their tissues, composed largely of water, are so incompressible that they do not expand. Less spectacular is the Great Lakes fish known as the pike-perch. When brought up in a net from a depth of one hundred feet, it swells so that it floats helplessly at the surface. If a hollow needle is inserted through the flesh into the air-bladder, the hiss of escaping gas can be heard, and the fish is able to resume normal swimming. The pike-perch is obviously supersensitive in this respect, for we all know of other fish which can come up from greater depths with no such alarming manifestations. The swordfish is a famous diver, but when we get it to the top it is by no means a helpless floater.

So far our glimpses of the air-bladder have been far from reassuring. To the fish which we have mentioned, it seems to be about as pleasant a possession as we should find a hand-grenade which we had to carry around in our pockets, equipped with a barometric fuse which would set it off and blow us to pieces if we climbed a high hill or went up in an express elevator. However, we have been considering arti-ficial conditions—abrupt, man-made changes. On the Pacific Coast the rock cod lives at a depth of 100 feet. Bring him to the top, and he is helplessly bloated, but let him spend a week in an aquarium, and he can reduce himself to normal. Another set of Pacific Coast residents, the lantern-fishes, have a family habit of spending the night at the surface of the sea but going down to depths of 600 feet for the day. Now, the pressure at 600 feet is nearly twenty atmospheres. If you bring them suddenly up from that depth, they are in a highly explosive state, and yet they make the round trip every day of their own volition—two changes of twenty atmospheres every twenty-four hours. The conclusion is that each of these two species can adjust the air-bladder to the conditions, but that it must be done gradually. The lantern-fish is quicker at it than the rock cod, but each has the capacity to accomplish it. The old theory is to some extent borne out, but appears in a new light. The air-bladder, instead of being something which helps the fish to change levels, is something which the fish has to guard against, to keep under control.

How does the fish make these adjustments? If he is one of the species which retain that tube leading from the gullet to the air-bladder, through which his ancestors used to take in air, it might be assumed that he uses this. It may be that in some cases he does, although at the time that he needs air most, to expand his bladder against increasing pressure as he descends, there is no air to be had, for he is under water; and further, it has been found that in some species the tube is so grown together, or so clogged with mucus, that there is little possibility of anything passing through it in either direction. Such fish, and the many species which lack the tube entirely, must have other methods. Principally, they depend on secretion of gas into, or absorption of gas out of, the air-bladder by the blood. This may seem like a mysterious and unnatural kind of operation, but it is a kind very commonly used in the life processes, both animal and vegetable. The fish's air-bladder has walls rich with thin-skinned blood-vessels, and these vessels have the ability to put forth gas into the interior of the bladder, thus pumping it up against external pressure, or to absorb gas from the interior of the bladder, thus preventing it from overexpanding when the external pressure is released. But the process is not, in most cases, a rapid one, and so the fish must have time to make the adjustment gradually.

At this point in their reasoning, a great light dawned on certain scientists, and they brought forth the theory that it was the duty of the air-bladder to keep the fish within certain depth limits, or to prevent it from making depth changes too suddenly. This is at first sight a tempting idea. Rapid changes of altitude bring about undesirable disturbances in our internal workings. And yet for us to go up to ten thousand feet from sea-level is no more, so far as change in pressure is concerned, than for a fish to come up from a ten-foot bottom to the surface, an act which he can accomplish in a few seconds. The air-bladder is there to prevent him from overindulging this ability and thus unknowingly injuring himself. If he comes up too far or too fast, the air-bladder expands and pokes him in the stomach. If he goes down too far or too fast, his stomach pokes him in the air-bladder. In either case, he has an ache in his insides which warns him that something is wrong, and that he had better go back where he came from.

There is no question that something of this kind does happen. An Italian experimenter found that if he increased the pressure in the air-bladder by injecting sterile, air-free water, the fish tried to swim up, and if he reduced it the fish tried to swim down. In other words, increased pressure gave the fish the sensation that he was too far down and had better come up, and *vice versa*. This proves that an air-bladder out of adjustment with the depth does warn the fish to seek a different level, but it does not prove that the same fish, if it had no air-bladder, would have any disturbance in its other organs at that depth. The whole theory of the air-bladder serving as a warning pressure gauge is wrecked by the number of fish which have no air-bladder at all, and which safely make great changes in their level just the same. The halibut sometimes lies on bottom at a thousand feet, sometimes feeds at the surface. It has no air-bladder. The chub mackerel has an air-bladder, the common mackerel has not. They are not only almost indistinguishable in appearance, but they frequently live side by side and school together. It is difficult to believe in the indispensability of an instrument which one of them gets along perfectly without.

At this point we have to stop and consider the connection which the air-bladder makes with the ear in some fishes. Controversy has gone on for years about this apparatus, one school of thought holding that it serves to keep the fish more completely informed as to the state of its air-bladder, the other, that it is a hearing mechanism.

In the cod and some other fishes, the connection takes place merely through forked lobes of the forward end of the air-bladder which rest against the auditory capsules. Much more complicated is the system found in a great group of fresh-water fishes which includes not only such familiar forms as the catfish, the carp, and the sucker, but also the characins so abundant in South America and in fish-fanciers' aquaria. Here there are four small bones linked together with movable hinges (see Figure 16). These are called, after their discoverer, the Weberian ossicles, but they are not to be confused with the ossicles in our ears, the hammer, anvil, and stirrup. The latter derive, as we have seen, from three bones in the fish's jaw, and the carp is still using them to eat with, whereas his Weberian ossicles he has improvised out of the forward end of his backbone. But, however different their origin, there is a similarity in their present action, for our ossicles form a bony linkage between our membranous ear-drum and our auditory capsule, and the carp's Weberian ossicles form a bony linkage between the membrane of his air-bladder and his auditory capsule. It is this similarity which first suggested that the Weberian ossicles might be used in hearing: the tense air-bladder would be well adapted to receive vibrations coming through water, and would use the ossicles to transmit them to the ear.

The opponents were quick to point out that while this might be all very well when the air-bladder was fully ex-

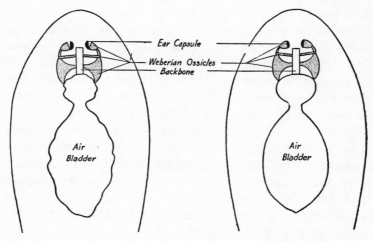

FIGURE 16. DIAGRAMMATIC REPRESENTATION OF THE AIR-BLADDER AS A SENSE ORGAN IN THE CARP

After Thilo.

panded, as in the diagram on the right in the figure, it would not work at all when the air-bladder, in the course of its hydrostatic duties, reached the shrunken state shown on the left. In that state, not only would the membrane of the bladder be so relaxed as to be no use in receiving sound-waves, but the ossicles would cease to press against the ear, and would be unable to transmit them. To these people it was evident that the system was a device to keep the fish informed as to its relative depth by the increase or decrease of the pressure transmitted by the ossicles from the air-bladder to the ear; and since the ears were known to have the equilibrating sense in the semicircular canals and their auxiliaries, it was thought not unreasonable to assume that they have this depth sense also.

The proponents of the hearing-mechanism theory offered two points in rebuttal. First, even if the air-bladder in these fish does change size with change in depth and pressure, which has never been proved, does it ever become slack (like the left-hand diagram)? For as long as the fish remains under water there will be pressure on the bladder, and as long as there is pressure on it, its walls will remain tense and will be capable of receiving and transmitting sound-waves. Second, of what use would such an elaborate depth-measuring or pressure-registering device be to these fishes? The great majority of them live in comparatively shallow waters, and their opportunity to change levels is thereby very much limited. For that same reason—because for a great many of them the bottom is so near the top—they might find a device which strengthened their hearing very useful, especially if it enabled them to detect enemies above the surface.

It remained for the German physiologist whose experiments were described in the section on "Hearing" (page 105) to settle the matter in a scientific manner. It will be recalled that he worked with a minnow, a member of the carp family, which is equipped with the Weberian ossicle connection between the ear and the air-bladder. He had found that his minnow had such an acute sense of hearing that it would show response to a tuning fork at a distance of 200 feet sounded so softly that a man under water (in the form of one of his students who volunteered to occupy the same tank with the fish) could hardly hear it. However, when he operated on the minnow and removed its air-bladder, its hearing became much poorer. It could still be trained to sounds, but they had to be a great deal louder. He found that the characins showed a well-developed sense of hearing; and that the mormyrids, Egyptian fish from the Nile in which the air-bladder makes a direct connection with membranes in the cranium, hear as well as the minnow. Other species which lack the ear-air-bladder connection heard much less acutely; they could be trained to sounds, but the sounds had to be much louder. From this the trout and black bass anglers may take comfort, for absence of the connection in these fishes may be taken to indicate poor perception of sounds made in the air.

So the controversy has been settled, and it is accepted that in many fishes the Weberian ossicles are a part of the hearing apparatus which serve to transmit vibrations to the ear from the air-bladder, which acts as a resonant sounding-board. And to complete the argument, it is now known that, at least in many of these fishes, the forward compartment of the air-bladder can be closed off by a sphincter muscle, so that it can be kept taut no matter what the condition of the rest of this organ.

Thus, while there are still things about the air-bladder that we do not understand, there are many things which we actually do know. In the first place we definitely know that it still retains to some extent its original respiratory function. This, its primordial duty, is still one of its most widespread and most important ones. In the lung-fishes, those five species of living fossils scattered through Africa, South America, and Australia, this is true to such an extent that *Protopterus*, the African form called by the natives *Kamongo*, can no longer breathe water through his gills. If caught in a net so that he cannot reach the surface, he soon drowns; and he can live literally for years in the cocoon of dried mud which he makes for himself when the waters of his swamp disappear, in Devonian style, during times of drought.

The tarpon has perfectly good gills, but it also has a fine large open tube leading from the upper side of its gullet to its air-bladder, and the inside of the air-bladder is well supplied with blood-vessels. Young tarpon are frequently found in lagoons which have been cut off from the sea by sand-bars for so long that their water is stagnant, brackish, even sulphurous, and the tarpon's ability to survive there seems with little doubt to be due to its ability to come to the surface and take atmospheric air into its air-bladder.

But aside from the fish which actually "breathe" air in this way, a great many others use the air-bladder as a sort of respiratory reservoir. Deep-sea fishes have an unusually high percentage of oxygen in the air-bladder, and in some species, the deeper the fish the more oxygen. The oxygen content of the water is low at these depths, and the fish extracts from the water more than its current requirements and stores it up in the air-bladder against emergencies. Further, when fish are experimentally suffocated, the oxygen in the air-bladder is greatly reduced, showing that fish do fall back on this reserve when the normal oxygen supply is cut off.

In the second place we definitely know that, in those fish which have it, the air-bladder plays a part in the permanent equilibrium between the fish and the water. This is self-evident, and has nothing to do with adjustment of pressure to changing levels. It has to do with density. If a fish has an air-bladder, that air-bladder must be of such a size that the total volume of water occupied by the fish will weigh just about what the fish weighs, if he is not to be in constant struggle with his environment. The actual tissue of which most fishes are made is denser than water, and all fish would weigh more than water and tend to sink if they did not have some way of buoying themselves up. The air-bladder supplies this need, but paradoxically, all fishes do not have to have air-bladders to keep them from sinking. The shark lives in the open sea, and rarely sinks to bottom. He has no air-bladder, but instead he has an enormous liver full of oil which keeps him afloat. The flounder, on the other hand, is a very solid fish. It has no air-bladder, and you can almost feel the thud with which it lands when it settles on the bottom. It is heavier even than salt water.

In the much lighter, less buoyant fresh water, it is impossible for any fish to carry enough fat or oil to keep afloat. Without exception, the fresh-water species which lack the air-bladder are bottom dwellers. To those which wish to carry on their lives on a higher plane, it is indispensable as a float. Without it the pickerel and the muskellunge could not hang motionless in the water, waiting for their prey; without it, the black bass could not hover over its nest, guarding its offspring against marauders; and without it the trout and its relatives could not lie for hours just below the surface, rising to take in the food drifting down the stream. Further, to those fish which go from fresh to salt water, or the reverse, the ability to *adjust* the air-bladder is indispensable. For a fish in proper adjustment in fresh water will find itself too light when it goes into the heavier salt water, and it will tend to float at the surface unless it can reduce its air-bladder, thus reduce its total volume, and increase its weight-to-volume ratio, its specific gravity, to that of salt water. In the same way, when a fish adjusted to salt water goes into fresh water it will tend to sink unless it can increase its volume. This does not mean that the former fish will be unable to get below the surface, as you are when you bathe in the Great Salt Lake. It does not mean that the latter will be unable to get off the bottom, as even the best human swimmer is if he falls into an oil-tank. The differences between natural fresh and natural salt water are not so great. What it does mean is that a fish in equilibrium in one will, if he goes to the other, have to work to keep below the surface or to stay off bottom unless he can make an appropriate change in his volume. Experiments with killifish, some of which are able to stand abrupt change from fresh to salt water or the reverse, show that when first placed in salt water they have to swim constantly downward to overcome their buoyancy, and when first placed in fresh water, constantly upwards to overcome their weight, but that in fifteen minutes they adjust themselves sufficiently to the changed density to maneuver without any perceptible difficulty.

In the third place we definitely know that the air-bladder has been turned into an efficient hearing aid in one way or another by many species of fish, including the predominating group, both in number of species and number of individuals, in all the fresh waters of the world.

In the fourth place we definitely know that some fish use the air-bladder to make noises. Best known is the weakfish and its allies. It has a peculiar muscle by which it can set the air-bladder into vibration and produce sounds. The male only possesses this muscle, and the male only can make the sound, from which we judge that it has something to do with mating; and so loud is this sound that it has been heard six feet above water when the fish is fifty feet under water.

So much for the positive side—for the things which we know that the air-bladder does do. As for the things which we know that the air-bladder does not do, while at first thought a summary of the negatives may seem of little value, it is undertaken here to dispel the many misconceptions which have been held in the past and which are to some extent still held.

We know that the air-bladder is not an active instrument for changing levels—that fish do not raise or lower themselves by increasing or decreasing their size. For this reason it seems to me that the name "swim-bladder," which is sometimes given it, is misleading. With locomotion in any direction it has nothing to do. True, the mixture of gases which it contains is not air, and it should really be called a "gas-bladder," but at least the name "air-bladder" is more indicative of its true nature than "swim-bladder."

We know that it is not even a passive help to the fish in making depth changes, as the first theory held. Fish without the air-bladder are almost incompressible, and therefore have an almost constant volume at all depths. If they are in equilibrium with the water at one level, they are in equilibrium at all levels. They change from one depth to another without disturbance. Fish with air-bladders are compressible. In order to maintain their constancy of *volume* they have therefore to increase or decrease the *pressure* in their air-bladders. The air-bladder has to work to overcome the weakness which it itself has introduced. It is in no way a help; it merely succeeds in overcoming the obstacle of its own presence. It is probably just as much of a nuisance to the fish, in so far as depth changes are concerned, as our lungs would be to us if we suddenly acquired gills and took to living under the water.

And we know that it is not an indispensable device to keep the fish from too rapid or too great changes of level. If such a pressure register were necessary to keep the fish within safe limits, the halibut with its great changes of depth would long since have perished.

And it may be that some day exceptions will be found to every one of the statements we have just made; but they will still remain in general true.

There is one more point about the air-bladder which is of interest to human beings. In most present-day fish the tube which connects the air-bladder to the throat opens into the upper side of the gullet; but this was not always so. In the

Devonian fishes it opened into the lower side, for the air-bladder or "lung" lay below the digestive organs. This seems mechanically unsound, since the bladder, being light,

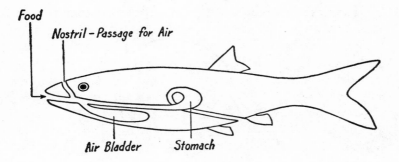

Food

Nostril - Passage for Air

Air Bladder   Stomach

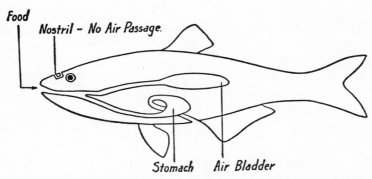

Food

Nostril - No Air Passage.

Stomach   Air Bladder

FIGURE 17. AIR AND FOOD SYSTEMS OF EARLY FISH (above)
AND MODERN FISH (below).

should naturally be above the stomach, and it is possible that the tendency of the bladder to rise is responsible for the present position of the opening. Anyway, whatever the reason, in the early fishes the opening was on the lower side of the throat. The nostrils, however, were on the top of the head, and when they succeeded in acquiring a passage through the skull into the mouth cavity for the fish to breathe through, the path of the air came to cross the path of the food. For the air came in at the top and went out at the bottom, whereas the food came in at the bottom and went out at the top, as in the upper diagram in Figure 17.

If the fish had moved that air-bladder connection around

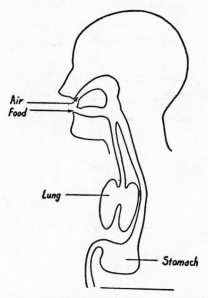

Figure 18. AIR AND FOOD SYSTEMS OF MAN

to the top of the throat before the land animals branched off from it, as in the lower diagram of Figure 17, it would have been much more convenient for us. We might then have succeeded in working out two separate passages, one leading from the nose directly to the lungs, one from the mouth directly to the stomach, with no trouble-breeding interconnections. But it did not. The result is that the land animals carried on that crisscross arrangement and never modified it, and handed it on to us. Our food and our air have to cross over (see Figure 18), and sometimes the food gets into the passage leading to the lungs. It "goes down the wrong way."

And so, when you choke over a piece of bread, it may, or it may not, be some consolation to you to realize that that particular bit of discomfort had its origin in the Devonian drought some three hundred million years ago.

CHAPTER VII

Internal Workings

DIGESTIVE SYSTEM

THE digestive system of a fish consists of a stomach and an intestine, with a mouth at the front end for taking in nourishment, and an anal opening at the rear end for disposing of used food. In addition to these elements common to all animals from the worm up, it has also some of the accessories which we are apt to think of only in connection with human beings, such as gall-bladder, spleen, and pancreas. That it has a liver is not likely to be forgotten by those who have had anything to do with cod-liver oil.

The fish's mouth is full of teeth. It has teeth on its jaws, and often on the roof of its mouth and on its tongue as well, but it does not use these teeth to chew with. This fact was borne in on me very clearly once when I found, in the stomach of a trout I had just taken, several intact salmon eggs of the preserved kind sold for bait. Either this fish had been an expert at stealing bait off the hook without getting caught, or some angler had dumped the remains of his egg supply into the water. In any case, the eggs looked as good as new. Out of curiosity I took one of them and put it on my own line. In a very few minutes I had another trout on the bank, and inside his stomach the same salmon egg which his dead brother had once eaten was still uninjured. Neither fish had chewed it at all; at this rate a deft angler would need no more than one salmon egg to carry him through a whole season.

As a matter of fact, if fish tried to masticate their food as good little children do, they would suffocate, for they would then be unable to pass the current of water through their mouths and over their gills which is necessary for their breathing. To overcome this difficulty, some of the vegetarians, and others which like to chew, have grinding-mills well down in their throats. These are called pharyngeal teeth, and are supported by bony arches similar to those which carry the gills. It is here that the "Fletcherizing," if any, is done.

Fish are largely carnivorous. Most of them, therefore, have sharp-pointed teeth in the mouth with which to seize their prey and hold it while it is being swallowed whole. Those which feed on tiny living organisms in the water, like the herring, have small delicate teeth. The rays live on shell-fish, and have great flat teeth like paving stones with which to crush the shells before swallowing them. Of the few that go in for a vegetarian diet some, like the carp, have no teeth in the mouth; while one of the strangest modifications is found in the "parrot." These large, brightly colored fish graze on the coral reefs, and their front teeth have all fused together to form a beak very much like a parrot's. With this beak they nibble the coral and the weeds, which are then ground up by the powerful pharyngeal teeth in the throat.

Many fish have an unlimited ability to replace their teeth, not being confined to two sets as we are. This is particularly evident in some of the sharks, whose mouths are bristling arsenals of teeth, row after row, in diminishing size, lying flat in readiness, waiting to take their turn in the front line as the ones in active use wear out.

As has been noted in an earlier section, the fish's tongue is a flat, immovable projection from the floor of the mouth. There is no salivary gland.

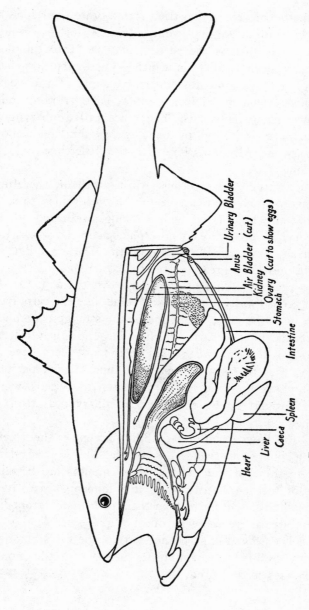

FIGURE 19. INTERNAL ORGANS OF THE STRIPED BASS

Drawn from a model by Dr. W. K. Gregory in the American Museum of Natural History.

Urinary Bladder
Anus
Air Bladder (cut)
Kidney
Ovary (cut to show eggs)
Stomach
Intestine
Spleen
Caeca
Liver
Heart

Behind the mouth is the pharynx. Here there is a constriction open only when food is passing through into the stomach. If it were not for this barrier, the fish's stomach would be continually flooded with water, and the digestive juices would be diluted and rendered useless. The stomach is generally U-shaped or in the form of a sack, and is highly distensible. The intestine in the carnivores is comparatively short, being hardly more than a straight tube leading to the anus, but in the herbivores, whose food is in a form not so readily assimilated, it may be long and twisted. In the carp it is eight to nine times the overall length of the fish. The majority of herbivores are fresh-water inhabitants.

Close to the stomach are blind pouches, like the fingers of a glove, known as *caeca*. They are found in no vertebrates above the fish, although they do superficially resemble our vermiform appendix. However, they attach to a much more forward portion of the intestine than our expensive organ does. The catfish and the pikes are without caeca. The flat-fishes have 2 or 3. Our childhood friend the sunfish has 7 to 10, and his relatives the black basses have about 14. The brook trout has 40 to 50, the Atlantic salmon 50 to 60, the steelhead 42 to 80. The Pacific salmons vary from as low as 45 in the silver to as high as 214 in the king. But the tuna and the swordfish head the list; in these species the caeca are described as "very numerous," which we may take as meaning that there are too many for a busy ichthyologist to bother counting.

The caeca probably serve to retain the food for digestive and absorptive purposes. Similar in action is the geometrically admirable spiral valve (see Figure 20), especially characteristic of the sharks and rays. It lies at the lower end of the gut. It works just as a long, twisted intestine would in providing more absorptive surface and greater storage capacity.

The liver is large, taking up a disproportionate amount of the body cavity. The gall-bladder and the spleen are clearly recognizable, but the pancreas is what is called "diffuse," which means that it is pretty well scattered about. It does

Figure 20. LOWER INTESTINE OF THE SHARK CUT OPEN TO
SHOW THE SPIRAL VALVE

From J. R. Norman, *History of Fishes.*

nevertheless contain something in the nature of the "islets of Langerhans" (the name given to the ductless glands in the mammalian pancreas from which insulin is obtained) for the discovery has been made that insulin can be obtained from fish pancreas. If this proves to be commercially practical, diabetics can look forward to an unlimited supply of this indispensable remedy at a low price.

BREATHING

The purpose of breathing is the same in all animals: to take the prime mover, oxygen, into the body, and to get rid of the waste-product, carbon dioxide. This is accomplished in the higher animals by exposing the blood, in vessels so thin that gases can get through their walls, to a source of oxygen. If there is less oxygen in the blood than on the outside, oxygen will pass into the blood. If there is more carbon dioxide in the blood than on the outside, carbon dioxide will pass out of the blood.

To man the source of oxygen is air, and because of its drying action the thin-walled blood-vessels into which the oxygen is to be absorbed must be placed in lungs where they can be kept alive and moist and permeable. To the fish the source of oxygen is water, and since water has no drying effect, the blood-vessels can be exposed on gills in the mouth. The gills are the red objects which can be seen by raising the gill covers and looking through the gill opening into the gill chamber underneath. They consist of a multitude of filaments full of tiny blood-vessels, arranged on bony arches somewhat as the flanges are arranged on the tubes of an automobile radiator. There are four of these gill arches in most fishes. Between them are openings, or clefts, through which the water passes. Since there is no opening from the fish's nostrils into the mouth cavity, as there is in humans, breathing has to take place through the mouth. The gill covers are closed, and water is drawn into the open mouth by expanding what might be called the cheeks. The mouth is then closed, either by the shutting of the jaws or by the automatic action of flaps of skin which act as check valves and thus block the orifice even though the jaws remain apart. The gill covers are opened, and the water is forced out over the gill filaments by contracting the "cheeks."

The normal rapidity of these movements varies. The human being takes from 20 to 25 breaths a minute. In comparison, the rate in fish varies from as low as 12 per minute in the wrasses to as high as 150 in the minnows. In the brook trout it is between 40 and 50. Under stress, such as when the fish puts forth unusual exertions, or when the oxygen content of the water becomes low in an aquarium with too many fish and insufficient aeration, the rate is accelerated and the fish "pants."

As the water passes through the gill chambers and out through the gill openings it is easy to see that the current might carry with it particles of food from the mouth which might injure the delicate gill filaments. To guard against this the gill arches are equipped with straining devices known as gill rakers. In fish which eat large animals the rakers are nothing more than knoblike protuberances on each side of each arch. In the herring they are fine, almost hairlike outgrowths, acting more as a sieve to prevent the escape of the minute organisms on which it feeds than as a protection for the gill filaments. In general, however, they are designed to prevent the food from interfering with the breathing, just as the valve called the glottis in our throat is designed to prevent food from getting into our windpipe. That these safety devices sometimes fail to work, in fish as well as in men, is evidenced by the body of a twenty-pound striped bass found with a three-pound carp stuck in its gill opening, its wiggling tail still protruding from its captor's mouth. The would-be diner had suffocated, but the intended dinner was still alive.

Some people are under the impression that it is the oxygen constituent of water which the fish breathes. Their inference is not illogical, since water, as we all know, is composed of one part of oxygen to two parts of hydrogen. What they fail to take into account is the fact that water

is one of the most difficult compounds in the world to break down. To dissociate the one part of oxygen from the two parts of hydrogen requires elaborate chemical processes. But water exposed to air absorbs oxygen from it, and this oxygen penetrates to the depths of the sea. It is this absorbed oxygen which the blood-vessels in fish's gills take from the water.

Fishes vary in their oxygen requirements. The trout, for instance, needs much more than the carp, which is why the trout like swift streams while the carp can live in a mud-puddle. The trout's *minimum* requirements are about 3.5 parts per million by weight,[1] but while it can exist under such conditions, it shuns water with less than 5 parts per million. The Federal hatchery at Leetown, West Virginia, has 10 parts per million, the Klamath River the same. This is pretty close to the saturation point, which is to say that the water has absorbed just about as much oxygen as it can possibly hold. Man, even if equipped with the gills of a fish, could not live in water, for he requires fifty times as much oxygen as a fish his own size. Air, with its 210 parts per thousand, is none too good for him.

Other things being equal, the colder the water is the more oxygen it can hold—which is one of the reasons why trout prefer cold water. The maximum temperature at which the brook trout can live comfortably is 70° F., the brown trout 76°, the rainbow slightly higher. Cold water being, within limits, heavier than warm, it sinks, which is why trout tend to stay on the bottom in hot weather. Exceptions to this are certain inland lakes in which, on account of their protected position, or their depth, there is very little circulation in summer. In the hot weather the surface becomes warm and light, the lower water cold and heavy. Two dis-

[1] 2.5 cubic centimeters per liter by volume.

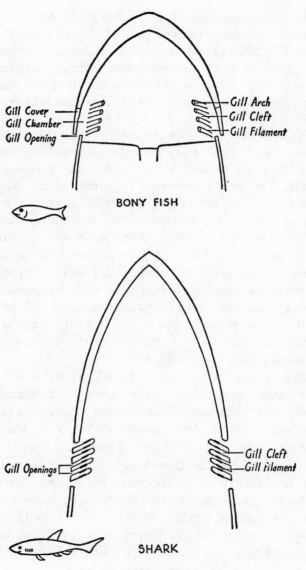

BONY FISH

Gill Cover
Gill Chamber
Gill Opening

Gill Arch
Gill Cleft
Gill Filament

SHARK

Gill Openings

Gill Cleft
Gill Filament

FIGURE 21. GILLS

tinct zones are formed, between which there is no inter-change of water, with the result that the lower levels, cut off from the oxygen supply, become depleted of that ele-ment, and uninhabitable to fish. Such lakes are said to have *thermoclines,* the name given to the dividing layer between the upper, warm, light, oxygen-rich zone and the lower, cold, heavy, oxygen-poor zone.

The sharks and rays breathe just as other fish do. They differ, however, in this way: that the clefts between the gills, instead of opening into a common gill chamber with a single external aperture for the escape of the water, open separately through the skin to the exterior (see Figure 21). There may be from five to seven clefts, with the corresponding five to seven slitlike openings in the skin so characteristic of the appearance of sharks. In addition, there is the small round opening in the top of the head, the spiracle, considered to be a degenerate gill slit. which we discussed in Chapter V.

EXCRETION

Excretion means the removal from the body of the un-usable or injurious products which have been formed by the operation of the bodily machine. It does not refer to the removal of that fraction of the food which, having no nutri-tive value, has been allowed to pass through the digestive tract without being absorbed.

In both fish and human a certain amount of excretion takes place through the respiratory organs and through the skin, but the principal method in both is by solution of the mat-ter to be excreted in water and its passage out of the body as urine. In both, it is the kidneys which prepare the urine, but the way in which these organs function is so unlike in the different forms that it brings about a startling dissimilar-ity in the way in which they go about getting their supply of water. The human does it by drinking fresh water. The fresh-water fish does not drink at all, but absorbs water. And the salt-water fish drinks salt water.

An explanation of all this in terms of osmotic pressure, hypotonicity, and the like, would turn our hair gray, but we can set up a few conceptions which, while they will probably turn the chemists' and physicists' hair gray, will give us an easy understanding of how the system works.

The first point is simple. A solution is a combination of water and some other substance. If the proportion of the other substance to the water is high, the solution is strong, or concentrated; if it is low, the solution is weak, or dilute. Both fresh water and sea water have salt in them, but the sea water is a much stronger solution. Now, if two solutions of different strengths are separated by what is called a semi-permeable membrane, they will tend to equalize. Water will pass through the membrane *from* the weak solution *into* the strong solution until they are of equal strength.

The second point is simple. Blood, both fish and human, is a stronger solution than fresh water. Therefore, fresh water will pass through semi-permeable membranes into blood. In man, such membranes are found only inside the body, and he must therefore drink in order to get water into the stomach where it can be absorbed. In the fish the semi-permeable skin is, as we have seen, normally rendered inactive by the slime, but the functioning semi-permeable gills are in constant contact with water. Through these gills fresh water constantly goes into the more concentrated blood and must be taken out of the blood by the kidneys and turned into dilute urine for excretion. The fresh-water fish does not have to drink.

The third point is also simple. The fish's blood is a weaker solution than sea water; therefore, sea water does not pass into it through the gill membranes. The tendency is for the reverse to happen—for water to pass out of the fish's blood through the gills into the sea. The only way, then, for the marine fish to obtain water is to drink. It actually takes large quantities of salt water into its stomach. This is absorbed into the blood, but since the kidneys of the fish, unlike those of the human, are capable of excreting only urine more dilute than its blood, it must separate the water from the salt in order to have dilute water to form its urine. This task is assigned to its gill membranes, which do what is called osmotic work by excreting the salt back into the sea. In other words, they force the salt to go in the direction of the stronger solution, in spite of its natural tendency to go the other way. This leaves the water free to be formed into dilute urine by the kidneys, and at the same time prevents the accumulation of too much salt inside the fish's body.

And so the fresh- and salt-water fishes have to have quite different excretory mechanisms. In the former, water constantly seeps in through the gills, and the kidneys must be able to remove it in large quantities from the blood stream. In the latter, water is taken copiously into the stomach to make up for what escapes through the gills; the kidneys must use as little of it as possible for the excretory solutions; and the gills must be able to get rid of the excess salts which the water brings in. Neither set of equipment is suitable for use in the other habitat, and so the salmon and the eel, which spend parts of their life in each, have to have both sets. However, switching from one to the other is not always a simple matter. Some species of fish can support a swift change, but a young salmon cannot be taken from a stream and dumped into salt water. It is only when the proper physiological moment arrives, signalized by the appearance of the silvery coating of guanin in the skin, that he can make the change safely.

The sharks and rays as usual do things differently. In them, the concentration of the blood is higher than sea water, so they are in the same position as a bony fish in fresh water. They absorb it directly through their membranes, and since it is more dilute than their blood, they can use it without alteration to form their urine. Sharks do not drink.

It is only recently that all of these facts were learned. They tell us at last what the difference between a salt-water fish and a fresh-water fish really is. They bring us a new understanding of the obstacles which have to be overcome by such fish as the salmon and the eel when they pass from river to marine life or the reverse. And they force us to modify our old expression about drinking like a fish. For, since sharks and fresh-water fish do not drink at all, if we want to have the phrase mean anything, we must qualify it, and say that a man drinks "like a marine bony fish."

Like the human being, the fish has a urinary bladder. This is an example of the incorrigible neatness of nature, for there seems to be no real reason for such an organ in an animal which is wet all the time anyway. Its existence, however, offers no material for the teleologist. It was not given the fish in preparation for evolution into a mammal, for the mammal's urinary bladder is formed from an organ which does not exist at all in the fish. In the marine fishes it seems to be particularly useless, for the amount of urine passed is very small. The fresh-water fishes, on the other hand, have a very large discharge—as high as 100 to 150 cubic centimeters per day per kilogram of fish. An idea of what this means can be had by realizing that if human beings operated at the same rate, a 150-pound man would have to excrete from 10 to 15 pints of urine a day. As man's bladder has a capacity of only about three-quarters of a pint, this would be highly inconvenient.

And one further comparison is of interest. In the fish, the anal opening is in front of the uro-genital, which is sometimes divided into two, whereas in humans the position of the two openings is the opposite. How we succeeded in reversing this relationship, whereas we were unable to do anything about the far more impractical windpipe-gullet business, is something which no one has yet explained.

CIRCULATION OF THE BLOOD

We now come to that system which ties together all the other internal workings. It is the function of the blood to carry to every living cell in the body the oxygen and the food which they need for their life-processes, and to carry away from them, to places where they can be disposed of, the carbon dioxide and the urea and the other excretory products resulting from those life-processes; and also to transport to the places where they are needed the regulatory hormones secreted into the blood by the ductless glands.

In principle the system is simplicity itself: a central pump, the heart, with a series of pipes to carry the blood, diminishing in size as they recede from the heart and increasing as they return. In actual construction it is very complex, only slightly less so than that of the human being, with an intricate network of thin-walled capillaries winding through the tissues to bring them their blood.

There is only one important difference between the fish's circulation and the human's, but that difference is so great that it accounts for many of the other differences between the two animals. In the human the blood goes from the heart to the lungs to be purified, and then this oxygenated blood goes back to the heart to get a fresh start for its trip through the rest of the body. In the fish, the blood goes from the heart to the gills to be purified, and then goes on through the body without any second impulse. The human has two blood circuits, the fish one, as shown by Figure 22.

The heart is a bag with muscular walls capable of rhythmic contractions. It is the pressure of these contractions which

forces the blood through the arteries and veins. The human
heart has two series of chambers, a right auricle and ventricle,
and a left auricle and ventricle. The right set receives used
blood from the body, blood which has given up its oxygen
and has absorbed waste products—so-called "venous blood"
—and forces it through the pulmonary artery to the lungs
where it is purified. It returns to the left auricle, goes thence

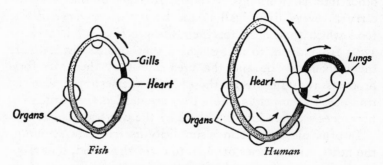

FIGURE 22. BLOOD SYSTEMS

to the left ventricle, and here receives the impulse which
starts it on its journey around the body. The right side of
the heart deals only with venous blood, the left side only
with pure blood.

The fish's heart lies close behind its mouth, and contains
only one series of chambers. Impure or venous blood enters
the base of the heart, and is forced out at the forward end
to go directly to the gills. Here it is purified, and then it
continues, forced by the pressure of the blood behind it,
to the head and other parts of the animal. The fish's heart
deals *only* with venous blood.

In the human, the stream of pure blood divides after it
has received its impulse from the left side of the heart. In
the fish, this division takes place only after the blood has
received its oxygen supply from the gills. The purpose of

the division is to give the brain a supply of the very best blood, for in both fish and human, one stream goes directly to the head and then, without being called on to do any further work, is returned to the heart for repurification. (This is not shown in the sketch in order not to complicate the diagram.) The other stream goes to all the rest of the organs. It goes to the muscles of the fins and tail; it goes through the kidneys in a network of capillaries known as the renal-portal system, where it disposes of some of the waste products of which it has relieved the other tissues; it passes around the digestive tract, where it absorbs nourishment; it goes through the liver in another capillary network called the hepatic portal, where it stores some of the excess nourishment; and it finally returns to the heart.

The fish's blood, like man's, is red in appearance because of red blood corpuscles, and these corpuscles, as in man, contain that substance hemoglobin, which is important because of its ability to attract, absorb, and transport comparatively large quantities of oxygen. Compared to man's, the fish's blood is thick, viscous. It does not flow as readily as man's does.

Now let us consider the combined results of all these characteristics of the fish's circulatory system. In the first place, because of the long circuit which the blood has to make on the impulsion of only one series of heart chambers, it is under much less pressure than is human blood. Cut a man's artery and the blood spurts out; cut a fish's artery and it just dribbles out. Because of this low pressure, and also because of its viscosity, the fish's blood does not flow so fast through its vessels. Because of this comparatively slow flow, and also because water has less oxygen to yield than has air, the oxygenation of the fish's blood is less than that of man's. But low oxygenation means low temperature; and the cooling of the blood by the surrounding water as it flows through the gills also means low temperature. So by a long process of reasoning we arrive at a conclusion which we already know: that the fish is a "cold-blooded" animal.

Or, if we wish to impress our friends, we can call it a poikilo-thermal animal. In either case, what we mean is that it is an animal whose body temperature is about the same as the surrounding medium. This is why fish are so sensitive to changes in the water. If it were not for the comparative constancy of their environment, it is hard to see how they could survive. Natural bodies of water not only undergo no sudden and violent changes of temperature, but their seasonal range is small, compared to what mammals often have to withstand. Mammals may have to face variations of as much as one hundred degrees between midsummer and midwinter, whereas fish rarely encounter a range even half as large. For the black bass the extremes are probably not over fifty degrees apart, for most of the trouts forty degrees, for the tuna thirty. And when the thermometer approaches what is for them the lower limit, many fish go into a state of hibernation. They lie at the bottom. No movement is made. No food is taken. The heart slows down, and all the life processes are at a low rate. The fish is very nearly in a state of suspended animation.

CHAPTER VIII

Reproduction and Growth

IN all animal species except the very lowest, each new individual starts life as an egg. The egg is a single cell produced by the female of the species. It cannot develop until it has been entered and fertilized by a single cell called a sperm, or spermatozoön, produced by the male of the species.[1] The egg contains nutritive elements which are drawn upon to build up the new individual. It cannot move. The spermatozoön is very much smaller than the egg. It is equipped with some form of tail, by which it is able to move itself through a liquid medium, just as a tadpole does. It is the active

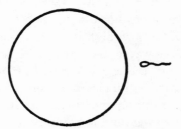

FIGURE 23. RELATIVE SIZES OF EGG AND SPERM IN THE
FLOUNDER

Magnification about 30 diameters.

---

[1] Exceptions, animals whose eggs develop *parthenogenetically* (without fertilization) have no bearing on this discussion and will not be dealt with here. These are all invertebrates; no vertebrate male has to suffer the indignity of being so ignored.

member, and its duty is to go out from its place of origin in the male, and to seek and enter the egg.

There are two basic methods for bringing about the union of the two members. In the first and simplest the egg is set free from the mother before it is fertilized. This occurs with the oyster. Millions of eggs and sperms are released into the water, and fertilization is entirely a matter of chance encounter. This method can be used only by animals which live in the water, for if the reproductive cells were released in this casual way on land the male member, being capable of movement only in a liquid medium, would be unable to seek the female, and both would soon die.

The second method, in use among both water- and land-dwelling animals, overcomes this difficulty. The sperm is introduced by the male into the body of the female, where it encounters and fertilizes the egg. This is a more efficient method than the one first described, because the reproductive cells of the two sexes are brought together in a restricted space where their chance of encountering each other is increased. It is found in such low forms as the flatworm, of which the tapeworm occasionally parasitic in human stomachs is an example, and in such high forms as the birds and human beings. There is, however, this great difference: in the tapeworm and the bird, the egg is released after fertilization to develop outside; in the human it remains within the body of the female parent during the embryonic stages of development, and the offspring does not emerge into the world until it is a more or less finished product. In the bird, the egg contains abundant nutritive elements in the form of a yolk, on which the embryo feeds during development; in the human and all other mammals the egg contains comparatively little yolk, and the embryo depends on the blood of the mother for nourishment. It is not true, however, as many people think, that the blood of the mother flows through the veins of her baby; what happens is that the blood vessels of the mother are brought into such intimate contact with the membranes surrounding the developing child that the necessary nourishment passes from one to the other through the very thin and permeable walls.

Boiled down to their elements, there are three basic systems: (1) external fertilization and external development; (2) internal fertilization and external development; (3) internal fertilization and internal development.

Fish are able to make use of all three of these methods. They are the only vertebrates, aside from the amphibians, which use method Number 1. They utilize method Number 3 in a form as fully developed as the mammals. And they have made modifications in method Number 2 until it is at times unrecognizable.

The great majority of them favor Number 1. Some of the species have made refinements on the old system, but others use it in all its original simplicity. That little cousin of the tuna, the mackerel, is an example: males and females come together in great schools at the spawning season and, indiscriminately and without any apparent mating, release their reproductive cells into the water. It is up to chance to do the rest. Whether sperm meets egg, and whether fertilized egg survives and develops into a new mackerel, is of no more concern to the parent mackerel than if it were an oyster. The term "poor fish" seems fully justified here, for there appears to be no consciousness of sex, no gratification from the sex act—nothing more than a relief from the pressure of overabundant sex products.

The trout do better. Here there is an unmistakable pairing, a preparation of the bottom for the eggs by the female, an accompanying defense by the male, and a collaborative sex act, as we shall see in a later chapter. When the whole process is finished the parents separate and go about their respective businesses, but at least during the few hours of spawning each was conscious that the eggs existed, that certain things had to be done in connection therewith, and that there was another individual who played an important part in the proceedings.

Among aquarium fishes there are some which, while still releasing the reproductive cells of both sexes into the water, take complicated measures to ensure the fertilization and development of the eggs. Betta, the Siamese fighting fish, is a well-known instance, and in this species, as well as in the paradise fish and other near relatives, the male is the leading spirit. When he feels the urge to spawn he advertises the fact by building a "bubble-nest." This is a collection of bubbles on top of the water, sometimes under a floating leaf, sometimes in an open space between several leaves. To construct it, the male comes to the surface, takes air into his mouth, retires to the chosen spot, and there releases little bubbles, one after the other, each covered with a sticky coating from his mouth which prevents it from bursting and makes it adhere to the others. This process he repeats until he has a dome of bubbles anywhere from one to two inches in diameter and protruding sometimes as much as half an inch above the surface of the water (see Figure 28).

He then takes his post under his nest, and attacks all intruders. With gill covers projecting, with stiffened fins, and with intensified coloring—all, it may be noted, tending to make him look larger than he actually is—he sidles threateningly up to any stranger. If the latter is a male, a fight ensues in which the home-owner, through some submarine working of the law of moral right, almost always wins. If the stranger is an unripe female she flees; but if it be a ripe female she refuses either to fight or to flee, and the only thing left to do is to make love.

The male swims around her and slaps her with his tail.

He goes to the bubble-nest and adds a few bubbles. He drives her off and then lets her follow him back. She begins to poke him in the side with her nose. This demonstration of affection is too much for him. He herds her under the nest. Their two bodies come close together. She pokes him once more. He wraps himself around her in a half circle, she turns on her back, and ten or fifteen eggs come from her vent. Quivering, clinging together, they sink slowly toward the bottom, then, still in the attitude of the embrace, their bodies drift gently apart. He recovers, takes in his mouth the eggs, which are also sinking, and carries them up to the bubble-nest in which he places them. After a short interval the embrace is repeated, and this continues until she is empty of eggs. Her parental rôle is now ended. She is not only at liberty, but actually under compulsion, to go on her carefree way, for the male no longer permits her to share his home. He drives her out, and mounts solitary guard under the nest. Here he remains, making such repairs as are necessary and replacing such eggs as fall out, until the young are hatched. For several days thereafter he continues to guard his wriggling infants, until he suddenly becomes fed up with the whole idea, turns cannibal, and those of his offspring which do not at once strike out for themselves are eaten.

The betta's courtship and mating all takes place in the space of a few hours, but some of the nest-building cichlids, of which the orange chromide, the scalare, the acara, and the jewel are the best known, have a more elaborate love-life in which both male and female take an active part. Readiness for spawning is indicated by a brightening of the coloring in both sexes, this being especially noticeable in the jewel, which changes from characterless sandy-beige to a brilliant red with sparkling blue spots. If the male has no mate, his next step is to stake out a claim on a piece of territory. From this domain he drives all other fish, using the same tactics of projecting gill covers and extended fins which we noted in the betta. Unripe fish, even though much larger, will make no attempt to stand against him. Other ripe males fight back, and the vanquished in the battle loses his bright coloring and retires from the field. A ripe female, as in the betta, will neither fight nor flee. There follows a prolonged courtship, often lasting several days. The two fish, both in brilliant coloration, join forces in defending the occupied territory. They slap each other with their tails. They stand on their heads in the sand and vibrate. They select some hard surface like a piece of rock, and clean it of all dirt and weed by polishing it with their mouths. They dig pits in the sand. At last the moment arrives. The female swims slowly over the rock, depositing on it a row of from five to twenty adherent eggs, and now the reason for the rock-polishing becomes apparent, for if the surface were not clean the eggs would not stick to it. She swims off a short distance and waits while the male moves over the same spot, fertilizing; then she returns to lay more. This goes on for about an hour, the unengaged member keeping all other fish at bay, until there is a beautifully geometric circle of several hundred fertilized eggs. (See Plate IV.) These the parents guard until they hatch. While the young are helpless they move them from place to place in their mouths. After they have learned to swim they herd them about and drive away enemies, quite like a hen with its chicks.

Aside from the fact that fertilization is external instead of internal, the parental behavior is every bit as complex as that of most birds. And even though copulation does not take place, the sex life of the parents seems to be as complete as that of birds, and certainly far more so than that of most reptiles and amphibia. For we have selection of mates, court-ship accompanied by brilliant courting colors and an elaborate pattern of activities, a prolonged period of fertilization, and a bond between the mates which often outlasts the period during which the young need care, and holds the parents together for another spawning. In some cases it is very difficult to persuade either member of a couple to accept another mate, even during the intervals between successive broods, and although absolute monogamy has never been proved there have been instances which seemed to bear all the earmarks of that sacred institution.

Method Number 2, internal fertilization with external development of the eggs, is used among more animal groups than either of the two others. It is common among the invertebrates, and it is the only method employed by the reptiles and the birds. It is not uncommon among fish, but only rarely does it occur in its pure and easily recognizable form, in which the fertilized egg is released from the body of the mother and hatches outside. In some of the rockfishes of the Pacific coast, this is the case, but in other species of this group the egg is retained inside the female and hatches there, and what emerges is a young fish. While this would appear to be a form of method Number 3 (internal development), it is not truly so as long as no nourishment is received from the mother. In the rockfish there is no more connection between the developing embryos and their mother than there is between a hen and the eggs on which she is sitting; the female fish's body is merely the nest in which the eggs remain until they hatch. She sits on her eggs not by covering them with her body but by keeping them inside her body. Her eggs, just like the hen's, draw upon their own yolk, not upon their mother's blood stream, for nutrition. Development of the eggs is external to her tissues, even though it takes place within her body cavity.

In *Gambusia*, the well-known mosquito fish, the process is similar; in the guppy of home aquarium fame, only slightly modified; and from there on we proceed through various gradations to pure examples of method Number 3, where the egg contains practically no yolk, and all nourishment for the developing young is received from the mother. The means by which this is accomplished are diverse. In some the young fish, free in the ovarian cavity, merely absorb maternal fluids. In others, processes are formed which bring the membranes of mother and child in close contact; or flaps grow from the mother's tissues into the gill openings of the baby, or from the anal orifice of the baby to the ovarian walls. And in one instance, the embryo actually feeds on the mother, for in its digestive tract have been found traces of her broken-down follicular tissue, and, in addition, of dead sperms which had entered the ovarian passages without fulfilling their mission, as well as the remains of other embryos which had presumably failed to survive after development had started. Here is cannibalism at an early age indeed!

Method Number 3, then—internal fertilization and internal development—has in fish evolved from Number 2. It has evolved separately and in different ways in different groups. And it is in the primitive sharks that it has most closely approached the mammal. Internal fertilization is common among sharks, the male introducing the sperm into the female with modifications of his ventral fins called "claspers." In many species the eggs are then extruded into the water, a pure example of method Number 2; but in some there is true internal development, and in at least one species the blood stream of the embryo and that of the mother have been brought into a relationship every bit as close as that found in the placenta of the mammal. If this primitive fish had some means of furnishing its infant with nourishment from its own body after birth it would be reproductively on a par with us.

However, this is a far-flung exception. In the great majority of fish, fertilization takes place in the water and the egg develops in the water. It is because of this that fish are practical subjects for large-scale artificial propagation. Such propagation falls into three general categories. The first, in which the parents are killed, is the simplest. This is used especially in connection with commercial fisheries, many of which concentrate on the fish at the time they are gathered together for spawning. "Ripe" females caught in the nets— meaning those in which the sex products are mature—are opened and their eggs removed and fertilized with sperm-bearing milt taken from the males. Sometimes this is done on board the fishing-boat, either by government agents or by fishermen who receive extra pay for the work. If the eggs are of the kind which float, they are returned to the sea to develop while drifting naturally; otherwise they may be sent to some kind of hatchery. There has been much debate as to the value of this work, its opponents maintaining that the number of young it produces is so small in comparison to the enormous numbers provided by nature that it is not worth while. When you realize that a single school of herring has been estimated to contain three billion individuals, while scores of such schools exist in the Atlantic and the North Sea; that commercial fishermen take from the seas of the world some forty billion pounds of fish yearly; that this catch is only a fraction of those which are left in the water; and that of those left in the water at least half are females each producing from twenty thousand to two and a half million eggs per year, you begin to understand the validity of the argument. The fact is that this type of work is now carried on less extensively than it used to be, except in cases where restricted numbers make it of value.

A variant of the system is applied to the salmon of our Pacific coast, especially in restoring the supply in streams where the natural run has been endangered by dams or other man-made interference. All these salmon die as soon as they have spawned once. Fish are caught as they ascend the rivers, and held in pens until they are ripe. The female is killed and cut carefully open. Her eggs are poured into a receptacle, fertilized with milt, and placed in a hatchery trough with flowing water. In due time the young hatch, and are returned to the stream. The corpses of the parents, while not inedible, have lost condition to such an extent that they are not marketable. However, they are not wasted. Their own young, and the young of trout, have no objection to them, so they are often preserved and ground up to feed to fingerlings which are being reared in hatcheries.

Most of the salmon caught for the commercial canneries have eggs not ripe enough for fertilization. These are not wasted either. Some are preserved and put in jars and sold to fishermen to use as bait. Most of them are made into salmon-egg meal, which is recognized by growers of trout as one of the best foods for the young. It is especially efficacious in bringing out those bright colors which delight the anglers who catch the fish after they have been released in natural waters. All in all, the Pacific salmon adds a lot to the trout fisherman's happiness.

The second method of artificial propagation is very like the first, except that the parents are preserved alive to spawn another season. The trouts are the outstanding example, and the process is practically identical in its application to the various species. The fish, whether wild adults trapped in natural waters, or hatchery breeding stock, are kept until they are ripe. One man with wet woolen gloves then holds a female by the head and tail while his partner massages or "strips" the eggs out of her into a receptacle. A fifteen-inch rainbow or brook trout will furnish over a thousand eggs, a thirty-inch steelhead over seven thousand. The female is replaced in the water, and a few drops of milt from a male, held in the same way, are expressed over the eggs and gently stirred into the mass. They are set aside for an hour to harden, for the eggs when they first reach the water are soft and slightly sticky. At the end of that time they can be placed in the flowing current of the hatchery troughs, where they remain until they hatch. The young can be put in the waters to be stocked as soon as the yolk-sac is absorbed, or they can be retained and fed until they reach any desired size.

Trout are particularly well suited to the artificial method for two reasons. In the first place the eggs, while not set free in the body cavity as has often been stated, are so loosely held by a thin membrane that the trained human hand can easily manipulate them along the troughlike duct and out the abdominal opening. (Both membrane and duct are so delicate that it is difficult to open a trout without destroying them, and they are therefore rarely seen.) And in the second place, the eggs are only very slightly adhesive even at first, and soon after extrusion absorb water to such an extent that they become hard and elastic.

There are other game fish in which artificial spawning is practically impossible. In such a highly desirable form as the black bass, the eggs, smaller and held by a much tougher membrane, are hard to "strip" from the fish. They are very sticky, and adhere to whatever they first touch. The term "artificial propagation" is almost a misnomer as applied to them, for the third method is artificial only in that the fish are confined in prepared ponds. Here the adults, either captured from the wild or raised for breeding purposes, are kept in a ratio of about two females to one male, and here they deposit, care for, and hatch out their eggs just as they would in natural waters. Either the fry or the parents can be moved to other ponds after hatching to prevent cannibalism, and if golden shiners or other small fish have been allowed to spawn in the water at the same time their offspring will furnish such excellent food for the little bass that the latter will grow prodigiously. The bass-raising pond bears about the same relation to the trout hatchery that a cattle ranch, where the animals breed on the range and forage for their own food, bears to a chicken farm, where the eggs are hatched in incubators and the chicks are fed by hand.

The time between fertilization of the egg and its hatching varies in different species. In the brook trout it may take as long as four to five months; in the muskellunge the time varies from six to twenty days; in the black bass twelve days is the upper limit, and in the striped bass two days suffices at normal temperatures. In general, large eggs require more time than small eggs. And it may be taken as axiomatic that in any species the warmer the water, within the supportable limits, the more quickly the eggs will hatch.

The size of the young when they emerge from the egg varies with its size, for it must be remembered that the fry have to be small enough to remain curled up inside until they hatch. Most of the better-known marine fishes have floating eggs of very small diameter—one-twenty-fifth of an inch and under—whereas the eggs of almost all the fresh-water fish sink, and are larger, reaching one-quarter inch and more in the salmon. From this it can be seen that the larger fish often have the smaller eggs, and that fish may be smaller as fry than the contemporary young of other species which they greatly surpass as adults. Trout fry are half an inch long or over, but little swordfish, whose mother may have weighed hundreds of times as much as the trout's, are only one-quarter of an inch long.

The young of most fish are at this stage by no means perfect. They have comparatively huge eyes. They have transparent bodies through which the beating of the heart can be plainly seen. Their fins are rudimentary, and often attached to each other by the "fin-fold" which later disappears. Most conspicuous is a semi-transparent, often bright red or yellow, globular mass extending along the under side of the body for half of its length, which so impairs navigation that the little animal is helpless to move, or at best can shoot forward a short distance by violent wiggling of its tail. This is the yolk-sac, and contains what remains of the egg material out of which the fish developed. The fry continues to live on this for some time; in some species the mouth has no opening at the time of hatching, and begins to function only after this rich embonpoint has been absorbed. Not until then does the fry have to start scratching for its own living. In fact, it is not until then that it is capable of moving enough to secure its own food.

In a few species there is a great difference in appearance between the young and the mature fish. An outstanding example is the common eel. Its young was for years thought to be a fish of an entirely different species, and the physiological processes which accompany its transformation to the adult condition are almost as complicated as in insect larvae.

But in the majority of species the young are enough like the adult to be easily recognizable. Most of them differ in color or in color pattern from their parents, and also in the proportions of the skeleton, but aside from the gradual changes in these features, about all that happens from the time a fish graduates from the yolk-sac until it reaches maturity is that it grows. Fish, unlike birds and mammals, never entirely stop growing. The habit of establishing a definite size limit, beyond which the animal does not go, and which comes to be looked upon as the normal size for that animal, seems to be associated mainly with warm-bloodedness, for in most of the cold-blooded groups such limits do not exist. You may speak of a full-grown man, or a full-grown horse, or a full-grown canary, but there is no such thing as a full-grown oyster or a full-grown rattlesnake or a full-grown trout. Fish, or most of them, anyway, continue to grow as long as they live and as long as they obtain food in a quantity greater than the amount necessary to maintain the body in a normal state of upkeep and repair. The rate of growth varies in different species, and varies within the species at different ages. In general, it is faster in young fish than in old fish, the most marked slowing-down coming at the age of maturity, by which is meant the age at which the fish is ready to spawn. From that time on the growth is apt to be much slower, probably because so much food is needed for the manufacture of sex products, and also because many fish take no food during the spawning period and therefore have to rebuild their depleted tissues, when they start feeding again, before they can add anything to their growth. Such fish may show only very slight annual increases in size after the age of maturity, but a definite and measurable increase can nevertheless occur every year.

The arrival at maturity—at that condition where the eggs or spermatozoa are ready, where the creation of new individuals is possible—is the great moment in the fish's life. It may come early, or it may come late, measured not only in absolute units of time but also in comparison to the life-span of the fish. Cichlids like the jewel are ready to spawn at the age of four months, when they are about two inches long; and jewels have been known to live five years and to reach a length of five inches. In other words, the jewel matures when it has lived only one-fifteenth of its possible life, and reached only one-fifteenth of its possible weight.[1] The golden trout in the upper Cottonwood Lakes of California matures

---

[1] Since in almost all species of fish, weight is proportional to the cube of length, a two-inch jewel weighs only about one-fifteenth of a five-inch jewel:

$$\frac{2^3}{5^3} = \frac{8}{125} = \frac{1}{15} \pm$$

at the end of the third or fourth year and at an average length of ten inches. One of the biggest recorded in recent years was fifteen inches long and six years old: it matures therefore when it has lived one-half to two-thirds of its possible life and reached about one-third of its possible weight. The king salmon spawns generally in its fourth or fifth year and dies immediately thereafter: it matures therefore at the end of its life and at its maximum weight.

Once a fish has reached maturity its insides become principally a factory for the production and storage of sex products. The basic elements are tissues called ovaries or testes, depending on the sex, which produce either eggs or spermatozoa. They form two masses, one each side of and above the digestive organs. In the trouts and their relatives, the ovarian walls do not entirely surround the eggs, and the ducts which lead to the genital aperture are open troughs, so that eggs can, and sometimes, especially in the process of stripping, do escape into the body cavity. Such eggs can never be extruded, and must be absorbed by the tissues. In most fish, however, the ovaries are complete sacs with closed tubes leading to the outside. This system seems more efficient than the mammals', for in the latter there is a gap. The mammalian ovaries are separate organs which have no connection with the uterus. The ova are thus set free in the body cavity, and it is up to slender arms of the uterus called Fallopian tubes to corral them and bring them in. For this purpose the tubes have funnel-like open ends located close to the ovaries, and a vacuum-cleaner suction to sweep up loose objects, but even at that an ovum sometimes lingers in the open spaces, and once in a while is caught and fertilized in this embarrassing position by a far-traveling sperm. "Extra-uterine" pregnancy is the result. The primitive sharks have the same gap between the ovaries and the oviducts, and it looks as though the closed system of the bony fishes is an improvement which they invented after they had branched off from the main line of evolution.

The amount of space taken up by the ripe sex products in most fish is comparatively tremendous. The ovaries of a cow form only an infinitesimal fraction of her total weight, whereas the ovaries of a salmon may make up from one-fourth to one-fifth of her total weight. In most fish the ripe eggs not only completely fill the body cavity but swell it out to a very matronly plumpness. In some species the whole mass of eggs comes to the state of ripeness at approximately the same time, and is released at one time, or at most over a period of a few days, immediately after which the process of forming new reproductive cells begins again. No sooner is one lot disposed of than another lot is on its way, so that the mature female has inside her eggs at some stage of fruition at any time except immediately after spawning. In other species not even this hiatus occurs, for the female carries several generations of eggs at once. Ripe eggs to be spawned in the immediate future, unripe eggs to be spawned in the next cycle, and the tiny rudiments of eggs to be spawned in years to come, are all present together.

The interval between spawning varies with the species. In some of the small tropicals it is astonishingly short: four days after the production of one batch of eggs the female is ready with another, while the male is apparently never unready to do his part. This rate cannot continue indefinitely. Longer lapses, and rest periods, occur. But the number of times which they are capable of spawning during their lives seems limitless.

The temperate-zone fishes proceed at a more deliberate pace. Most of them have definite breeding-seasons, and spawn but once a year. The number of spawnings therefore depends on the length of life of the fish. In the trouts it is limited by this factor to a maximum of seven or eight, with a total life-span of fifteen years not unknown. Some fish live much longer—figures of thirty years for the striped bass, sixty years for the carp, are mentioned—and therefore spawn a greater number of times.

As for the number of eggs, it depends on the size of the body cavity of the fish and on the diameter of the egg. Within any species the diameter does not vary greatly, and small females will therefore have fewer eggs than large females of the same species. However, there is a much more significant variation, of which the relative size of body cavity and of egg is only an expression. It is a variation found throughout the animal kingdom, and it is dependent on the extent to which the parent provides for the survival of its offspring.

In the oyster, where fertilization is a matter of luck, and where survival of the fertilized egg to maturity is precarious, the number of eggs produced by each individual at each spawning is in the millions. In the human being, where parents give much more care not only to fertilization, but also to the protection of the offspring until it matures, only one child—normally—is produced at a time.

The same principle holds for the fishes. The cod, with floating eggs which drift in the open sea, may produce as many as nine million; fertilization and survival are largely a matter of chance. Trout, as we shall see in the next chapter, prepare nests, choose mates, and provide for a certain amount of postnatal care of the young: their eggs number in the lower thousands. And in the guppy, where the young remain in complete safety in the body of the mother until they can fend for themselves, fifty at a time is considered a good-sized family. The greater the parental care, the smaller the number of eggs necessary. For preservation of the species is the great object, and any form in which an average of at least two offspring do not reach maturity for every pair of parents is inexorably doomed to vanish from the face of the earth.

CHAPTER IX

Trout and Salmon

TO write a book about either salmon or trout would be easy. To write a chapter on both is difficult. More is known of the natural history of the two types than of any other fish in the world. More has been written about them than any other fish, but, aside from the literature designed for scientific consumption, it has been mostly about fishing rather than fish. To keep ourselves within the limits of what even the most liberal-minded would call a chapter, it will be necessary for us to confine ourselves here to the high points of the latter subject only.

Trout and salmon are much alike. They are members of the family *Salmonidae*. Natives of the northern hemisphere only, they are spread through Europe, Asia, and North America. They have taken up their abode in Corsica and Sardinia and Switzerland, in the rushing torrents of the Pyrenees and the quiet brooks of Normandy, in the clear English chalk streams and the rough Welsh currents, in the smiling Loire and the majestic Rhine. They have entered the rivers of Scotland and Wales. They have made Restigouche and Beaverkill and Nepigon and Gunnison and Klamath great names in the American fisherman's geography. But they have never crossed the equator. If the New Zealander and the South African are able to share in their English cousins' piscatorial pastimes, it is only because the trout and the salmon have been transported by ship across warm equatorial waters which they have never penetrated under their own power.

TROUT

The most widely accepted theory about the salmonids holds that they originated in the Arctic as migratory fish. When the ice came down across the parts of the world in which we now live, they came with it. When the ice retired and the seas grew warm again, colonies of them which had become fresh-water dwellers were trapped in the cool streams they had entered—some as far south as the Atlas Mountains in North Africa—and have remained there ever since. Cut off from each other in these streams, the differing conditions brought out different hereditary tendencies. And from this arose the bewildering number of species and subspecies and races and varieties of trout which make life difficult for the taxonomist—the man whose job it is to interrelate and classify and name the forms of animal life. For the trouts, as we have said in an earlier chapter, are still in a state of evolutionary fluidity. Species and subspecies are still being formed, and only a few years ago a new one was described, the beautiful little *Salmo seleniris* Snyder, the "moon-rainbow" trout, inhabitant of the headwaters of a small stream-system in California.

Up to a few years ago zoologists felt that it was desirable to seize on comparatively minute differences to split trout up into different species. If these "splitters" had continued on their way, it would not have been long before every stream and lake had its own distinct species. Recently the trend has changed. Splitting is looked on with less favor, and the tendency is to take all trout which are not separated by clear-cut, permanent differences and lump them together in one species. The "lumpers" now believe that all the English trouts, from the smallest inhabitant of the smallest burn to the largest ocean-going "sea-trout," are nothing but variations of one and the same species. They likewise believe that the more than fifteen species of trout formerly recognized in California are really variations of not more than three or four distinct species. The lumpers perhaps go to extremes, even as the splitters did, but their influence is salutary.

This classification of the trouts is a puzzle which I have no intention of inflicting on the reader, but a general idea of their interrelationships can be had without suffering. The two best-known groups are the genus *Salvelinus*, to which belong the eastern brook trout and the Dolly Varden, and the genus *Salmo*, to which belong not only all the trouts of the rainbow and cutthroat series, but also the Atlantic salmon and the brown trout. The lake trout is isolated in the genus *Cristivomer*.

The distinction which anglers make between the Loch Leven and the brown trout has no support among scientists, who now look upon the former as merely a variation of the latter. And the word "char," current in England, is little used in the United States. The English maintain, generally with a note of implied disparagement, that our eastern brook is not a trout at all but a char. Webster's International Dictionary tells us that a char is "any trout of the genus *Salvelinus*." According to this definition, "char" is a particular word describing one form of a group called by the more general word, "trout." A char is a trout although a trout is not always a char. The brown is a trout but not a char; our eastern brook and our Dolly Varden are both chars and trouts.

Once upon a time, all the country now known as the United States was divided into two parts as far as trout were concerned. In all the waters draining into the Atlantic, the eastern brook trout ruled the waves. The Atlantic salmon made annual migrations into the streams to spawn, and established scattered non-migratory colonies which we call landlocked salmon; but the fresh waters were essentially the domain of *Salvelinus fontinalis*.

The Pacific seaboard was the domain of the genus *Salmo*. Not a single eastern brook trout was to be found between the Mississippi basin and the west coast. His cousin, the Dolly Varden, *Salvelinus malma*, abounded in Alaska, and trickled south as far as northern California, while the Pacific salmon, a different genus from the Atlantic, made annual invasions from the ocean. But the Rockies and the Sierras, and all the streams flowing out of them, were the stronghold of *Salmo clarkii*, the cutthroat, and *Salmo gairdnerii*, the rainbow. And it is in these groups, and especially in the latter, that the worst complications arise. For it is easy enough to tell the eastern brook and the Dolly Varden and the Pacific salmon apart, but the rainbow in all his manifestations—Kern River trout, Kamloops trout, golden trout, steelhead—is a puzzle. He is an impressionable creature with whom evolution is still having its way, cutting him off in isolated groups from his brothers and sisters by geographic barriers, and bringing about the changes which, little by little, separate such colonies into distinct forms. Were it not for the interference of man, mixing the waters of different streams and watersheds with his engineering works, and mixing the different strains of trout with his hatchery fish, nature's processes could be expected to continue until clear-cut distinctions became evident. As it is, the taxonomic situation appears to be growing more confused, and we shall not attempt to untangle it here.

There is one question, however, which we must answer, and that is the old one, What is a steelhead? It is really very simple, and apparently the only reason why it keeps baffling people is that they refuse to believe what science tells them. The steelhead is a rainbow trout which goes out to sea for part of its life and returns to spawn in fresh water. The man who has given the most study to the subject in California recently has in essence this to say:

The only difference between a steelhead and a rainbow is in the migration to salt water. The adult steelhead is a trout that has spent part of its life in the ocean, with the increase in growth which accompanies such life. Young steelhead are the offspring of these fish. Steelhead streams are those in which the majority of fish are of this type, but may contain trout which have reached maturity without leaving the stream. And it may be that the hatch from eggs of this latter type can become migratory.

I know of no more complete answer to the old question. To render it in terms of the Atlantic coast, the rainbow is a "landlocked" steelhead.

Further, it is now held that the dominant trout of the Canadian Pacific coast, the Kamloops, is a form of the rainbow. The principal difference between them is the number of scales, and it has been found that by raising the temperature of the water during the embryonic period Kamloops can be produced with as few scales as the rainbow. The two are merely climatic variations of the same fish. If we admit this, we can tell ourselves a very complete, though entirely hypothetical story.

A certain fish at one time lived in the Arctic. He moved south into the waters between Europe and America, and there came to be called the Atlantic salmon. He moved south to our Pacific coast, and there came to be called the steelhead. He entered the streams of California and was known as the rainbow; he entered the streams of British Columbia, and was known as the Kamloops trout. He is at present engaged in turning himself into several distinct kinds of fish, but the distinctions are not yet very clear. Some day, unless man interferes, they may be. The intergrading links will then have disappeared, and we shall have sharply defined species;

but at the moment the Atlantic salmon and the Canadian Kamloops are still almost the same fish, and all the evolutionary steps are for once visible to us at the same time.[1]

To return to our United States and its partition between the eastern brook trout in the east and the rainbow-cutthroat in the west, that division no longer holds. You can no longer tell, from the fish that you take out of the water, whether you are angling in Vermont or in California; you may get eastern brook, rainbow, or European brown in either, or you may take all three fish out of the same stream. It is man who has altered the situation, and while he has made some mistakes in the way of unnecessary adulterations of native stock, he has on the whole been moving in the right direction. For the great lament that has been going up all over the country about the passing of the wild trout is not without foundation. Gasoline is easy to tax and gasoline taxes go into roads. Roads are being built into the most inaccessible corners of our land, and where roads go automobiles go, and where automobiles go fishermen go. And so the regions where wild trout still hold their own are being invaded, and there is no escape from the fact that eventually the greater part of the country will be reduced to the condition in which the thickly settled middle Atlantic states already find themselves. There each season's fishing strips the popular streams bare. Hardly a fish is left at spawning-time to produce another generation. If it were not for the state and Federal hatcheries, there would be few trout and little trout-fishing.

For their natural spawning, most trouts seek gravel beds in the shallow reaches of swiftly flowing streams. Instinctively they move against the current in their search for such regions,

---

[1] The only constant anatomical character by which the Atlantic salmon can be distinguished from the trout of the rainbow-steelhead series is the shape of one small bone lying deep within the skull.

river fish going up tributaries and lake fish ascending inlets, but some forms, including the landlocked salmon and the golden trout, will also go down into the outlet of a lake to spawn. The eastern brook trout, although normally seeking stream gravels, can spawn successfully in lakes if there are spring seepages in the bottom, and the lake trout or mackinaw spawn only on lake bottoms, without need of any current.

Many people have watched trout on their natural breeding-grounds, but early observers apparently confused courting and nesting activities with the true spawning act. Their descriptions have been so widely accepted in the past and have so firmly established certain misconceptions that it is worth while to summarize here the reports of more recent and more thorough observations.

The steelhead may be taken as a typical example. The female chooses the location, which is usually at the lower end of a pool where the still water just begins to break off into a riffle, and often where it is so shallow that her dorsal fin or even her back is visible above the surface. In leisurely fashion she digs a pit in the gravel. This is accomplished by turning on her side, pressing her tail against the bottom, and flapping it vigorously several times. The movement loosens the bottom materials, which are carried downstream by the current, and at the same time forces her upstream several feet. She returns to the spot, sometimes at once and sometimes after an interval, and continues operations, from time to time dropping down into the hollow and appearing to test it with her anal fin. Her mate remains in close attendance, a little to one side and a short distance to the rear. He does not help with the digging, but occupies himself in driving away the other males who invariably try to join the party, and in courtship. The latter consists partly in swimming around and over the female and nudging her with his snout, but most especially in coming close alongside her and

Base

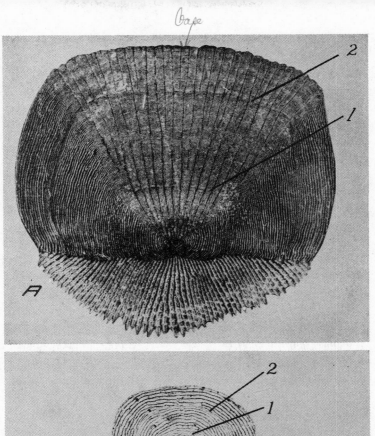

2

1

A

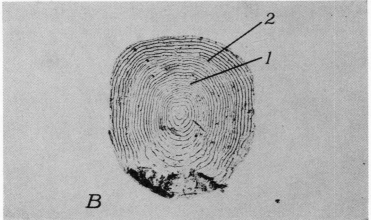

2

1

B

PLATE I. SCALES

A, ctenoid scale of 15-inch striped bass, in its third year, showing teeth on exposed rear part of scale. By permission of E. C. Scofield and the California Division of Fish and Game.

B, cycloid scale of 12-inch trout, in its third year. The points 1 and 2 on this scale, as in A, mark the annual checks at the end of the first and of the second year.

PLATE II. STEELHEAD SCALE

Scale of 28-inch specimen at end of fourth year, showing two years of stream life and two years of ocean life, with spawning at end of first year of ocean life. The scale was taken from the fish when it returned to the stream to spawn a second time.

Photomicrograph (40×) by Leo Shapovalov

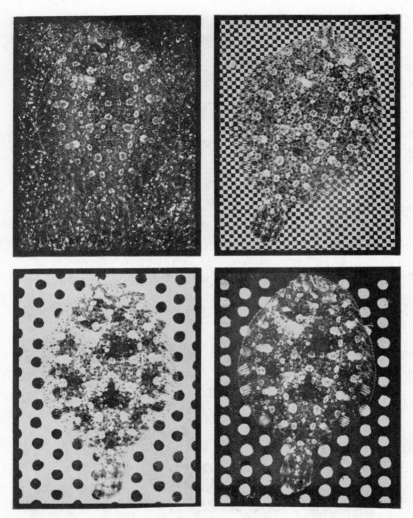

PLATE III. CHANGES IN THE COLOR PATTERN OF THE FLATFISH

Photographs of the same individual on various backgrounds,
by permission of Dr. F. B. Sumner.

SPAWNING JEWEL-FISH

The male is fertilizing the eggs while the female is swimming forward
to lay again.

American Museum of Natural History, New York

FEMALE JEWEL-FISH BROODING EGGS

American Museum of Natural History, New York

PLATE IV

PLATE V. CUTTHROAT TROUT AT MOMENT OF SPAWNING

The white "cloud" of milt is filling the pit and has spread beyond the female (nearer camera).

Osgood R. Smith

PLATE VI. BONNEVILLE DAM FISH LADDER
Salmon passing through Bradford Island counting station.

Portland District, Corps of Engineers, Photo

quivering, or vibrating his body rapidly. This is an outstanding courting act not only throughout the salmonid family, but also in entirely different species such as the jewel described in an earlier chapter. Since a very similar vibration accompanies the actual deposition of the sex products, the layman would be inclined to think that the male is putting on a "pseudo-spawning" or simulated spawning act in order to induce the female to do likewise in earnest, but no scientist could allow himself such a thought without suffering the accusation of unseemly anthropomorphism.

These activities may go on from one to eight hours, depending on the diligence of the female and her nesting standards, but eventually a depression some four to eight inches deep and about her own length has been completed which seems to satisfy her, and she suddenly drops into the center of this pit, with her vent and anal fin well down in the deepest part. The male immediately moves up into position alongside, with his vent opposite hers, and heeled over so that his abdomen is close to hers. With downwardly arched bodies quivering, with open mouths testifying to the muscular strain of the act, they discharge the eggs and milt at exactly the same instant. (See Plate V.) This is important for two reasons: first, because otherwise the milt might be carried away by the current without reaching the eggs, and second, because, although the eggs remain fertilizable for several minutes, the sperms lose their potency within forty-five seconds after they have entered the water.

Often one or more of the other attending males rush in and take part in the fertilization, the cloud of milt settling compactly about the bright pink eggs as they stream into the nest. The whole process takes about two seconds. The males then disperse, the dominant one returning to his original post. The female starts covering the eggs by digging slightly to the side and forward of the pit, the material displaced by her being carried into it by the current. Within a minute or two the eggs are well covered, and she moves upstream a short distance and begins a new nest. As she works on this, sand and gravel are carried downstream over the first excavation until it is turned into a mound projecting above the stream bed, and the eggs are protected by a layer of gravel four to eight inches deep. Steelhead characteristically start at the bottom of a suitable spawning area and work upstream, placing their egg-pits almost in a straight line with the current in a manner highly efficacious for the utilization of hydraulic forces, but other species do not always do so, the later nests sometimes being to the side of or even below the earlier ones. In all cases, work is done at the first site to cover the eggs; the protecting over-layer of gravel is not merely the fortuitous result of a later upstream spawning, but is definitely the completion of the spawning act at that point.

This process of nest-building, courtship, and spawning is repeated several times and may continue for anywhere from a day to a week before the female is rid of all her eggs. Mother and father then forget about family life and go their separate ways.

The whole spawning pattern is essentially similar in the rainbow, the cutthroat, the brown trout, and the various species of Pacific salmon, but in the eastern brook there is one variation which may have considerable significance. The female covers her egg-pit not by going upstream and flapping up gravel which the current carries over it, but by using her anal fin to sweep gravel over the pit from its edges. This is a much less efficient method than that described above where the current did a large share of the work; but it can be seen that it would produce a protective mound even where a current was lacking. Now, you will remember that the eastern brook is able to spawn successfully on a lake bottom with a spring seepage, where the other species are not. It is not at all impossible that this is the secret: that the trouts which depend upon a current to carry the protecting gravel over their eggs cannot operate where the only flow is upward; but that the eastern brooks, doing it the hard way, give their eggs the necessary gravel protection without the aid of a current, while the upwelling water suffices to bring the necessary oxygen for the young to develop.

Steelhead start spawning in the late fall, when the rains which follow the long dry season on the Pacific seaboard bring enough water down the coastal streams to permit them to ascend from the ocean, and continue until spring. Rainbow spawn in the early spring, and cutthroat slightly later. Brown trout, Dolly Varden, and eastern brook spawn in the autumn and early winter. The eggs of all lie for a long time developing under the gravel which protects them against enemies and light and yet permits the oxygen-bearing water to reach them; even after they have hatched, the little fish remain in the gravel until they have absorbed the nourishment in their yolk-sacs, when they are at last ready to wriggle their way up out of the bottom and start life on their own in the open water. These developmental processes take longer in cold water than in warm, but aside from that there is a difference between the species which seems to have some correlation with their life histories. Brook trout eggs develop more slowly than rainbow, even at the same temperature. Brook trout spawn in the fall and their low developmental rate, together with the cold winter water temperatures, keeps the young fish from coming up out of the gravel until the ice is off and food has begun to be plentiful in the early spring; whereas rainbow, spawning in the early spring, develop rapidly enough in the warming water to get the benefit of the full summer's feeding.

SALMON

All salmon, except for the "landlocked" races, are, like the steelhead, anadromous—meaning that they are born in fresh water, go to the ocean to live while growing up, and return to fresh water to spawn. This applies equally to the Atlantic and the Pacific species.

All the salmon in the Atlantic, whether they come from Norway or the Bay of Biscay or the Saint Lawrence River, are one and the same species. Their name runs trippingly off the tongue. It is *Salmo salar*, "Salmo the leaper."

The salmon of our Pacific coast are five species, and they range from the Asiatic rivers to the Sacramento. They belong to the burdensomely named genus *Oncorhynchus* ("hook-nose"). The five species labor under excruciating names taken from the Russian vernacular, such as *tschawytscha, gorbusha*, etc. We shall have nothing to do with these, and shall refer to them simply as the king or chinook salmon, the silver salmon, the pink salmon, the chum salmon, and the sockeye or red salmon.

The difference between the Atlantic salmon on the one hand and the whole group of Pacific "salmons" on the other is that the former does not necessarily die after it has spawned once, whereas the latter unquestionably and inevitably does. And the unforgettable similarity between the two is that the adults in both species, after years of wandering in the ocean, find their way back at spawning time to the identical stream in which they were born.

There is also on the Atlantic coast the landlocked salmon or "ouananiche." Some people claim that it is a distinct species, but I find it hard to believe that it is anything more than a non-migratory, fresh-water variety of *Salmo salar*. It often survives spawning. And on the Pacific coast our old friend the steelhead, *Salmo gairdnerii*, also often survives spawning, and from this and other similarities to the Atlantic form among which is the fact that it will take a fly on its way upstream to the spawning-beds whereas *Oncorhynchus* generally will not, it could be called the true salmon of the Pacific.[1]

Salmo salar used to be enormously abundant on our Atlantic coast. Dwellers along the Hudson and the streams further north had no trouble in catching all the fish they wanted from the great annual salmon runs. Now it is practically extinct—except in its landlocked form—south of the Canadian border, and to catch it you must travel hundreds of miles into remote country, and then probably pay a king's ransom for the right to put your fly into the water.

The Pacific salmon used to be enormously abundant in the Sacramento River; here it, too, has been greatly reduced by the progress of civilization, although surviving in sufficient numbers to provide a significant fishery. However, in the rivers further north, and especially in Alaska, the annual spawning migrants are still counted in almost astronomical figures. The capture of them is a great industry, and for this reason they have been much studied. In Norway and England, *Salmo salar* is still numerous, having been more carefully conserved in those old countries than it was on our Atlantic coast; and there, being the basis of both a sport and a commercial fishery, has received much study. Combining these two sources, the two forms of salmon have received more attention than any other fish. Experienced men, working for governmental and state agencies, have been reading their scales for years. They have "marked" them by cutting off one or more fins so that all members of a certain group

---

[1] It used to be firmly believed that none of the Pacific salmons would take a fly. It is now realized that under suitable conditions some species will,—especially the silver or coho and the chinook. Eventually ways may be found to capture all of them in this manner.

could be identified when caught again. They have "tagged" them with numbered metal plates or plastic disks so that individual fish could be identified when met with later. They have studied their metabolism and their birth rate and their growth rate. The result is that the natural history of the Atlantic and Pacific salmon is better known than that of any other fish, and what is set forth in the following paragraphs has a mathematical certainty about it which cannot often be attained in biological matters.

Aside from the essential difference in survival after spawning, the Atlantic and Pacific species lead quite similar lives. Both hatch out of eggs buried from five to ten inches under the gravel in the shallow, swift, upper reaches of streams. Both live for a certain length of time in these rivers. The pink salmon and the chum salmon of the Pacific stay only a few weeks, the others may remain anywhere from a few months to as much as three years, and this period varies not only between species, but also within each species, depending on the conditions and on the individual. All grow slowly during river life, few reaching a length of more than six inches in fresh water. All eventually go to sea, and there grow at a tremendously accelerated rate due to the enormously greater amount of food available. The record is held by an English fish which, according to the data, gained 27 pounds between May, 1905, and August, 1907—at the rate of a pound a month. The Pacific salmon rarely grow so fast.

Some of the Atlantic fish, especially the males, return to fresh water to spawn after only a few months at sea. They are still small, and are what the English call "grilse." Most of them remain longer in the sea, some being six or even seven years old on their first return. Such fish have had a chance to eat on a gargantuan scale, and it is probable that all very large individuals are in this category. Of the Pacific salmon, the pink all return at the end of their second year to spawn and die. The king mature anywhere between the second and sixth year, by far the greater number in the fourth and fifth years. The other species, including the steelhead, may be anywhere from two to five years old at maturity.

On entering fresh water they all cease to feed. Various explanations for this have been offered: that they have other things on their minds; that they are not equipped to eat the food available in fresh water, any more than a St. Bernard dog is equipped to catch mice; that their digestive juices cease to function and their stomachs shrink into hard little shells. This last change undoubtedly takes place, but it may be effect rather than cause. Why *salar* and the steelhead and some of the Pacific salmons none the less rise to the angler's fly is a question which we shall avoid discussing here on the ground that it has to do with fishing rather than with fish. In any case, most Pacific salmons go in for no such by-play, and thus come to sensible deaths in nets, and get shipped around the world in cans, instead of dying on the end of a sportsman's line and being eaten by his somewhat bewildered and supposedly admiring friends. But it must not be forgotten that a small proportion of them do yield to the sport fisherman's lures, both in sea and river, and escape the can in this way.

From the time they enter fresh water until they spawn, the fish must live on the reserves accumulated in earlier years in the form of fat and muscle. These reserves must not only provide the material for the eggs and sperm, which are largely manufactured after entering fresh water, but also must furnish the energy to carry the fish to the spawning grounds. The Atlantic salmon in America usually have a comparatively short journey, but in such a river as the Rhine they may spend as much as a whole year on the trip—without a bite to eat! It has been calculated that they lose, in body substance and in sex products discharged, between 40 and 45 per cent of their weight. Since death by starvation is known to occur in many animals when the loss in body weight exceeds 40 per cent, it may be assumed that those Atlantic salmon which survive spawning are the fortunate ones which have lost less than the average. The fact is that most Atlantic salmon in most localities do die after spawning. Only a small percentage survive to spawn a second time, and of those that have spawned twice only a few survive to spawn again. Fourth spawnings are exceedingly rare; in general eight years of life and three spawnings are the limit. In very short streams the spawning-beds are more quickly and easily reached than in the longer ones, the strain on the fish is not so great, and more of them survive. The survivors, having less distance to cover on their return journey to the sea and less depletion to make up, are more quickly ready for another spawning. The result is that the fish of such streams spend more time on the aggregate in fresh water, less time in the ocean sopping up good food, and therefore do not grow very large. This is one of the reasons why smaller streams usually have small salmon. The really big fish, as we have said, are the old "maidens"—the fish which do not come in from the feeding grounds for their first spawning until they have had a chance to do a lot of growing.

While some of the Pacific salmon travel only a short way, some have tremendous trips to make. Spawning-beds in the Yukon are two thousand miles from the sea, and, since the time between the disappearance of ice in the spring and its reappearance in the fall is so short, the distance must be covered with great speed. Records show the fish making the first fifteen hundred miles in thirty days—a rate of fifty miles a day, against a current which probably sets them back at least that amount. In other words, they cover what really amounts to three thousand miles in thirty days. By the end of the trip they are so thin and bruised and battered that they must be quite content to lie down and die as soon as they have done what they came for. In fish with much shorter journeys to make, it seems to be just a habit. They die also.

The spawning act of the Atlantic salmon has been scientifically reported as identical with that described for the steelhead. The spawning act of the Pacific salmons, according to those who have visited their breeding areas, is in a general way similar. The landlocked sockeye, also called "little redfish" or "kokanee," has been observed and recorded in close detail, but not the sea-run salmons on their natural breeding grounds. In the throngs of fish milling around, with dead bodies strewing the banks for miles, with new fish swarming in to dig up the eggs already laid in their search for nesting places, and with Dolly Varden trout darting about to prey on unprotected eggs, it is probably difficult to make out just what does happen. Somehow the eggs do get fertilized, and the next generation does get produced. Between generations, however, the waste is tremendous. It has been estimated in one case that, out of over seventeen million fertilized eggs, only five to six thousand fish survived to become parents of the second generation—a survival to maturity of only one fish for every three thousand eggs.

We now have reached the point where we can gaze with proper appreciation upon one of the great wonders, one of the outstanding unsolved mysteries, of the zoological world. This is the fact that the salmon, after years in the wide ocean, find their way back to spawn in the very same stream-bed out of which they once wriggled toward the light of day.

When and where human beings first began to suspect that this might be happening is uncertain. It was long ago, for the inquisitive Izaak Walton tied ribbons on the tails of fish in the hope of finding out where they went. It seems likely that small boys, or poachers, or fishermen, feeling sure that they recognized the same old salmon back in the same old pool, first got an inkling of what was happening. It seems likely that scientists at first laughed at them, and classed the suggestion with folklore and old wives' tales. Like many another old wives' tale, it has proved to be truth. Science has come to have more respect for old wives' tales than it once did.

When scientists took up the serious study of the salmon on account of its fisheries' value, they themselves began to find evidence in favor of the theory. They found that the fish in certain streams year after year showed strong racial characteristics—such as size, or fat-content, or coloration, or age at going to sea, or length of time spent at sea, or age at maturity. They found that with experience they could come pretty close to telling what river a fish was taken from just by examining its scales. They felt that these traits were probably hereditary. If fish from other parts, with different traits, came into the stream, how could these differences continue to exist? Only if the fish born in each stream returned to that stream to spawn could the racial differences be maintained.

They found that if the run of fish in a given stream were destroyed or prevented for several successive years, so that salmon ceased to be born and to grow up in that stream, the salmon did not return to it, even though conditions might be highly favorable for spawning. They found that in many rivers the pink salmon have a very heavy run every other year, a very light run in the intervening years. As we have seen, pink salmon all mature at two years. If fish came in from other streams, there would be no reason for this alternation; but if they did not, there would. For it is obvious that this year's heavy run would produce a large egg supply, which would result in a heavy run year after next, whereas last year's light run would produce a small egg supply, which would result in a light run next year, and so on *ad infinitum*.

Such facts as these were far from conclusive. At best, they were circumstantial evidence, but they were enough to spur scientists on to find incontrovertible proof of the matter, one way or the other. In this they were aided by the economic aspect of the question. Government agencies were trying to preserve the salmon by limiting the fisheries. Each fisherman was objecting that there was no point in saving the fish in his particular waters just to let them spawn a new generation somewhere else for someone else to catch. If it could be shown that the adult fish always returned to the stream in which they originated, it could be made clear to the fishermen that saving fish in his waters would be for his own benefit, not someone else's, and that if the fish in his waters were exterminated, he himself would be the one to suffer.

And so Great Britain and Canada and the United States all undertook to find out the truth. They initiated great marking programs. In the Welsh and Scottish rivers, and in the streams of North America, hundreds of thousands of little salmon lost fins. Before they went out from their natal waters to the sea, they were seized upon and their home address was unalterably fixed upon them. In one stream the adipose and one ventral fin were removed, in another both left fins, in a third the diagonals, in a fourth the anal and right pectoral, and so on. Then careful watch was kept of the fish returning to spawn. And the amazing fact was proved that they do return to the stream in which they grew up. The proof is overwhelming. On this continent the number of fish which have been marked is close to four million. I do not know the number in Great Britain, but it is large. And while some fish have been found other than in the stream where they belonged, they are so few in proportion as to be negligible. Fish do stray, as no one doubts —even humans make mistakes—but the general truth of the principle is not to be questioned.

Most of us can look upon this phenomenon with a satisfying degree of wonder and humility. However, scientists are by nature and training skeptics. They must, if they are to be good scientists, never accept things at face value. They must look for flaws and possible loop-holes. They must determine whether what seems to be cause and effect is not really due to chance. And some of them pointed out that chance might play a large part in the return of the salmon.

According to this hypothesis, salmon go out from the estuaries into the sea, follow along the submarine river-beds until they get to the point where the bottom slopes off steeply at the edge of the continental shelf, and there remain to feed and grow until the time for spawning. They then seek the nearest fresh water, and this is the river out of which they came, whose "influence" they have never left.

Most of the men closely involved in the salmon studies had to admit the possibility of this hypothesis, but felt that it did not jibe with things which they knew almost certainly to be true, but could not prove to be scientific facts. In the meantime another government program was piling up evidence in their support. This time it was not a matter of cutting off fins, but of numbering the fish. Men went to sea in ships, caught salmon in nets all up and down the coast, and fastened to each fish a small plate with a serial number on it. When these numbered fish were recovered on their spawning-runs, it was possible, by looking in the records, to find the exact spot in the sea where each had been marked. It was found that some fish had wandered as far as fifteen hundred miles from the mouth of their "home" estuary. It was found that most of the chinook taken by the fishermen from the mouth of the Columbia to Sitka, Alaska, are Columbia River salmon. And it was found that salmon tagged all at one spot in the ocean turned up in widely separate streams at spawning time.

All of which the skeptics agreed was most interesting in showing that some fish did go to distant places in the sea, but failed to agree that it proved anything about "homing." That a salmon which was caught and tagged in the ocean later came to spawn in a stream hundreds of miles away failed to demonstrate, they claimed—and quite logically—that it had been born in that stream. The total number of fish tagged was but a fraction of all the salmon in the seas; it might be that all the tagged ones were strays. It might be that the fish which were marked by fin removal before they left their native streams and which later did return there to spawn, never got beyond the continental shelf and the influence of their own streams, and that the others which went further and which were tagged with numbered disks far at sea, never did get home, but became the strays. For conclusive proof, it would be necessary for a little fish to be marked by fin removal with its proper address before it left home, to be recaptured far away in the ocean by one of the interested agencies and numbered with a tag, and then to return to its own stream and have the fortune to fall into the hands of someone who would recognize the importance of *both* the missing fins *and* the tag. That such a series of coincidences could occur outside of fiction seemed, by the laws of combination and permutation, of a likelihood so remote as to be for all practical purposes impossible.

And yet the impossible did occur. In 1938 a young Atlantic salmon had its adipose fin removed on its way down the Northeast Margaree River, Cape Breton Island, to the ocean. In June of 1940 this fish was captured off Bonavista on the east coast of Newfoundland, 550 miles away by sea. It was given a numbered tag and released. Ninety-six days later it was taken by an angler in the Northeast Margaree River. Bonavista is alongside the Labrador current, and entirely remote from any conceivable influence of the Margaree River; but the fish had come home to spawn. And in 1943 two pink salmon which had been fin-marked in Morrison Creek on Vancouver Island in the spring of 1942, and which had been captured and tagged in the ocean earlier in 1943, one at a point 45 miles to the north and one 115 miles to the south, returned to Morrison Creek to spawn, and reached the counting weir on the same day. These fish had not been so far as the Atlantic salmon, but they had come through strong tidal currents where any influence of their native water must have been entirely obliterated. Little ground is now left for the skeptics to stand on.

To add further to the wonderment, of layman and scientist alike, it has now been proved that the fish return to spawn not only to the general river system where they grew up, but to the exact identical small tributary stream. Steelhead marked in Fall Creek near the Oregon-California line have gone down the Klamath River to the Pacific (ocean life showed clearly on their scales), and after three years have re-entered the Klamath, swum up it 200 miles past the mouths of numerous other tributaries until they came to Fall Creek, and there turned off, just as you turn off the highway when you get to the corner that leads to your house, and entered it to spawn. This is hard to believe, but it is true. It has been found to be true in other cases, where salmon have come back not only to the same river but to the same brook where they were born. And both Atlantic salmon and steelhead have been known to enter the wrong stream, make a brief stay there *without* spawning, and then leave and go to the right one.

This has been called the "parent stream theory." It is no

longer theory but fact. Moreover, the word *parent* is misleading. The fish do not necessarily return to the stream of their parents, or even to what might be called their "parent stream." They return to the stream in which they themselves *grew up*. Sockeye eggs were brought from Alaska and hatched at Bonneville on the Columbia River. The little fish were marked. They went out to sea, and when they returned to spawn, they went not to Alaska but to the Columbia River. They not only entered the Columbia, but they swam up it one hundred miles to Bonneville and there they deposited their eggs. Their young grew up, were marked, went out to sea, and in due time this second generation also came back to Bonneville to spawn. They had adopted this water as a "foster-parent."

How are these astounding feats of home-finding accomplished? This question has several parts, susceptible of different answers. In the first place, the fish must find his way through trackless ocean waters to the mouth of his own river. Other animals perform similar voyages: birds fly vast distances between summer and winter quarters, flightless penguins swim with infallible precision from the Antarctic to South America and back, adult eels find their way across the ocean to their breeding grounds near the West Indies. All we can say is that some powerful directional sense is at work, and it may be that there is something in the hypothesis that it is the action on the semi-circular canals of the ear and their associated sense-organs of the so-called "Coriolis force"—a resultant of such geo-physical factors as the rotation and angular velocity of the earth, the velocity of a body relative to the earth's surface, and the angle between the body's direction of motion and the earth's spin axis.

Assuming that some such force does exist to keep the salmon on the proper compass course, how does he distinguish the waters of his own river system from the others with which he comes in contact? And how does he pick out his own small tributary as he ascends a large river? Does he remember landmarks so clearly that he can retrace his route years later? Or is it true, as some scientists suggest, that he has a chemical sense which enables him to pick out the chemical composition of his own water from all the other currents which he meets, and with some of which it mingles? Aside from the fact that his own home water probably differs from itself in chemical composition at various times of the year more than it differs from other near-by streams at the same time of year, it is harder for me to believe that the salmon's chemical memory can retain for years his home stream's composition than to believe that his visual memory can retain the landmarks. One needs, like Alice in Wonderland's queen, to be able to believe at least three impossible things before breakfast. We know that birds, after a several-thousand-mile round trip to their wintering grounds, return in the spring to the same nest that they occupied the previous year. We find ourselves capable of believing that their memory enables them to do this, although we could not do it ourselves. We know that a salmon can travel a thousand miles from his own stream and still find his way back to the small tributary of that stream in which he was born. If we are not capable of believing that he does this by means of a topographic sense stronger than any we ourselves know, then we must believe that it is by means of some sense of which we do not even conceive.

Baffled in their efforts to solve the "parent stream"—preferably the "home stream"—problem, zoologists have turned to the question of what makes the salmon leave salt water and come into fresh to spawn. It is easy to say that it is instinct, just as it is instinct which makes a bird build a nest before it lays its eggs. Scientists are no longer satisfied with that answer. They want to know how instinct works. Scientists always want to know more than they know now. The unknown is the food on which they live.

They have found that in some cases what has been called instinct is in reality a definite reaction to definite conditions. It is this kind of reason which they have tried to find for the spawning migration of salmon. One theory is that the fish seek lower temperatures, choosing always the stream with colder water. This has the defect of not always harmonizing with the facts, any more than the theory that they always choose the stronger current.

A second hypothesis is very complete. It holds in the first place that, as spawning-time approaches, the salmon's metabolism is accelerated, it needs more oxygen, and it therefore ascends those rivers in which oxygen is more abundant than in the ocean. Theoretically the oxygen content increases the higher up a stream you go, and this would lead the salmon on up to the spawning-beds. Actually there are often stretches where for a short space the oxygen content remains stationary or even decreases. If, then, this theory were true, the salmon would cease to advance at such a point. The second part of the theory deals with the descent of young salmon to the sea, which it accounts for by the fact that when they change from their dark parr coloring to their light smolt shade, they become exceedingly sensitive to light, and seek the deeper ocean waters for protection against it. This double-barreled theory should be the delight of those who like to explain everything on purely mechanistic grounds.

A very engaging hypothesis is the argument that a salmon is practically forced to return to fresh water by the buoyancy of the fat which he stores up. He comes down from the river a thin little fish, well adapted to the heavier salt water he is about to enter. For a year or two his food goes into growth. Then, in the last year before he matures, he starts to put on fat, and he eventually becomes so buoyant that he seeks the less dense fresh water in order to be able to handle himself with more comfort. This fails to take into account the grilse which mature and come into fresh water before they have reached the stage of great obesity.

Still another theory is that their keen sense of smell leads salmon into those streams in which there are at the moment young salmon. This is based on an experiment in which salmon fry were placed in a stream which had once had a salmon run, which had then been closed by a dam, and which even after the dam had been out ten years had failed to attract a run. That very summer adult salmon entered the stream and spawned—brought in, according to the theory, by the smell of the little fish. This sounds convincing, but it is not conclusive: a group of lost fish may have strayed in. Further similar experiments are needed to prove that coincidence played no part.

And the most recent theory, based on deep study of physiology, osmosis, metabolism and chemistry, and set forth with elaborate and convincing technical detail, maintains that the carbon dioxide content of the water holds the true answer, and that the salmon is absolutely obliged to follow a carbon dioxide gradient which leads him unfailingly to spawning grounds in fresh-water streams.

Now, any or all of the reasons advanced in these various hypotheses may have something to do with the salmon's migration into fresh water. But the fact remains that none of them tell us how the salmon finds its home stream. And the fact remains that trout carry on the same migration in a minor key, but may go upstream or down, into cooler or warmer water, into water higher or lower in oxygen; and their sense of smell can play no part in a downstream movement, and their fat content can play no part in a movement which begins and ends in fresh water. When they come to a gravel fine enough to keep enemies away from their eggs and coarse enough to let water in, and a current swift and cool and well-aerated enough to let their eggs breathe, they are satisfied and they spawn. If the trout can go through this cycle of behavior without any of the influences set forth in the foregoing hypotheses, it seems reasonable to believe that the salmon can do the same; and if that is so, then the theories fail to explain.

CHAPTER X

Other Game Fish

A GREAT many fishes furnish excellent sport for anglers. It being manifestly out of the question to consider them all, we shall, with apologies to those passed over, confine ourselves to the few species dealt with in this chapter. Of some, such as the black bass, the natural history is well known. Of others, for instance the tarpon, our knowledge is expanding rapidly. And of still others, such as the swordfish, the life-story is almost a closed book, and to try to set it forth is interesting primarily in that it shows how little of it we know.

TARPON

The tarpon has been well treated by the taxonomists, for they call him, quite simply, *Tarpon atlanticus*. He is a good example of a primitive present-day fish; ventral fins placed well to the rear, no spines, and air-bladder opening into the gullet by a tube. It would be unkind to him and to his devotees to call him a glorified herring, but just as the lordly salmon is a distant relative of the lowly smelt, so is the mighty tarpon a distant relative of the little fish which appears on the breakfast table as a kipper. For he belongs to the order *Clupioidea*, and to this belong not only his cousin the bonefish, but also the alewives, herrings, shads, and sardines. In vindication of his character, it should be pointed out that he is the purest of all game fishes, for as a table delicacy he is a total loss, and it is solely in the name of sport that man pursues him. Ulterior motives might be assigned

to the trout and salmon fishermen, even to the hunters of
tuna and swordfish, but not to the tarpon-angler.

The tarpon has been found on the west coast of Africa,
and strays as far north as Massachusetts, but his center of
abundance is the Gulf of Mexico, where he spends much of
his time among the shoals and passes and keys which line
the coasts of Florida and southern Texas. He also goes

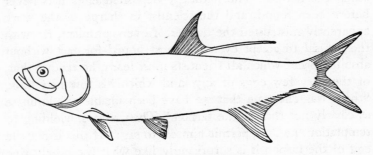

FIGURE 24. TARPON

From Jordan and Evermann, *Fishes of North and Middle America* by
permission of the United States National Museum.

readily into fresh water; he is a well-known visitor to Lake
Nicaragua. He eats mullet, pinfish, sea catfish, sardine,
shrimp, and crab. His enemies are the shark, which he can
outrun, and the porpoise. He is hooked mostly at a depth of
about forty feet, whereupon he rushes to the surface and
leaps what seems to be about forty feet into the air. Uncon-
cerned observers have estimated that his jump is in reality
not over twelve feet high and twenty-five feet long.

Studies begun only ten years ago have thrown much light
on hitherto dark passages in the tarpon's life. Up to that time,
no one had ever seen this fish spawn, and where such activities took place was purely a matter of conjecture. Now spawning has been observed; in May, June, and July, between the
islands of the Florida keys, pairs of fish, or sometimes three

(the eternal triangle—presumably, two males and one female) have been seen milling around in the shallows, with
white clouds of the milt emitted by the males appearing in
the water.

The next step in the study was to recover some of the eggs.
Since it was known that the nearly ripe eggs taken from
captured females sank, a very fine-meshed net was towed
along the bottom. The naturally deposited eggs had never
before been found, and the scientist in charge of the work
apparently mistrusted the danger of over-optimism, for with
the refusal to accept even the most hoped-for fact without
absolute proof which all scientists must learn, he reports that,
of the very few eggs of any kind which his tow nets took,
"there was one type that we have been unable to eliminate
as clearly not that of the tarpon." Then, almost yielding to
temptation, he does permit himself to say: "If this is not the
egg of the tarpon it is surprisingly like what the nearly ripe
eggs must approach on full development."

These eggs were one-sixteenth of an inch in diameter, as
compared to less than one-thirty-second of an inch for the
eggs found in the nearly ripe ovaries; but the latter swell to
the size of the former when permitted to stand in water—
a process known as "water-hardening," whereby water per-
meates through the egg surface and enters the space between
the inner and outer membranes, thus providing a cushion
which protects the developing embryo against shocks. The
prized eggs were taken to the laboratory and hatched in
basins in the hope that their development would give sure
proof of the species to which they belonged, but it was found
impossible to keep any of the little fish alive for more than
three days. During this period they shrank in size instead of
growing, and the most advanced laboratory stage showed
"characters not unlike those seen in the pre-leptocephalid
larvae of apodal fishes."

"Apodal fishes" are eels, and the very young differ from the adults so much that they were once thought to be a separate species and given the name *Leptocephalus*. The name is now used to describe the stage in the young of other species in which their larval appearance is very like the little eel, and unlike their own species. The bonefish or ladyfish, famous game fish of Florida waters recently discovered to be a resident of Southern California, is definitely known to go through this larval stage. It starts life as a thin ribbon, with

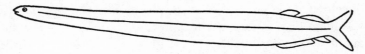

FIGURE 25. LARVAL OR LEPTOCEPHALID STAGE OF
BONEFISH

a tiny head at one end and the dorsal and anal fins crowded together at the other end (see Figure 25). It is almost transparent, and in open water the spot formed by its eye is about the only thing that can be seen. It grows in this form until it is over two inches long. Then a metamorphosis sets in. Its growth goes into reverse, and it starts to get smaller. It shrinks rapidly until in ten days it is less than an inch long, and at the same time it abandons its disguise and changes into a miniature of the adult fish.

Elops, the ten-pounder, also has this leptocephalid stage. The close relationship of it and the bonefish to the tarpon has led zoologists to believe that very possibly a like stage may occur in the development of the tarpon. Support for this theory came in 1934, when a little fish one inch long from near Beaufort, North Carolina, was tentatively described as a tarpon in transition from the leptocephalus to the adult form. This specimen was unfortunately destroyed before it could be drawn or preserved, but recent analysis of the de-

scription has shown a discrepancy in the number of rays in
the dorsal and anal fins, and raises strong doubt whether
this actually was a tarpon.

If the tarpon does have a leptocephalus stage, why has it
never been found, when this stage in the ten-pounder is
common? The fate of the little fish hatched from the hypothetical "tarpon" eggs in the laboratory provides a clue to
the answer. The water in which they were held, taken from
the nearby shore, was found to be full of minute crustaceans
which were so voracious that they set upon the little fish and
devoured them as soon as they were out of the egg, and it
was impossible to raise them even to three days of age without first filtering out these predators. The "green" inshore
water where the tarpon have been seen to spawn is also alive
with these crustaceans; the "blue" outside waters are almost
devoid of them. In these "blue" waters larval stages of other
known fish have been found which are absent from the inshore waters. Piecing all of these facts together, the following hypothesis emerges: Little tarpon which hatch in the
"green" water succumb to the tiny crustacean predators.
However, the smooth round eggs are immune to such attacks; if some of these are carried by currents into the "blue"
water before hatching (and in the denser "blue" water they
float), the larval tarpon then have a chance to survive. Or, it
may be that adult tarpon spawn in the "blue" water as well
as in the "green." That the larval tarpon has a leptocephalus
stage and that this stage is passed in the "blue" waters is the
conjecture which fills in the gap in our knowledge. The fact
remains, however, that neither in these "blue" waters nor
anywhere else has anything been found which could be positively identified as a larval tarpon.

With the very doubtful exception of the Beaufort specimen, tarpon under two inches long have never been seen.
From two to eight inches, numerous individuals have been

obtained, mostly well up rivers or from landlocked waters formerly connected with the sea. These specimens, and others of larger size, have been studied, and good evidence obtained that their age can be assessed from the annuli which appear on their scales. When it is realized that the water temperature at Boca Grande, Florida, ranges from a high of 93 degrees in summer to a low of 59 degrees in winter, and that there is a seasonal change in the availability of the various food forms, it is not surprising that there is a change in the growth rate which would show on the scales.

According to scale readings, tarpon reach a length of ten inches at the end of the first year, twenty inches at the end of the second, thirty inches at the end of the third. They probably start spawning in their sixth or seventh year, when they are about four feet long, and it is at this time that they play the largest part in the catch. However, there is evidence that angling is not heavy enough to deplete their numbers to a dangerous extent. Ten-year-old fish are not uncommon, and average five feet in length. The oldest fish found in the course of scale examination had reached its fifteenth year.

One of the most startling facts recently discovered about the tarpon has to do with its air-bladder. As we have seen in Chapter VI, this is well supplied with blood vessels and has an open connection with the gullet which enables little tarpon trapped in landlocked lagoons where the water is almost devoid of oxygen to survive by coming to the surface for air. Experiments have now shown that even in well-oxygenated sea water these fish rise periodically for air—adults on the average of five times per hour, younger fish more frequently. If prevented from coming to the surface, they perish—in the experiments, within from seven to 128 hours. Like human beings, they must have air; if held under water too long, they drown.

TUNA

The tuna is a giant relative of the common mackerel. The name is used for several species, but the one which is of most interest to sportsmen is *Thunnus thynnus*, the blue-fin tuna. This animal has the less frigid regions of the whole world for its home. In the North Sea, the North Atlantic, the Mediterranean, the Caribbean, the North and South Pacific, and off Madagascar, the same species has been caught. Its relations with man go back into antiquity, for its pictures figure in Greek designs. In spite of all this, very little is known about it. However, to avoid giving a wrong impression, let me specify that it is its life history that is little known. Its insides—its anatomy, its physiology, its chemistry —have been well explored; it is the habits of the beast which remain in darkness.

Tuna are believed to mature at three years of age, when they weigh about thirty pounds. Spawning presumably occurs between December and July, varying with the locality; spawning areas are not definitely known. Eggs, of the pelagic or floating type, have been found in the Mediterranean. They hatch in two days into larvae less than one-quarter inch long. Larvae have been found in the Mediterranean and in mid-Atlantic. Fish under six to ten pounds are unknown on the shores of North America. Large tuna feed on mackerel, herring, dogfish, squid, flying fish. On account of their size and speed, they have only one effective enemy, *Orca*, the killer-whale, which they greatly fear.

Migrations northward in summer and southward in winter are characteristic of the tuna. In California it makes its appearance off the southern coast in May and moves northward as the season advances. In December it vanishes, and from December to May its whereabouts is unknown. It reaches a weight of five hundred pounds and is subject to a great commercial fishery. It is easily caught in purse seines when the water is relatively warm, but cooler water makes it wary and active and often drives it down from the surface. More recently, the primitive hook-and-line has largely replaced the net, the big new boats, which sometimes spend weeks offshore, being designed primarily for this kind of fishing. When a school of tuna is found, the fishermen clamber over the sides onto racks around the stern of the vessel. Each man wields a stout bamboo pole with a short line and a feathered "jig" with a barbless hook. Almost in one motion, the hook strikes the water, is seized by the fish, and is heaved backward and upward, so that the startled tuna flies through the air and lands on the deck behind the fisherman. The barbless hook comes out and is immediately cast back into the water. When a school is biting fast, action is almost continuous. If the fish are too large for one man to handle, two work together, one hook being fastened by a twin line arrangement to two poles which are lowered and raised in perfect unison. For big fish, three men with three poles must join forces, and for the biggest four, and sometimes even five. To see those bamboos bend as the giant fish rises and sails through the air is a spectacular sight. As may be guessed, a strong back is an essential for a commercial tuna fisherman—but in few activities does a strong back gain a higher financial reward.

The tuna is in California also a great sport fish, for it was at Santa Catalina Island that a hardy, pioneering gentleman first conceived of the possibility of catching this huge animal on rod and line, and did actually take one on tackle which would now be looked on as pitiable. This was the inception of the famous Tuna Club. It was also in California that the most effective method of getting tuna on a troll hook was invented—attaching a kite to the line, which pulls the lure out of the wake of the boat, and makes it skip over the surface in simulation of a flying fish.

In this connection, the natural relation between the flying fish and the tuna is of interest. The tuna is, as we know, one of the fastest of fishes: it can make at least thirty miles an hour. In the water, the flying fish can attain no such speed, but it has been estimated that in the air it sometimes glides more than one thousand feet at a rate of forty miles an hour. When it does this it leaves the tuna far behind. Therefore a single flying fish can escape a single tuna if it makes a good flight; but if it makes a poor one, or if it is surrounded by a school of tuna, it has little chance.

One other feature of interest in connection with the tuna's speed is its high body temperature. Unlike most fish, its insides are consistently six to eight degrees warmer than the surrounding water. The explanation is thought to lie in the smallness of its viscera. This great big bouncing fish is almost all muscle, with its stomach and intestines tucked away in a comparatively tiny space. To furnish the energy necessary for the animal's swift propulsion through the water, a great amount of food must be consumed. With its small capacity, the only way to accomplish this is to pass the food through the digestive organs with great rapidity. In other words, the fuel must be burned very fast, and the result is a high body temperature.

On our Atlantic coast, the tuna follows the example of many vacationists, and goes to New England for the summer. On account of the immense size which it reaches in these waters—one thousand pounds is not uncommon, and a ten-foot fish weighing sixteen hundred pounds has been recorded—the New England fishermen used to call it the "horse mackerel," and for a long time had little regard for it as a food-fish. More recently they have come to realize that the Mediterranean peoples have for centuries considered it highly edible. Recently, also, east coast sportsmen have awakened to the fact that the fish which they had been traveling to California to catch had a summer colony in their home waters, and one of them has taken a tuna weighing over nine hundred and fifty pounds. But, as one Massachusetts ichthyologist has remarked, "No one has yet succeeded in subduing a really large tuna on rod and reel." This is perhaps the New Englander's quiet way of pointing out to the Californian that his tuna do not compare in size with those found on the effete east coast. But, regardless of size, the tuna disappears from New England when winter comes just as completely as from California, and its spawning is just as much of a mystery.

SWORDFISH

The swordfish is the greatest fighter of them all, for it not only fights to get away from the fisherman, as all good game fish do, but it sometimes turns and carries the fight to him, especially when harpooned. It has been known to swim at his boat and drive its sword through the planks. Whether this attack is intentional, or just happens in the course of its blind rushes, we do not know, but in any case it gives the fisherman a thrill. The psychology of these animals is difficult to understand, for it is hard to see why they should attack ships, and yet there are indisputable records which prove that they do, One rammed a China clipper so violently that she leaked, and there was great to-do in the law courts as to whether the resulting damages should be paid by the insurance companies, or whether it was an act of God not included in ordinary marine risks. And there are records of a ship's hull being penetrated to a depth of eight inches by a swordfish sword. The speed and weight which could drive the weapon this far into wooden planking at a single blow can only be imagined.

The broadbill swordfish rejoices in the merry name of *Xiphias gladius*. *Xiphias* means "sword" in Greek, *gladius* means "sword" in Latin. The scientist who labeled it was evidently impressed with the fact that it has a sword. This is a flat, sharp-edged projection of the upper jaw which may

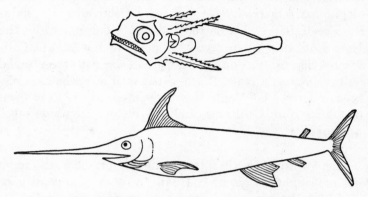

FIGURE 26. SWORDFISH, YOUNG (much enlarged) AND ADULT (much reduced).

After Ch. Lütken.

The little creature at the top of this figure was first thought to be the young of the sailfish, but was later classed as a swordfish. The matter is not yet completely settled, but in either case the young has no sword, the adult has.

reach a length of five to six feet, and the fish has been known to attain a length of fifteen feet overall and a weight of one thousand pounds. Like the tuna, it roams throughout the world, avoiding only the regions where the water is really cold. It feeds on schooling fish such as menhaden, mackerel, even bonito, and is said to strike right and left with its sword in a school until it has incapacitated several of its prey, which it then eats. The larger sharks are its natural enemies. Like the sharks, it often carries remoras, those small fish which use the suctorial disks on the tops of their heads to attach themselves to their large hosts and thus obtain free rides to the meals provided by the latter.

Stories of swordfish banding together with thresher sharks to attack larger animals are to be looked on with suspicion. It is possible that both species have in the course of history attacked the same animal at the same time, but actual co-operation between them is unlikely.

Swordfish spawn in the vicinity of Sicily and Cuba, and very probably in other locations not yet discovered. The eggs are minute, round and buoyant, and hatch two days after fertilization. The very young fish are wistful-looking little things, with scales and teeth, but no sword. As they grow, scales and teeth disappear, and the upper jaw develops the sword.

The spear-fish or marlin, so-called because its sword is round like a spear or marlinspike, belongs to a different genus from the broadbill. It has ventral fins, which the broadbill lacks, and it has teeth and scales in the adult form. The sailfish is a close relative of the marlin, and gets its name from its long, high, sail-like dorsal fin.

STRIPED BASS

The striped bass is native to our Atlantic coast from the Saint Lawrence River to the Gulf of Mexico. He lives, according to books, in tidal estuaries, but he is frequently caught in the ocean surf, and he goes up rivers into fresh water to spawn. He is a natural wanderer, but his longest voyage was anything but natural. This occurred back in 1879, when 135 young striped bass journeyed by train from the Navesink River in New Jersey to San Francisco Bay. Three years later, 300 more followed in the footsteps of the pioneers. From these small beginnings the species has spread up and down the coast for five hundred miles, and is now abundant in the Sacramento River, where it is held in high esteem as a game fish. Tampering with nature often has unhappy results. The English sparrow imported to this country to combat caterpillars, the rabbit taken to Australia to provide food, have turned into intolerable nuisances. But unless the striped bass's occasional habit of eating young steelhead and salmon turns out to be a real boomerang, it can be said that its introduction to California has brought only happiness to all concerned, and the same thing is true of the shad, which was shipped west at about the same time, and which is now more abundant there than in its native waters in the east. These two immigrants furnish food and recreation which would not otherwise exist, and, with the above-mentioned reservation, the men who conceived and brought about their importation may be looked upon as benefactors of humanity.

The striped bass is a typical modern fish with all the advanced features. Its ventral fins are located under the pectorals, its dorsal is double with the forward part supported by stiff spines and the after part by soft rays, its scales are ctenoid, its premaxillary bone forms the upper lip to the exclusion of the maxillary, and its air-bladder has lost its connection with the gullet. It belongs to the *Serranidae*, and is therefore more closely related to the sea-bass and the grouper than to the large- and small-mouth black bass, which are members of another family.

Its natural history is fairly well known. It spawns between the months of March and July, when temperatures range between 60 and 75 degrees. It may spawn in brackish water, as has been reported, but certainly much more often in fresh. It chooses channels where there is a definite current— sometimes not great, but sometimes very considerable. One of its best-known spawning grounds on the Atlantic coast is in the fast-flowing, rock-strewn rapids of the Roanoke River. On the Pacific coast it spawns in the comparatively slow-moving tidal currents of the Sacramento-San Joaquin Delta and also well up the Sacramento in more rapidly moving waters.

Its spawning activities, called "rock-fights" in the east where the name "rock-fish" is current, involve large numbers of individuals splashing about at the surface. Anywhere from five to thirty appear, mill around for a few moments, then all head up- or downstream and roll over on their sides at about a 45-degree angle, throwing water in all directions with their tails. These groups are usually composed of one female and many males, the female being larger than her consorts; and many such groups are in sight at one time. That this is actually reproduction, and not courtship, is proved by the fact that fertilized eggs can be collected from the vicinity which are only one-sixteenth inch in diameter, having not yet "water-hardened"—a process which, while taking only one hour, swells them to about one-eighth inch in diameter.

The eggs sink but are what is called "semibuoyant," meaning that they are so near the same specific gravity as water that the slightest disturbance will lift them off the bottom. They hatch in seventy hours at 60 degrees, in forty-eight hours at 67 degrees. The young absorb the yolk-sac in a week, and form scales when about half an inch long. They grow rapidly, averaging four to five inches at the end of the first year, fifteen inches at the third, twenty at the fifth, thirty-two at the tenth, forty-two at the fifteenth. This is when food is abundant and temperatures favorable, but it appears that even under optimum conditions growth takes place only between May and October, and that during the remaining months of each year there is no increase in size. They live to be at least twenty-five years old, and have been known to reach a length of six feet and a weight of 125 pounds. They eat herring, sand-launce, menhaden, crustaceans, mussels, and small fish.

Males reach maturity in the second or third year, females in the fourth or fifth, and they spawn annually thereafter. They do not give up feeding during the spawning period, so that growth is not interrupted at this season, and the scales show no spawning-mark. The number of eggs is large: about one million for a ten-pound female, ten million for a seventy-five pounder. Males are smaller than females of the same age, and this is a fact which holds true for many of the bony fishes. Males are often smaller and brighter-colored than their consorts.

BLACK BASS

The black bass is a typically American fish. He belongs to a family native only to North America, the *Centrarchidae,* which includes also the crappies and the sunfishes. His character embodies traits which we like to think of as typically American: adaptability, gameness, individuality. And one of his first appearances in history is also typically American: it consisted of a journey in the water-tank of a locomotive.

The black bass was originally confined to the Saint Lawrence and Mississippi basins, and to the South Atlantic states and the territory near the Mexican border. He was not to be found in the New England and Middle Atlantic states, and in the days of slow travel it was impossible to transport him. At that time there lived a gentleman named William Shriver who could not get over the fact that a careless god had done everything imaginable to make the Potomac a paradise for black bass, and had then neglected to put any of the species in that body of water. When the Baltimore & Ohio Railroad was completed across the Alleghenies, the event had one significance to Mr. Shriver: man had provided the link which nature had omitted. He procured a large bucket, punched it full of holes, filled it with bass, and then hung it in the water-tank of the locomotive while the train puffed down to the shores of the Potomac. There he released his fish, and there have been black bass in the Potomac ever since.

Since that day, many other shipments of this fish have been successfully completed, both by government agencies and by individuals. The ease with which it is kept alive, and its adaptability, have favored its artificial distribution. It is now to be found all over the United States, and it has been successfully introduced into Cuba, Great Britain, continental Europe, and even South Africa.

It can survive under conditions which trout would find insupportable, and if deforestation, irrigation, flood control, and power projects continue to change the nature of our lakes and streams, the bass will take the place of the trout in many of our more populous areas. This is bad news for the trout fisherman, but since the trout seems doomed in these localities anyway, we can be thankful for so desirable a replacement. That bass exterminate trout when introduced into the same water has never been conclusively proved, but observation shows that where conditions are equally favorable to both, the bass often become the dominant fish. Where the advantage is distinctly on the side of the trout he is generally able to resist the inroads of his rival, although sometimes even in cold waters he goes down before hordes of stunted bass. The introduction of bass into trout water should therefore be carefully guarded against unless it has been definitely decided to give that water over to the spiny fish.

So far we have spoken of the black bass as though it were one species, which is obviously untrue. There are two species: [1] the small-mouth, *Micropterus dolomieu,* and the large-

[1] A third, the spotted or Kentucky bass, *Micropterus punctulatus,* is now recognized, intermediate between the other two.

mouth, which the systematists changed from the genus *Micropterus* to the genus *Huro* some years ago, and have now decided to restore to *Micropterus*. *Micropterus salmoides* is now once more its name. The two are so much alike that it is sometimes difficult for the fisherman to tell which he has caught. Such distinctions as "smaller" mouth, "darker" color, do not help much unless one has the two species side by side. Some people look for the notch between the spines of the forward portion of the dorsal fin and the soft rays of the after portion; this is much deeper in the large-mouth. There is one difference which, while requiring more labor to determine, is exact. It is in the scales, which are smaller in the small-mouth than in the large-mouth. The former typically has eleven horizontal rows of scales between the lateral line and the base of the dorsal fin, the latter not more than eight.

In habits the two fish differ more than in appearance. The small-mouth is restricted to cooler waters. He frequents rocky streams, or the gravelly shoals and the bottom springs of lakes. In addition to the insects, larvae, frogs, etc., which both forms eat, he is addicted to crustaceans, especially crawfish. Whether this is because they abound in his favored habitat, or whether he favors that habitat because of his dietary preference, is still to be decided.

The large-mouth is hardier. He gets along in either moderately cool or in very warm water, and he therefore has a wider geographical range. If given the chance, he will hang about sunken logs in rivers, and will stick to the reedy parts of lakes. Although seeming to this extent to prefer a more sheltered life than the small-mouth, he is more aggressive in his feeding, for the minnows on which he specializes certainly require more active pursuit than crawfish. It has been long the fashion to rate him as inferior to his brother in gameness, but sportsmen well acquainted with both state that this is an illusion, and that under equal conditions he is just as good a fighter.

The spawning processes of the two species are essentially similar, and their domestic life is much more elaborate than is found in any other of the game fishes. It is suggestive of the jewel described in Chapter VIII, although the mating is much more perfunctory, and the care of the young is not so prolonged.

Spawning does not take place until the water temperature rises above 60 degrees. The season therefore varies with the latitude, and may begin as early as March in the south, as late as June in the north. In both species the male alone makes a nest. The small-mouth chooses a sandy or gravelly bottom, from eighteen inches to six feet deep, on which he prepares a circular, concave, saucer-like depression, its diameter about twice his length, with sand and small stones in a ring around the edge, larger stones in the center. The large-mouth can utilize a muddy bottom, where he sometimes makes a foundation of sticks and stones cleaned of mud.

Although nests may be quite close together, each male looks upon his nest as his own very private property, and allows no other male to come within his territory. Fights among the males occur, especially when females enter disputed or borderline regions. Having provided what the female wants—a home—he makes no effort to pursue her, but takes up his post there and waits for her to make the advances. When she enters his territory, he comes out to meet her with raised fins. After a brief courtship, consisting of advances and retreats, they begin to circle inside the nest, she laying a few eggs at a time, he fertilizing them. The minute laying is over, he throws her out, and is at once ready to take in another prospective mother and do what is necessary for her. As many as three females have been known to lay in one nest in quick succession. A two-pound female contains about six thousand eggs, and although it is probable that all of these are not deposited at one time nor in one nest, these successive marriages build up quite a family. Ten thousand eggs in one nest is not unusual.

The hatching period is short. At 72 degrees it is only two days; at 66 degrees, five days. During this time the male remains on guard, driving off all hungry intruders, and spending much time over the nest, which he fans with his fins. The resulting current of water presumably aerates the eggs and keeps them free of fungus, parasites, and other microscopic predators. His care continues until the yolk-sac is absorbed, which takes from one to two weeks depending on the temperature, but as soon as the fry begin to swim he deserts them. Up to this point they have been his joy and pride and the darlings of his heart, but from now on he ceases to recognize them. They are just little fish, and all little fish are good to eat. Parental instinct, at this stage in the evolutionary scale, has made a brave beginning, but it lacks endurance. It breaks down under temptation.

The little fish are now over half an inch long. They live on larvae and tiny crustaceans. By autumn they have reached a length of from two to six or even eight inches, and are eating insects and the fry of smaller fish. Within a year the more precocious ones may attain a length of ten inches, but it is the end of the second year before most of them have reached the eight- to twelve-inch range. Under highly favorable conditions they mature and spawn at the end of the first year, but more often it is at the end of the second, and sometimes of the third.

What we have described above is the family life of the bass when all goes smoothly. However, aside from the mishaps and mortalities which all fish are subject to, there are two natural phenomena which may cause disaster to the bass. Roily water affects the eggs, and may kill them. In this case the father builds another nest and begets another family, but recurrence or continuance of the condition may wipe out a whole season's crop. Chronically roily water is therefore unfavorable for bass, but even otherwise suitable water may be roiled by freshets, or—and here the villain enters—by other animals. The carp, that unadmired immigrant from China via Europe, does little direct harm to game fish. His babies furnish excellent food for his betters, and there is no evidence that he is guilty of feeding on their young. He is largely a vegetarian, but it is in this very fact, innocuous as it seems, that he causes trouble, for in his search for his preferred foods he is continually rooting up the bottom and roiling the water. The carp can in this way be a menace to the bass.

The other natural disaster which can overtake the bass family is a sudden lowering of the temperature after the eggs are laid and before they hatch. Under these conditions the eggs die, and father knows it is no use, and abandons his nest, to try again later on. This sensitiveness to and dislike of cold weather extends to the adults. When winter comes and temperatures go down, they go down with them. They burrow into the mud, or pack themselves in crowds into crevices in the rocks. They cease to move, they cease to eat. They literally spend the winter in hibernation—except in Florida and in certain parts of California, where the mild climate keeps the large-mouth, the species which thrives best in these regions, active and eating all through the year, and brings him sometimes to a weight of over twenty pounds, as compared with a maximum of six to eight in less favored regions.

Further, this distaste for cold weather may bring on a fit of sulks at any season. For whenever the temperature drops below 50 degrees both species, according to reliable authorities, sink to the bottom and become inactive. At such times there is no use in fishing for them. If this is true, the thermometer should be an indispensable part of every bass fisherman's equipment. It would protect him against waste time, waste effort, and unnecessary disappointment. For when he found the water below 50 degrees, he could with a clear conscience take down his rod and quit work.[1]

MUSKELLUNGE

This fish can be spelled in almost any way, and authority can be cited to back the choice. The above form is used here because it has been adopted as the official common name by a committee of ichthyologists appointed for the purpose. To me it has always seemed that maskinonge was the most logical spelling from both the practical and scientific point of view: the Indian words *mas kinonge* mean "great pike," and the scientific name of the fish is *Esox masquinongy*. The argument in favor of the prettier spelling *mascalonge* or *maskallonge,* based on the theory that the early French settlers called the fish *masque allongée* ("long face"), is unconvincing. Of the family *Esocidae* five species are native to this country: three pickerels, muskellunge, and pike. The last-named, strangely enough, occurs in Europe also. It seems unlikely that the voyageurs would have called our gigantic relative of the pike by any other than the latter's French name, *brochet.*

The family is a primitive one. The ventral fins are well behind the pectorals, the fin rays are all soft, the scales are cycloid, and the air-bladder has a connection with the gullet. The five species look much alike, but differ in size. There are also more exact anatomical distinctions. In the pickerels the opercle, the bony plate over the gills, is com-

---

[1] Certain anglers have recently reported occasional catches of large bass in winter. They advance the thought that it is only the smaller bass which hibernate completely, and that the big ones do have feeding periods throughout the cold season. To what extent if any this applies to brief cold spells which occur during the warm season is not known.

pletely covered with scales, as is also the whole cheek forward of the opercle. In the pike, the cheek retains its full quota of scales, but the lower half of the opercle is devoid of them. In the muskellunge only the upper half of the cheek retains the scales, its lower half being scaleless; authorities differ as to whether the whole of the opercle is scaleless, or only its lower half, as in the pike.

The muskellunge lives in the Saint Lawrence and Great Lakes regions. It spawns from the time ice goes out until late April or May. One female may produce from one to three hundred thousand eggs in the course of a season. They hatch, in from twelve to twenty days at 50 to 60 degrees, into fry one-quarter to one-half inch long. At first they feed on larvae such as the "blood-worm," but by the time they are five weeks old and two inches long they have graduated to small minnow fry. They have a tendency to creep up on their victim, curling before they strike, and perhaps it is this slowness of movement which accounts for their very high mortality in the early stages. They may find each other easier prey than minnows.

At one year they average 8 inches, two years 16 inches, three years 22 to 24 inches, six years 35 inches, twelve years 48 inches—with variations depending on local conditions. Sexual maturity comes in the fifth or sixth year. The maximum age recorded is twenty years; maximum weight, 110 pounds. The adults eat fish, frogs, and aquatic mammals.

The hardiness of the family equals that of its distant relative, the Alaska blackfish, described in an earlier chapter, for a well-known and highly respected fisherman tells of catching pike through the ice, laying them aside until frozen stiff, and then thawing them out in the bathtub at home until they revived and splashed about lustily.

CHAPTER XI

Fish and Fishermen

FISH have little interest in man and little in common with him. When the two meet, it is usually man who has made the advances which bring them together. The old adage, " 'Dog bites man is not news' but 'Man bites dog is news,' " must be reversed for fish. Men bite fish millions of times every day—in fact, in some islands they live on little else—but when a fish bites a man it calls for headlines.

Man's interest in fish has two major phases: food and sport. Their relative importance varies between individuals and nations. To one man, fishing may be an insufferable bore, while to his brother it may be a consuming passion. To a nation like the United States, where food is so abundant that at times crops are plowed under, fish as a form of nourishment is relatively unimportant. To a nation like Japan, which has never been able to produce within its own boundaries enough to feed its people, fish is a major item of diet, and the oceans have been studied and explored and exploited to keep the nation from starving. Since fish are not equally distributed throughout the length and breadth and depth of the seas, but are concentrated in the comparatively shallow waters around the margins of the continents, Japanese fishermen have been led far from home in their quest, and have in the past invaded such areas as the salmon fisheries of Siberia and Alaska, thus adding to the frictions which sometimes lead to wars.

FOOD FISH

The great bulk of food fish comes from salt water. There are to be sure fresh-water food fisheries, but their total production is comparatively small. Vast stores of nourishment exist in the ocean which are available to us only in the form of fish and which we have never learned to utilize in any other way, as we have learned to utilize the nutritional resources of the soil through agriculture. We are completely dependent upon fish to go out and collect this nourishment and concentrate it in bodies large enough for us to capture and consume. If there were no fish, it would be lost to us. Even with their help, there is much loss, for many forms of fish life cannot be reached, others are inedible, and still others, while edible, are not considered marketable. This is especially true in the United States, where fish which would be eaten in other parts of the world are discarded when taken in the nets. The little puffer, or blow-fish, which swells up like a balloon when disturbed, belongs to a group many of whose members are poisonous. Until recently it was tossed out when found in the nets. Now it has been discovered that it is a great delicacy, and it is much in demand in the markets of New York and Boston.

Once in a while a hitherto unheard of species is revealed by nature and offered for man's edification. The tilefish, spectacularly hued in brilliant reds' and golds and reaching a weight as high as fifty pounds, had never been seen by human eyes until encountered in 1879 by a fisherman at a depth of a hundred fathoms on a previously unexplored bank south of Nantucket. Brought into the Boston market, it proved highly edible and marketable. Found in abundance near the coast, it was soon being caught in large numbers, to the profit of fishermen, fish markets, and consumers. Three years later, with all the drama of a major catastrophe, a storm of gale intensity swept out across the sea and in its wake dead tilefish were scattered at the surface over an area 170 miles long by twenty-five miles wide. It was estimated by careful observers that they numbered no less than one billion, four hundred million. Scientists believed that it was not the storm which killed the fish, but a "straying" movement of the Gulf Stream in which it shifted its course to the eastward, and allowed the bottom where the tilefish had lived in the warmth of its current to be invaded by chill waters. This "cold wave" was lethal to the tilefish. Although complete and total extinction was believed unlikely, no tilefish were seen for years. Then gradually the Gulf Stream moved back to its former course and they began to be found again. By 1915 they were considered to be as abundant as ever, and in 1937, one of the last good pre-war years, three million pounds were caught valued at one hundred thousand dollars.

Other examples of "natural" destruction of a fish which man looked upon as his property are not unknown, the most recent being the Great Lakes smelt, which has almost disappeared due to what is believed to be a virus disease. However, in many cases not nature, but man, is the villain. Over-exploitation by man, "over fishing," is believed to be at least one of the factors in the extreme fluctuations of the populations of such species as the menhaden, the halibut, and the sardine. Whoever or whatever is to blame, severe reduction in numbers of any important fish means that a certain amount of the nourishing elements of the sea which it formerly turned into food for human beings is no longer being utilized, or is being utilized by forms which we cannot catch or do not find edible.

To study such problems and the methods whereby fish populations can be maintained in a state of utility to the human race is one of the fields of endeavor of a comparatively young science called fisheries biology. The "maximum sustained yield" is the ideal sought. If a species is fished too heavily, too many mature fish will be removed and too few will be left to reproduce sufficient young to maintain the population. The numbers will decrease until not enough remain to make fishing worth-while, and the species will no longer contribute to the well-being of humanity. Eventually, if left alone, nature will in most cases restore the numbers to the point where it can again be utilized, but for a time it will be out of the game. On the other hand, it is conceivable that a species may be so lightly fished that a great many of the individuals die of old age or other "natural" causes (meaning almost any form of death not brought about by man). This, from the human point of view, is undesirable waste.

The "maximum sustained yield" concept is complicated in detail and in practice, but in theory it is simply that for each kind of fish there is a surplus produced over and above that needed to maintain the population at an optimum level, and that that surplus, no more and no less, is the number which should be taken by fishing. To determine the maximum sustained yield is a highly difficult problem, involving the study of, among other things, life history and numbers caught. Once an estimate of the maximum sustained yield has been made, it is an equally difficult problem to evolve methods whereby the catch may be held at the desired number and to put those methods into practice.

The halibut fishery of the Pacific Northwest is a classic example of the realization of these objectives. Years of poor catches had brought the fishermen to such a state of despair that they asked for an investigation to see if any remedy could be devised. The resulting program of research included continuation of the life history studies which had already been made of this large, long-lived fish, and analysis of the log-records of their catches which many fishermen had fortunately kept for years. It solved the "maximum sustained yield" problem to an extent at least sufficient for practical purposes. The next step was to formulate regulations in keeping with the findings. And the third step was to enforce them —particularly difficult in this case because the fishery was carried on by citizens of both the United States and Canada and in waters belonging to both countries. However, a commission was set up, regulations were promulgated, the fishermen had the good sense to give them a fair trial, and the result is that more halibut are landed now with less fishing effort and therefore with more profit than ever before.

One small detail in the story of the halibut deserves highlighting: it was only when conditions became desperate that the fishermen were willing to accept the results of biological investigation. This is often the case. Fishermen are human. As long as they make money, they react with a violent negative to any suggestion of regulation. When they cease to make money, they want help.

The Pacific sardine industry has now reached this stage, after a history that can be called truly spectacular. Practically unknown in 1900, the Pacific sardine came to the fore during the food shortages of the First World War. By 1920 production had reached one hundred thousand *tons* (two hundred million pounds), and the canneries could not come near to using all the fish which the fishermen could bring in. Transformation of the excess into sardine meal solved that problem, and the catch continued to increase until by 1937 it had reached eight hundred thousand tons—the biggest in the whole of the western hemisphere.

All this time the fishery biologists—without the blessing of the industry—were working on the case. They studied scales and found that the sardine had a maximum life span of at least fifteen years (surprisingly long for so small and abundant a creature); that it began to spawn at three years; and that while in the early twenties the catch had been composed mostly of ten-year-old fish, in later years it was made up largely of three- and four-year-olds. They caught sardines at sea, made incisions in their bellies, and inserted numbered metal tags. Some of the fish died as a result and some of the tags came out, but enough remained in and were recovered from recaptured fish by electro-magnets in the cannery processing lines to give information on the migrations of the species and on the rate at which the industry was removing its stock in trade. The biologists also found that there were large year-classes and small year-classes—that in some years, due to natural conditions which have not yet been identified, spawning was phenomenally successful, and enormous numbers of young fish began to grow up on their way to the cannery; while in other years spawning was poor and the young were few.

All this time the biologists were issuing words of warning which, as the catch continued to rise, went unheeded. But 1937, with its eight hundred thousand tons, was the peak. The curve turned down; in the 1947-1948 season the catch did little more than equal the one hundred thousand tons taken in 1920. And, while one hundred thousand tons was highly satisfactory then, it is not sufficient to satisfy the greatly increased numbers of men, fishing craft, and plants existing in 1948. The call for help has gone out. Because the investigations were begun years before they were asked for, the material for help is at hand; otherwise, it would take years to assemble. The trouble is believed to be a combination of over-fishing and a succession of poor year-classes. Poor catches will discourage fishing and thus relieve the over-fishing; nature will sooner or later produce a good year-class; and the sardine fishery can probably stabilize at something less than half of its peak. This will mean fewer canneries and fewer fishermen, but with a stable living, as compared to the ruination which faces the large number of canneries and fishermen under conditions as they exist now. What regulations can be devised to bring this about is the question.

One fishery where regulation can be carried out without difficulty along whatever lines are indicated as best for the long-range interests of both the fish and the fishermen is the Alaska salmon. Alaska being a territory, federal agencies have complete control and have been able to carry out their program of providing for an "escapement" of fish to the spawning-beds equal in numbers to the catch. For years they accomplished this by actually counting the fish through weirs. With the information obtained in this way on the sizes and times of the spawning runs they have recently been able to regulate the escapement by closed seasons, with continuing counts at but a few points to provide a check on the success of this method.

The salmons are among the most valuable of fishes, and at the same time the most vulnerable. Their value on the market in dollars and cents is high, but even higher is the value of their habit of life, for they go out into the ocean, spend years there collecting its nutrient elements, and then bring back all that nourishment in concentrated form and deposit it at our very front doors. No plowing, no planting, no cultivating is necessary; not even a sea voyage to seek out and harvest the crop, as in the case of other fishes. The fact that many salmon are caught at sea does not invalidate the last statement. There can be no doubt that the most efficient way to harvest the salmon crop would be to carry on all fishing at the mouths of rivers, take the "maximum sustained yield" at these points in the shortest possible time, and allow the necessary spawning escapement. Such a scheme could be put into effect only in a fully regimented society. That much salmon fishing is now carried on in other and less efficient ways is a necessary concomitant of democracy and a free competitive system; it is the price we gladly pay for our freedom from regimentation.

This life habit which makes the salmon so valuable is also what makes it so vulnerable. No widely distributed marine species could conceivably be exterminated by man, even though he be admittedly the most dangerous predatory animal that has appeared in the whole history of evolution. But destruction of the salmon by him is not only conceivable, but seems at times probable. For the salmon must come up the streams to reproduce, and man makes this ever more difficult. Pollution has played an important part in the past, particularly on the Atlantic seaboard: rivers in which *Salmo salar* used to spawn and be captured in apparently inexhaustible numbers have been rendered unfit for all fish life and *salar* has vanished from them. The dangers of pollution and means for its control have now been established, and it can and should cease to be an exterminator of salmon runs. The major threat at present lies in man's desire to take water out of rivers for purposes of his own, principally for irrigation and power. To do this, he must build high dams and in some cases leave long stretches of river bed below them with little or no water; either or both of these exploits impede the salmon's efforts to reach the spawning areas.

In the early days, when the country was new, there were many localities where irrigation and power projects could be constructed with much benefit and with very little damage. Governmental agencies were created and given money to carry on these works. As time went on the favorable locations became fewer, but the governmental agencies did not. Their job was to build dams, and if no dams were planned they ceased to exist. The incentive has inevitably been for all such agencies to comb the country for locations which might possibly serve as dam sites and to count heavily on the support of the local interests which profit from dam construction no matter what the over-all effect. That many of these projects have unquestioned merit in no way gainsays the truth of this statement. If, in the future, man learns to harness atomic power to domestic and industrial machinery, water will no longer be needed for hydroelectric plants; and if he learns to do what the simplest blade of grass can, namely, to produce the chlorophyl in whose presence carbon dioxide and water react to form food, water will no longer be needed for irrigation. Man's only need for water will then be to drink and to wash with, the dam-building agencies will presumably cease to exist, and the atomic and chlorophyl agencies which succeed them will probably not interfere with the habits of the salmon—if by that time any are left.

In the early days the dam-building agencies paid little attention to fish, and their work at times resulted in the large-scale destruction of creatures which another set of agencies was hard at work trying to conserve. All this has now been changed. The dam-builders are now required by law to consult with the fish-conservers and to include in their projects in so far as practicable the fish-saving measures recommended by the latter. One of the first and most widely publicized of these co-operative labors was the Bonneville Dam. This barrier lies 140 miles from the mouth of the Columbia, but above it the river stretches its winding channel back into the continent for 1,100 miles more, partly in the United States and partly in Canada, and it is in the waters above the dam site that the major part of the immensely valuable salmon run finds its spawning-beds. Not only do greater numbers go above the dam, but individual fish in this part of the run are commercially more valuable because, having the furthest distance to go to the spawning grounds, they run earlier and carry a much larger reserve of fat than those which spawn near the sea. That means could be provided for these multitudes of fish to rise sixty-five feet from the level below to the level above the dam, and for the resulting offspring to get safely back to the ocean, was gravely doubted by many people. To the men charged with carrying on the work, there was little alternative; they had to accept the gamble and to do everything conceivable to win.

They prepared a project which called for the expenditure of over six million dollars, along with the corresponding man-hours of brain-work to make the plans and of muscular work to carry them out. They placed their main reliance in two gigantic fish ladders sweeping down from the top of the dam in impressive curves like the imperial stairway of the Fontainebleau Palace. Each pool in these ladders was forty feet wide by sixteen feet long by six feet deep, and only one foot higher than the pool below it. A one-foot jump is nothing for a salmon, especially with deep water and a long run to give it a take-off; the record leap is over eleven feet; but, to make it easier, submerged openings from one pool to the next were provided so that the fish could make the entire ascent under water if they preferred. To supplement the ladders, elevators with twenty by thirty foot shafts were built, into which fish would be attracted by outflowing water currents at the bottom for a free ride to the top.

By May of 1938, when the sluice gates through which the fish had been moving during construction were closed, everything which the best engineers and fisheries experts could think of to ensure passage of the salmon over the dam had been done, but no one could guarantee success. The fish ladders were certainly perfect from the physical point of view, but would the fish enter them, or the elevators? Would they follow the currents flowing from these sources, or would they prefer the tailraces from the turbines and sit down in front of these blind alleys and stay there until they rotted, and all their unborn children rotted with them?

Only time could give the answer, and to make sure that the true answer was obtained a long-range counting program was immediately started. Picket barriers were set up in each fishway with gate-controlled openings two feet wide and submerged platforms over which the fish pass (Plate VI). It being known that upstream spawning migrants move very little at night, the gates were kept open only during the daytime when observers were on duty to count and identify the fish. Each observer had to be provided with a battery of tallies, for in addition to the various salmons and the steelhead trout, it was found that large numbers of suckers, squawfish, and lampreys were using the ladders, as well as smaller numbers of carp, shad, sturgeon, various minnows, and even a few black bass and crappies. As may be imagined, this counting work requires a quick eye and mind and agile hands, for as many as 4,300 fish have been recorded up one ladder in one hour. The mental strain involved is shown by the fact that the workers—mostly women, who have proved better at the job than men—only work forty-five minutes out of every hour, with a fifteen-minute rest period. Intensive advance training is necessary, and to help the newcomers learn the different species and at the same time to provide means of examining doubtful specimens, devices have been installed which can stop any fish at any time and bring it up to the surface for examination.

When the end of the first season came it was found that some 470,000 salmonid fish had passed up through the ladders, and this did not include the spring salmon run and some of the steelhead which migrated before the dam began to act as a barrier. It was found that the fish passed upstream with no significant delay and that most of them used the submerged openings instead of making the jumps. And, since the lad-

ders had been so outstandingly successful, it was found unnecessary to use the elevators, and they never have been
used except experimentally.

The planners began to breathe more easily. The ladders
had done all that they had hoped in passing the spawners
upstream, but would the little fish be able to return successfully to the ocean? If they did not, then the whole project
was a failure. Would they find their way down through the
backwaters, reaching forty-five miles upstream, with only a
very weak current to guide them? Would they safely nego-
tiate the dam? Bypasses had been provided to carry them
down, but the flow of water through these was infinitesimal
compared to that which went over the spillway and through
the turbines. If they entered the turbine headgates, what
would happen to them? The runners are twenty-three feet
in diameter, with a minimum opening of one foot between
the blades, and revolve only seventy-five times per minute.
Would the hope that the little fish could go through them
unharmed prove well-founded?

Again only time could tell. Fish going upstream the first
season were the offspring of generations that had spawned
above Bonneville unhindered by any dam. But by the end
of the fourth year, practically all the upstream migrants
would have to be descendants of fish that had succeeded in
passing over the dam in both directions. How would their
numbers compare with the earlier years?

Ten seasons have now elapsed since the dam was completed. Ten counts have been made. There have been fluctuations, and some years, when the counts were low, the
situation has looked ominous. But the latest available figures,
those for 1947, show over 787,000 salmonid fishes passing
up over the dam on their way to spawn, a greater number
than has ever been recorded before. In the face of those figures there can be no further doubt: not only do the spawners

succeed in passing up over the dam, but the young succeed in reaching the ocean. We can have both a Bonneville Dam and a salmon fishery on the Columbia River.

Whether we can have the salmon fishery as well as the other dams which are scheduled for the Columbia is another question. One of these, Grand Coulee, already constructed some 600 miles from the mouth, is 550 feet high—far beyond the limits practicable for fish ladders as well as for the safe passage of young fish returning to the ocean. Solution of this problem has centered around the transfer of the runs by trapping the adults and either allowing them to spawn naturally in streams tributary below the dam, or spawning them artificially in hatcheries and planting the offspring in such waters. The program has been under way long enough to show that new generations of salmon are coming back to these "adopted-home" streams, but not in as large numbers as had been anticipated. Eleven dams in all are proposed for the main stem of the Columbia, entirely aside from projects for its tributaries. When these eleven are completed, all but eighty-four feet of the total drop of 1,288 feet below the Canadian boundary will have been utilized for power developments. The river will be a series of dams, with the backwaters reaching from the crest of one to the toe of the next. Will the current in these lakes be strong enough to guide the spawners up and the ocean-bound young down? And what about the spawning areas submerged by these impoundments?

The problem at Bonneville was a great one because of the magnitude of the river and the magnitude of the runs of spawning fish, but it was free of two major complications which exist on many of our other salmon streams. At Bonneville the whole river passed either over the dam or through the turbines. There were no irrigation diversions and no impoundment of water. Frequently conditions are less favorable.

In the San Joaquin River unit of California's Central Valley Project, to take an outstanding example, so much of the water is withheld from the natural channel for these two purposes that it becomes dangerously low and as a result dangerously warm. Furthermore the young fish tend to follow the main flow, which leads them out into the diversion canals and eventually to the farmers' fields. Fish screens to prevent just such mishaps were invented long ago and have been in use for years. Cylinders of fine wire mesh which revolve in such a manner as to pass debris over the top, let the water through, and hold the fish, can be built, but on large diversions they are extremely costly to install and to maintain. Electrical "screens" can be built, devices which produce a shock strong enough to repel fish without killing them; but when little fish are seized with the desire to go to sea they are apt to keep making attempts at such a screen until they become paralyzed, so that they drift with the current through the electric field and into the diversion ditch. Supersonics have yet to be tried. Maybe these high-frequency waves, which are said to induce in human beings almost unbearable discomfort and fear, will have a more powerful effect on the fish than the call of the sea.

Whatever the type of "screen" and however effective it may be, an indispensable requisite is a place for fish to go other than through the screen—a flow of water leading toward safety and a life in the ocean rather than toward danger and a death in the alfalfa fields. Even when an alternate path is provided the little fish may accumulate in front of the screen if most of the water is flowing through it. To overcome this attraction of the major current and to guide them to where they should go even though it be a comparative trickle, moving lights are being tried. While this may sound at first like the product of an unbalanced mind, it is based on the following reasoning:

All fish tend to be attracted by lights at night. Downstream migrant salmon, unlike the upstream spawners, travel mostly at night. If a screen be placed in the mouth of a canal diverting water out of a river, and lights move along its face in the direction of the flow in the natural channel, the little fish should follow in the same direction and get a start on the proper path. This scheme has not yet progressed beyond the experimental stage; whether it will be a real contribution to the preservation of the salmon remains to be determined.

It must not be thought that all dams are harmful to all fish in all ways. Where no anadromous species are involved the effects may be largely beneficial. Even to the salmon benefits have accrued in some cases, as at the Shasta Dam on the Sacramento River. Before the dam was built none of them spawned below its present site because the section was too warm; they merely passed through it on their way to more suitable areas further up. Now, chill waters from the depths of Shasta Reservoir flow through the channel below and have turned it into an excellent spawning area where many salmon breed successfully. However, the benefit here is no more than an offset to some of the damage caused by the dam; it is too high for a fish ladder, and it cuts the fish off from the spawning-beds above it which they used to use. Furthermore, when the project is in full operation the reservoir surface will in dry years be very near the bottom, and there will be no cool depths from which to draw water.

Why is there this struggle to preserve the salmon's spawning-beds when it is so easy to strip eggs from ripe females, fertilize them with milt from the males, and produce little salmon in hatcheries? The answer is that while it is easy in theory and with small numbers, it is not easy in practice and with large numbers. When they first enter fresh water the salmon are in most cases not ready to spawn; they seek "resting" spots where they can remain quietly until the sex products ripen. Resting spots must have cool, unpolluted, well-oxygenated water. Spots where large numbers of fish can be held artificially without high mortality are extremely hard to find. If that difficulty can be overcome, there remains the matter of cost. The number of eggs necessary to produce the number of salmonids which run annually up the Columbia River comes nearer to being expressed in billions than in millions. If to the expense of building the hatcheries we add the annual outlays for handling the products, the cost of *maintaining* such a run year in and year out by means of hatcheries alone is prohibitive—even if it can be done, which has never yet been proved. The federal government built many salmon hatcheries in Alaska. They have all been closed.

SPORT FISH

The greatest of all the sport fishes are the large marine species—the swordfishes, the tunas, the sailfish, the tarpon. About these man can do little except to catch them, and his pursuit of them in sport is comparatively innocent and has but an insignificant effect upon their populations. It is the fresh-water game fishes which can be most affected by his actions, either for or against, and of these the various trouts and the black basses and their relatives are the most widespread and the most popular.

The trout is more susceptible of manipulation by man than any other fish. With almost equal ease he can destroy or he can create whole populations. The philosophy of his dealings with trout has, in this country, passed through three distinct phases. First came the phase of introductions. The last half of the nineteenth century saw man indulging in a passion for meddling with nature, for transplanting animals from parts of the world where they had evolved to other parts where they were unknown. It took him some time to realize how dangerous this might be, to learn that a species which in one place had proved beneficial (to man) might go out of control in another place where the natural checks on its numbers were missing. The present unpopularity of the carp, which was brought into North America with such enthusiasm, attests the damage which can be done and the difficulty of undoing it.

Fortunately, trout introductions have done very little harm and considerable good. These fish have been found to be among the easiest of all animals to transplant because they can be shipped almost any distance in the form of "eyed" eggs—eggs which have developed to the point where the eyes of the embryo show as black dots through the enveloping membrane. At this stage they are very hardy and do not need to be in water. Packed in damp moss, they will survive for weeks. For journeys of very long duration, advantage can be taken of the fact that the development is greatly slowed by lowering the temperature. Brook trout eggs take 44 days to hatch at 50 degrees Fahrenheit, 100 days at 40 degrees, 145 days at 35 degrees. Rainbow take only 30 days at 50 degrees, 86 days at 40 degrees. With the aid of refrigeration it was possible, even before the days of air travel, to ship brown trout eggs from Europe to America, rainbow from America to Europe, New Zealand, and Africa.

While the intercontinental transplantations are the most spectacular, important introductions have been made on a much smaller scale. The simplest and shortest occurred when California cattlemen took a dozen of the famous golden trout out of the limited stream system in which alone that form was found and carried them in a coffee pot four miles across a divide to dump them into an entirely different watershed. From these rudely treated forebears have come all the golden trout which have been planted in other parts of California to bring joy to the hearts and beauty to the eyes of many more sportsmen than could ever have seen them in their very limited native habitat.

Few people realize how great an extent of excellent trout water in North America was barren of fish before the white man came, particularly in the rugged, geologically new, western part of the continent. Here glaciation had created numberless lakes so high in the mountains that they were inaccessible to fish; introduction of trout has created fishing where there would otherwise be none. Strange to say, it is the imported eastern brook which has given the best results in many such lakes. The reasons are two. The eastern brooks are natives of colder regions than the other species, and therefore grow faster in these high lakes with their short summers, long ice-bound winters, and correspondingly cold water. And they are, as we have seen, capable of spawning successfully in spring seepages, and thus are able to propagate themselves in these lakes without tributaries, where the other species would have to be maintained by restocking. In contrast, the rainbows of the west have replaced the brooks in some of the eastern streams which have been rendered uninhabitable for the aborigines by the increased water temperatures brought about by deforestation and erosion; and the European brown has proved better able than either of the Americans to stand up against the pollution, crowding, and other human activities which help turn the wheels of progress.

The second phase in the way of man with trout derived from the fact that for many years many men believed that natural spawning was highly inefficient. Someone had blundered. Someone had gone off on the wrong track, and all the others had followed blindly. Someone had misinterpreted what he saw, and all the others had accepted, and had come to the belief that the tail-flapping of the female which we now know to be a nest-digging movement was part of the act of egg-deposition, and that the ensuing approach of the male which we now know to be courtship behavior was the act of fertilization. Under the circumstances it is not surprising that one fish-cultural authority made the statement in print that only two out of every thousand naturally spawned eggs were able to complete their development.

In contrast, it was known that with proper handling over ninety per cent fertilization resulted from artificial spawning. Man could do far better than nature. So he proceeded to build hatcheries, and to take every spawning trout that he could lay hands on, strip it of its eggs or its milt, hatch the eggs in his troughs, hold the offspring until they had absorbed the yolk-sac, and then place these tiny creatures back in the natural waters from which he had taken their parents. Only, since this work was so much more efficient, it was not necessary to replace them all in those same waters; he could place a part of them there—perhaps only a small part—and use the rest to stock other waters. The trout fisherman could be happy. His sport was assured forever; in fact, he could look forward to expanding into new waters, and having more fish than ever before.

How long it took people to begin to see the fallacy in this program is not exactly known. As the results failed to meet expectations, efforts were made to raise the fry to larger size before releasing them on the theory that this increased their survival. But it also cost more for fish food and handling, and more of the fingerlings died in the troughs— partly because the longer period gave time for more deaths to occur, and partly because it gave time for disease to take hold in epidemic form. Sometimes, in spite of almost perfect fertilization, the number of young fish planted was less than ten per cent of the number of eggs taken. Thoughtful fish culturists wondered whether the extra money and labor were not being wasted; whether planting the fry the moment they were ready to begin feeding did not give just as good survival as holding them until they were three inches long. If you could hold them until they were six inches long, get them through that period when in natural waters they were preyed on by a host of enemies, you might bring about a really significant increase in their survival; but the added cost would be so great as to offset the improvement.

A series of experiments and observations has led gradually to the third and present phase of the trout culturist's philosophy. Repeated creel censuses with marked hatchery trout have shown that anglers catch on the average not over four per cent of the fish planted as fingerlings—and for practical purposes "fingerling" may be defined as fish which will have to pass through a winter after planting before they are of a size to be caught. Careful observers have corrected the misunderstandings about the mechanics of natural spawning which had led to the belief in its inefficiency; and painstaking work digging up areas where natural spawning has occurred has demonstrated its efficiency by showing that as high as ninety-nine per cent of the eggs had been fertilized. It began to be realized that if an appreciable number of adult trout remained in any water after the angling season, they could, if they had access to proper spawning areas, produce all the young fish which the water could support; that to take the eggs from them, raise them in hatcheries, and return the little fish to the water, probably added little to the total production; and that if instead of returning the little fish to their parent water a large proportion of them were placed elsewhere, the parent water was being "robbed" and its population gradually reduced.

The first corrective step was to permit the wild trout to spawn naturally, and to do everything possible to improve spawning conditions for them. The second step was to replace the wild trout with hatchery-reared brood fish as a source of eggs, so that the resulting offspring would be an addition to the native stock, not merely a processing of the native stock by man instead of by nature. The third step was to find ways of increasing the survival of the hatchery fish after they were placed in natural waters, the most obvious way being to plant them at a much larger size; and here a radical change in thinking had to come about.

As long as the principal object of the hatchery was to hatch a great number of eggs and turn out a great number of small fingerlings, no large volume of water was needed, and the belief that the best source was a pure spring with a temperature of around forty degrees was justified by the high percentage of hatch and the freedom from disease. But at that temperature growth is painfully slow; rainbows, for instance, held throughout the summer after hatching and the whole of the following winter, will not have reached catchable size by the opening of the fishing season. At sixty degrees they will, if properly fed, attain that size in less than six months. The hatchery man has had to change his ideal. The small, pure, forty-degree spring gives way to a source of water with a constant temperature of around sixty degrees and a large volume of flow. Such sources, it may be added, are very few and hard to find.

Strains of fall-spawning rainbow have been developed and maintained in hatcheries as brood stocks; under ideal conditions eggs taken from them in October turn into catchable fish at the opening of the season in the spring. These fish cost more to produce than the fingerlings—they eat more and are more susceptible to disease. Inexpensive foods and methods of mass disease prevention and cure have had to be developed. The diehards have argued that even under the best conditions, the cost of producing the large fish was so great as to more than offset their higher survival. Experiments have proved that this is not so. The catchable fish may cost on the average five to six times as much as the fingerlings, but under heavy fishing ten times as many are caught. This means that a fish in the angler's creel has cost one hundred percent more if planted as a fingerling than if planted at catchable size. It must be emphasized that this is *under heavy fishing pressure.* Where anglers are few, many of the catchable fish would go unharvested, and the cost per fish caught would increase correspondingly. If such waters must be stocked at all, fingerlings are still the most economical.

Man now seems to have the hatchery part of his trout problem well in hand. Just as important is the other part: what happens to the fish after they leave the hatchery and to the fish which have never been in a hatchery? Most of man's activities are detrimental. Deforestation, whether for lumber or for other needs of civilization, leads to silting and to higher water temperatures. Dams drown sections of trout streams. The resulting reservoirs may provide fishing if they are stable, but often their levels fluctuate to such an extent that the bottoms, alternately flooded and desiccated, produce very little trout food. Below them, stream flows may be so reduced that the water becomes too warm for trout, or at least so warm that it is invaded by undesirable species which crowd out the trout. Once in a while, to be sure, the reverse is true; the muddy Colorado River has become a clear trout stream for many miles below Boulder Dam because it has dropped its silt load and reduced its temperature in the reservoir above.

To help trout in natural waters man has thought up some ingenious tricks. He places deflectors in streams to force the current to scour silt accumulations off potential spawning gravels or to dig pools where fish may rest or hide. He builds dams in high mountain valleys to catch the rainfall and release it gradually over long periods into stream chan-

nels which would otherwise go dry. He has tried the trans-
plantation of beavers in the hope that their dams would
accomplish the same result, but whether the net effect of
this animal is helpful or harmful to trout has not yet been
decided. He has tried introducing certain organisms which
form fish food into lakes where they were absent, but without much success. A body of water, like a piece of land, has
a limited capacity to produce. Efforts in a more fundamental
direction, fertilization, he has also tried, but so far without
proven results in natural waters. One of his most successful
inventions is a method of nullifying the effects of the sportsmen's own negligence. Trout lakes sometimes become over-
run with minnows which have been brought from other
waters for bait. When this happens, the whole fish population—usually a very few trout and hundreds of thousands of
useless fish—is poisoned with a chemical which is comparatively cheap, does no harm to warm-blooded animals nor to
many of the invertebrates which form trout food, and loses
its effectiveness in a comparatively short time. The lake can
then be re-stocked, and if catchable fish are used not one
season's fishing need be missed. All goes well until the undesirable minnows return through the carelessness of anglers
and again over-run the lake.

The present-day thinking of trout culturists and conserva-
tionists may be summarized along these lines:

1. Brood stocks, hatchery-reared and maintained, should
be the main sources of egg supply. Eggs should be taken
from wild fish only where facilities are inadequate for them
to spawn naturally.

2. The most economical method of stocking heavily fished
waters is with catchable-sized fish planted just before and
during the season. Fingerlings are more economical for
lightly fished waters.

3. The old type, cold spring hatcheries must be retired

just as rapidly as sources of water can be obtained suitable for producing catchable fish—retaining enough of the old hatcheries to meet fingerling needs.

4. Effective disease-control measures, low-cost foods, and means of reducing expenditures on apparatus and installations must be constantly sought in order to raise more catchable fish with the money available.

5. Unceasing vigilance and constant effort are needed in order to use every reasonable means to preserve trout waters against the demands of dam-builders, lumbermen, road-builders, farmers, and miners; otherwise we shall find ourselves with hatcheries full of trout and no water to put them in.

6. Wild trout must receive all possible protection through improvement of their habitat and through wise conservation regulations. It still remains true that they can produce more, better, and cheaper little trout than man is able to do.

Trout are among the easiest fish to breed and distribute artificially. By this I do not mean that skill, care, intelligence, training, and experience are not necessary for successful results. I mean that we have learned to handle them in great numbers more easily than any other game fish. With the "warm-water" species such as the black basses and their relatives the sunfishes and the crappies, the picture is quite different. The eggs cannot be successfully removed from the females and hatched. The young are not receptive to prepared foods. The accepted method for "artificial" production of black bass is: Let the adults spawn naturally in suitable ponds; remove the young to other ponds to prevent their ingestion by their parents after the guarding stage has passed; see to it that these rearing ponds are well supplied with insect larvae, daphnia, and the like as food for the bass in their very early stages, and with small fish as forage for them when they grow larger. Under these conditions, it can be seen how impossible it would be to produce black bass in numbers sufficient to permit the large-scale and widespread stocking that is practical with trout.

Fortunately it is now realized that such stocking of the warm-water fishes is not necessary. They are much more prolific than trout, and they take care of their young for at least a part of the most critical period of their existence. *Stocking for seed but not for maintenance* has become the slogan. Even in a lake that appears to be "fished out" there are generally enough adults left to produce all the young fish that it will support. Once they have become established in a water, only a catastrophe or a state of extreme unbalance should make further stocking necessary. Under-fishing is more apt to cause trouble than overfishing.

This is particularly true in the "farm ponds" which have become so popular. Farmers are being encouraged to store water for livestock and for irrigation by building small dams, and, as a corollary, to place fish in them for their own sport and food. Black bass and bluegill sunfish form the best combination for these small ponds, the bluegills feeding on the invertebrate life and the bass on the bluegills. Production under favorable conditions may reach as high as four hundred pounds per acre—far more than the farmer and his family use. Under-fishing results, particularly for the bluegills. The bass, being more highly prized, are removed in greater numbers until they no longer keep the bluegills under control, and the latter multiply to the point where there is no longer enough food for them. They fail to reach a size fit for human consumption, and they are so numerous that they prevent the bass from spawning. Heavy fishing throughout the year and the retention of all fish caught without regard to size or species is the program which keeps the farm pond healthy.

Recently a somewhat similar formula has been tried on

large bodies of water. The Tennessee Valley project has proved that, where anadromous species are not involved, dams can be extremely beneficial to fish; the great impoundments have provided vastly more and better fishing than existed on this river before they were built. Experiments have led to the conclusion that here many more fish die of old age than are caught by anglers. To prevent this waste, to permit anglers to harvest the crops at the time the fish are most easily taken—in the spring of the year—closed seasons have been completely abolished. The numbers of fish caught, and of happy fishermen, have increased manyfold, without any visible reduction as yet in the total fish population. It is not claimed that this program would be successful everywhere. Trout present a problem of a quite distinct nature; even bass may react differently under different conditions. But other states are beginning to eye the Tennessee Valley, and to take steps toward following in its lead. The closed season for warm-water fishes may be on its way out.

CHAPTER XII

Habits and Adaptations

ADAPTATIONS in the world of fish are numberless. Some
are insignificant. Some are important but unspectacular. And
some are so startling, so incredibly fantastic, that they leave
the imagination in a state of collapse, mumbling to itself the
hackneyed old line about truth being indeed stranger than
fiction. Could anyone be expected to believe in a fish which
renders itself blind by its own activities, but overcomes the
handicap by using those same activities in a radar-like apparatus wherewith it finds its way about? And yet this is
just what the electric "eel" does. Its principal output is an
electric current so strong as not only to stun enemies and
prey, but also to cause cataracts on its own eyes. Its secondary
output is an almost continuous series of much weaker electrical
discharges. On its head are sensory pits which receive the
reflections of these weak currents from surrounding objects;
and so delicately are they adjusted that they orient the eel
after it has become blind and guide it wherever it wants to
go.

An adaptation, in the simplest possible words, is the modi-
fication of an organ, or of a whole animal, so that it is used
for a different purpose from the one which it originally
served, or so that it serves the same purpose in a different
way. When you use your hand to hold this book you are
benefiting from an adaptation, for hands were once front
paws and served only to walk on. Far below us in the scale a
somewhat similar adaptation has taken place, for the humble

248

sea-horse now uses his tail to grasp stems of seaweed, whereas it was once as much an organ of locomotion as mammals' paws.

This particular adaptation is a protective one. It helps the sea-horse to shelter itself among the weeds. In general, adaptations help animals to survive. Fish must have oxygen, food, mates, and, in most species, shelter from enemies,

FIGURE 27. SEA-HORSE

in order to live. It is probably safe to say that these requirements are to be found in greatest abundance in the shallow parts of the ocean. Why did not all fish congregate there and stay there? Why have they moved into the open seas, into the cold black abyssal depths, into tide-pools above low-water mark; into rivers and mountain-streams, and swamps that dry up; into lightless caves and artesian waters; into pools that stagnate, into muddy roadside ditches, into rice-fields flooded only part of the year; even into thermal springs in such desert regions as Death Valley, where the water temperature rises to 100 degrees Fahrenheit?

Competition is the answer. Competition drove human beings out of settled countries into new lands where new methods had to be found to provide the necessaries of life— which, it may be observed, are much the same for humans as for fish: oxygen, food, water, mates, and shelter from enemies. Competition has driven fish into all kinds of waters where these necessities could not be had without new adaptations. And so it is in connection with the obtaining of one or the other of these essentials that practically all of the adaptations which we find in fish show themselves. Whole books have been written on them; we shall mention only a few.

Betta, our old friend the Siamese fighting fish, is a good example of adaptation, and of an adaptation of an adaptation. He, as well as such aquarium favorites as the paradise fish and the gourami, belong to a group which are called labyrinth-fishes because they have modified some of the tissues on each side of their heads into labyrinth-like breathing chambers. They live in Asia and Africa, where the water in their small pools gets foul in the dry season, and because of the resulting lack of oxygen they have formed the habit of coming to the surface to take in mouthfuls of air which they store in these auxiliary chambers. This they use not only for breathing, but also to make their bubble-nests described in an earlier chapter, for it is from this store of air that the indispensable bubbles are formed. An adaptation originally connected with the need for oxygen has been readapted to suit the need for shelter of the young. And if you want to carry the matter one step further you might consider the way in which the upward-slanting mouth of this fish is so placed as to make it the perfect instrument for releasing bubbles and for inserting eggs into a nest overhead.

Betta is a case of one adaptive structure serving two purposes within the same species. In the ray and the flounder, on the other hand, we have one adaptive form occurring in two dissimilar species for two different purposes and in two fundamentally different ways. Both have the body so flattened that they are able to live on or very close to the bottom. In the ray this brings the mouth down to where it can easily scoop up the shell-fish which form its food. It is, therefore, mainly a feeding adaptation. In the flounder, however, it is more in the nature of a camouflage, for it permits him to lie flat on the bottom where, with the help

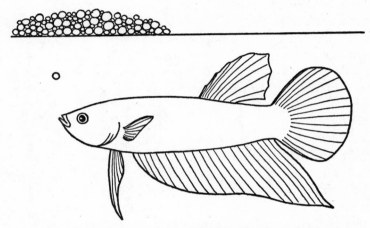

FIGURE 28. MALE BETTA UNDER HIS BUBBLE-NEST, RELEASING ANOTHER BUBBLE

of his changeable coloring, he escapes the notice not only of his own prospective food but also of those forms which look upon him as food. It is, therefore, both a feeding and a protective adaptation.

These explanations of purpose are, it must be admitted, conjectural. But in determining the method by which the adaptation is arrived at there is no need for conjecture. The anatomical evidence is all there. The ray is a highly depressed shark. It is compressed from top to bottom, just as if you had taken a clay model of a shark and squeezed it between two horizontal plates until it is almost flat. The ray, like

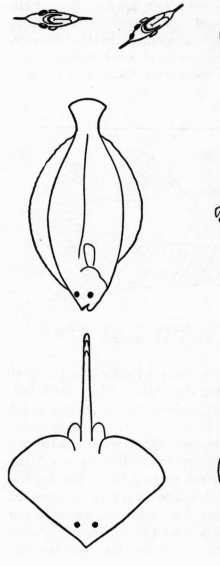

The young flounder swims upright (top view). Gradually it leans to one side, and one eye moves, until it swims in the position shown in the bottom view.

The flounder is flattened from side to side, and lies on one side with both eyes on the other side.

The ray is flattened from top to bottom, and lies on its stomach, as shown above.

FIGURE 29. RAY AND FLOUNDER

Young flounder, on right, magnified; other figures much reduced.

most fish, rests on its stomach, with its back uppermost. The adult flounder, on the other hand, lies on its side and swims on its side, and to achieve this position it goes through a strange transformation. An article which I once came upon in the public press describes it briefly, clearly, and without undue solemnity:

"The flounder is the ichthyological acme of lassitude. He begins life swimming in an upright position like any normal fish. Before he is many weeks old, however, he begins to tire in the cosmic struggle for existence. He sinks to the bottom, stretches out on his side, and refuses to get up again. In this position he finds himself with one eye staring in a futile fashion into the mud.

"The eye, apparently tiring in its efforts to pierce the primordial ooze, behaves in a manner still unexplained by science. It moves around and joins the other optic, fortunate enough to be on top. This results in the flounder being one of the silliest looking of all fishes, but it also enables him to achieve his aim. In piscine indolence, he lolls on the bottom with his misplaced orb and its fellow peering upward for any food that may drift down to him. Even this occasionally wears on the flounder, and when it does he buries himself in the mud where he doesn't even have to look."

The unknown author is to be congratulated not only on his sense of humor, but on a degree of accuracy not often found in journalistic ventures in biology. However, the sequence of events is not exactly as he narrates them. It is true that the flounders start life like any other young fish, moving along in the conventional upright position. At this time they are unbelievably tiny, for they, and the other flatfish like the sole, dab, plaice, and turbot, which have similar life-stories, come from eggs about one-twenty-fifth of an inch in diameter. The eggs develop in less than two weeks, and the fry are only about one-eighth of an inch long when hatched. These infinitesimal animals, like any other young fish, have a yolk-sac, which it takes them about ten days to absorb, and they develop an air-bladder. They swim around, like any other young fish, with one eye on each side of the head, but at an early age they stray from the conventional path. They begin to grow flat, but instead of being flattened from top to bottom like the skate they are flattened from side to side. They begin to lean over more and more to one side or the other, and at the same time the eye on the side to which they are leaning begins a migration. It may travel across over the top of the head, or it may travel *through* the head, but it eventually lands alongside the other eye— unless, as sometimes happens, it gets lost inside the head and never appears again. In general, all the fish of the same species use the same side to see out of. Most of the flatfishes we eat in this country are "dextral"—they have the eyes on the right—while many of the tropical flatfishes are "sinistral"; but there are some species in which both right- and left-sided individuals occur. In any case, it is only after the migration of the eye that the fish settles on the bottom. The under side then becomes colorless, and the air-bladder disappears. The end result is a fish which lives on its eyeless, colorless right or left side, and presents to the world its left or right side which contains both eyes and which is colored to match its background. And the surprising point is that the whole transformation takes place within the first six to twelve weeks of the fish's career, and that in most of the species the little animals are not yet an inch long when the change is completed and they give up wandering to settle on the bottom for the rest of their lives. However, they do not "refuse to get up again," as our journalist suggests, for their food does not "drift down" into their mouths. They are carnivorous, and have to spend a certain amount of time pursuing their prey.

Many fish, like the flounder, seek protection in imitating their background, but there are others which protect themselves by passing most of their lives in unlikely or inaccessible places. One tiny inhabitant of Brazilian fresh waters actually lives inside other fishes. It is so small that it can slip into the chamber which houses the gills, presumably doing this when the gill cover is open to let the water escape, and in this extraordinary spot it makes its home. The natives call it the *candiru*, and are in great dread of it when they go into the water, for it has been known to enter the excretory orifices of human beings, from which it cannot be extracted on account of its sharp, backwardly pointing spines.

It may be assumed that this is an error on the part of the fish. Entry into the organ is supposed to occur during urination by the human under water, when the outgoing stream presumably resembles, to the candiru, the expiratory current from the gill chamber of a fish. Certainly no fish would deliberately enter a hole from which there was no way of emerging, and to be stuck in the human urethra must be most unpleasant for the candiru, but it is even more unpleasant for the human, and the only way to prevent the intruder from reaching the bladder and causing death is to perform an immediate operation.

There is one fish which has even odder ideas about the way to protect itself from its enemies. The candiru by mistake sometimes lands in strange places, but this creature, which rejoices in the operatic name of *Fierasfer*,[1] deliberately chooses them.

Fierasfer lives in tropical shallows. In the same waters there lives a member of the starfish group called a holothurian. It has so altered its shape that it looks like nothing more nor less than a gigantic and rather dirty cucumber. In

[1] Ichthyologists have recently changed this to the unromantic sounding *Carapus*.

fact, in common language it is known as "sea-cucumber," and some of its species, when properly dried, are esteemed as table-delicacies by the Chinese under the name of trepang or bêche-de-mer. Now, the ordinary starfish has one aperture in the middle of his under side which serves him both for mouth and anal opening. And through this aperture he breathes. The sea-cucumber has advanced to the point of realizing that it is considered more decent to have the mouth at one end and the anal opening at the other, but, confronted

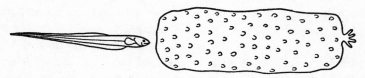

FIGURE 30. FIERASFER ABOUT TO ENTER HIS
HOLOTHURIAN HOME

with the choice of which of these two openings to breathe through, he chose what, from our point of view, is the wrong one, however logical it may seem to a sea-cucumber. He breathes through his anal opening.

And that is Fierasfer's opportunity. When the sea-cucumber is doing a little innocent breathing, Fierasfer pops in and makes himself at home. Believe it or not, he literally lives in the rectum of a sea-cucumber. What the sea-cucumber thinks of it no one knows for sure, but since he is noted for his habit of pettishly throwing out all his internal organs when he is annoyed, we can only conclude that he has no objection.

Fierasfer's form is a model for anyone who wishes to avail himself of holothurian hospitality. His body is elongated, his tail is pointed, and his vent is located so close behind his head that he can eliminate his waste products without polluting his home merely by sticking his head out of the door. Further, he has done away with his ventral fins, which might otherwise make him unpopular by tickling the insides of his host. Fins, it may be noted, are a favorite subject for adaptation. If not done away with entirely, as in this case, they are put to all kinds of uses for which they were not originally intended.

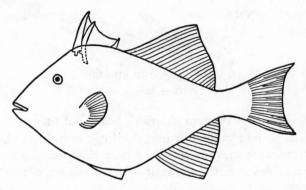

FIGURE 31. TRIGGER FISH
The dotted lines diagrammatically show the locking mechanism of the fin-spines.

In the common sea-robin, for instance, the pectorals become frail legs on which it creeps over the bottom. In the little mud-skipper, which spends much time out of water, they have developed into such sturdy limbs that it can hop about quite agilely on land in pursuit of its prey. In the flying fish the pectorals have been modified into planes which operate like the wings of a glider. They do not move the animal forward. The forward motion is obtained in the water, whereupon it shoots into the air and glides, falling back into the water when the initial impetus is lost. In the trigger fish the spines of the dorsal fin have been transformed into a fairly complicated machine for defense, one

spine fitting into a notch in the other in such a way as to hold
it against all pressure until the fish wishes to release it.

In the angler-fish the dorsal fin has an even more subtle
use. Part of it is prolonged into a flabby pendant which

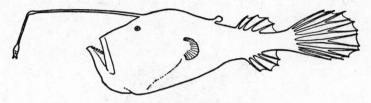

FIGURE 32. ANGLER-FISH
After Regan.

dangles over the front of the fish's head, and literally serves
as a bait to lure other fish into the huge mouth just below.

In several species the fins have been changed into suckers.
In the gobies it is the ventrals which function in this way,

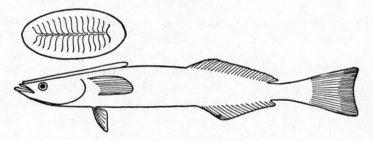

FIGURE 33. REMORA
From Jordan and Evermann, *Fishes of North and Middle America* by
permission of the United States National Museum.

permitting the little animals to cling to rocks when the surf
washes over them. In the remoras, fishes which reach a
length of three feet or more and are commonly known as
"shark-suckers," it is the dorsal fin, moved forward to the

top of the head, which has been modified into a mechanically quite beautiful suction disk. With this its owner attaches itself to the skin of a shark, and is given a free ride from place to place, letting go to feed when the shark does, returning to its carrier when the shark moves on. The sucker is extremely powerful, so much so that the natives of some of the islands in the Pacific use the fish to catch turtles with. They fasten a line to the remora, release it close to a turtle, and then let it cling inexorably to the shell while they tow it to shore.

And fins are also used in some species in mating. The tiny guppy uses his anal fin to direct balls of sperm at the female's vent; the great shark uses his ventral fins to introduce the sperm into her body.

In fact, mating and reproduction being the most important functions of fish, as of all animals, it is not to be wondered at that the most numerous and most interesting adaptations and habits are those which have to do with these processes. Most famous are the spawning of the salmon and the eel. The salmon's migrations, which we described in an earlier chapter, are more widely known because of the fish's sport and commercial importance, but the spawning activities of the eel are in some ways even more remarkable. They were for centuries a complete mystery, and the discovery of their breeding-grounds is one of the outstanding scientific achievements of the first quarter of this century.

The eel which we are speaking of here is not the moray nor the conger, but the common eel found in fresh water on both sides of the North Atlantic, the snaky fish with no ventral fins. In this country fishermen are inclined to look upon it as a nuisance when they find it on the end of their line, as a menace when they learn that it eats young bass, pickerel and even trout. They overlook the fact that, in exchange, bass, pickerel, and even trout, make many a meal off young eels.

On the other side of the Atlantic the same animal exists— although set off in a different species because it has an average of 114 vertebrae in its backbone to only 107 for the American —but the situation is different. The European has always looked upon the eel as a highly desirable food. For centuries he has been intent upon its capture and has, therefore, been interested in its mode of life. And for centuries its method of propagation baffled him, for it disappeared from his rivers in the adult stage, and reappeared in the young stage, but no ripe eels and no eggs were ever seen. Folklore provided theories ranging all the way from spontaneous generation to the transformation of horsehairs into little eels. The actual solution of the problem is an illustration of how halting the steps of progress sometimes are, and of the way in which different men in different lands at different times can unknowingly work together to write a complete scientific detective story.

The first step was taken by a German named Kauf in 1846. He discovered in the sea a little ribbon-like fish with a tiny head which he labeled *Leptocephalus brevirostris*. Science looked at this small animal without undue excitement, put it away in a bottle of alcohol, and forgot about it.

Fifty years elapsed before the next chapter was written. This time the collaborator was an Italian named Grassi, and the scene was the Mediterranean. Here Grassi found, in 1896, specimens of Kauf's little fish which were busily engaged in ceasing to be *Leptocephali*. They were in transition stages, and he succeeded in proving to his own astonished eyes, and to those of other scientists as well, that what they were doing was turning themselves into little eels. Kauf's *Leptocephalus* was the larva of the eel, almost as different from the adult as the caterpillar is from the butter-fly.

The preliminaries were now over, and the stage was set and waiting for the entrance of the master mind. This turned out to be a Dane named Johannes Schmidt. He had two clues to work with: the adult eels left the rivers and went out to sea, and the young larvae came in from the sea. Obviously the eels spawned at sea, but was it in the open ocean, or off some unknown coast or island? Did they go to different places, or did they all spawn at the same place? Schmidt burned with a great desire to find out. To follow the adults was impossible; they disappeared into the sea and were never seen again. But the little larval forms could be picked up by towing nets at the surface of the ocean. And the larvae were growing, at the same time that they were moving from their birthplaces toward their future fresh-water homes. Therefore, the smaller the larvae found in any part of the ocean, the nearer that part of the ocean must be to the spawning grounds. Schmidt's reasoning was simple enough in theory, but its practical application was stupendous.

In 1906 he put to sea, and for fifteen years he towed nets up and down the ocean. From the English Channel to Chesa-peake Bay, from Greenland to Puerto Rico, he collected and surveyed and mapped, and correlated sizes and seasonal numbers. And at last his maps began to make sense. For he found that as he went westward from the European coast the larvae grew progressively smaller, and the same thing happened as he went south and southeast from the American coast. And he was finally able to announce with absolute certainty that the spawning grounds of both species are between 20 and 30 degrees north and 50 and 70 degrees west, with the European spawning-beds to the east of the American. This area lies northeast of Puerto Rico, southeast of Bermuda. It is for all practical purposes the area of the

Sargasso Sea, where, according to song and story, the Gulf Stream comes into being, and where abandoned ships drift in a sad circle of their companions until they sink quietly beneath the waves—a perfect setting for the final chapter of one of the greatest of all scientific detective stories, a fitting place for the eel to spawn and die after its long journey across the seas.

And so the question "where" is answered, but let no ambitious young zoologist be discouraged by lack of worlds to conquer, for the eel problem is still full of "whys" and "hows." The eggs hatch in the late winter or early spring, and the leptocephali of both species start life with a length of about one-quarter of an inch. They start in very close proximity to each other in the Sargasso Sea, and yet one year later those of the American species appear off the American coast, and three years later the little Europeans appear off the European coast. Both have drifted with the Gulf Stream, both have now attained a length of two and one-half to three inches, both are still in the larval condition. How have they managed to separate, and find their respective homes? Each now metamorphoses, in a period of about two months, into a transparent miniature of its parents—a so-called "glass eel." How is it that the larval life of the American species takes only one year, just the amount of time necessary to cover the distance to our shore, whereas the larval life of the European takes three years, the amount of time necessary for it to reach the European coasts? In both species, metamorphosis occurs at the proper spot, and the glass eel makes for fresh water in the same continent which its parents inhabited. It is a beautiful arrangement of variables into an equation in timing, in which the speed of the Gulf Stream, the distance from the Sargasso Sea, and the length of time required to reach the stage of metamorphosis, have all been perfectly correlated.

The little fish now swarm up the streams. The word "swarm" is used advisedly. The numbers which survive to reach fresh water can be only a small percentage of those born in the Sargasso Sea, yet at times there are what appear to be solid ropes of elvers ascending our rivers. One authority speaks of getting fifteen hundred in a single scoop of a small dip-net as something not at all unusual. Those which survive this upstream passage—and the number eaten by fish and other animals must be enormous—settle down to live and grow in fresh water. They are voracious, but grow slowly. Scales form, in the American species, at three to four years. They are so deeply sunk in the skin that people often think of eels as having no scales, but they are there, and they are readable. Eels kept in captivity have been known to live for fifty years, but they never breed in fresh water.

Normally, the males grow to sixteen inches, the females to three feet. Age at maturity varies from eight to fifteen years; it is earlier for males than for females. But whatever it may be, there comes for each an autumn when something irresistibly impels it to go down to the sea. So strong is the urge that if the water in which it dwells has been isolated by drying streams, it will travel overland, choosing damp nights for such excursions. Arrived in salt water, its sex-organs begin to develop, it ceases feeding, and it starts on its slow journey back to its birthplace. A French zoologist has estimated that eels do not travel ordinarily faster than one-half mile an hour. At this rate it would take the American eel from one to two months, the European eel about six months, to make the journey. Great armies of eels, endless processions of eels, from Maryland and Maine, from England and France, from Cadiz and Trieste, solemnly wriggle across the Atlantic at this funereal pace. They reach the Sargasso Sea, they go down into its dark depths, and there, a thousand feet below the surface, they spawn and die.

And so it may be seen that the eel's life-cycle is the reverse of the salmon's. The latter is born in fresh water, goes to sea to live, feed, and grow, returns to fresh water to spawn and die. The former is born in salt water, goes into fresh water to live, feed, and grow, and returns to salt water to spawn and die. It is difficult to conceive how the salmon finds its way back from the sea to its home tributary; but it is even more difficult to conceive how the eel finds its way back across the trackless ocean to the Sargasso Sea.

A very different kind of spawning migration is that of a little smeltlike fish six inches long called the grunion. The grunion lives along the sandy California beaches, and it has worked out an equation in timing in which the movements of the sun and the moon are the variables.

The moon, as we all learned in school, is the principal cause of the tides of the sea, but the sun also plays a part. The moon moves in an orbit around the earth which it takes a little more than twenty-nine days to complete. At one spot in that orbit, the moon is directly on the line between the earth and the sun, and the pull of moon and sun then combine to make the tides higher than average. Some fourteen days later, when the moon has gone half-way around the earth, the moon is on the opposite side from the sun, and the two astral bodies pull in opposite directions, with the same result. In plain words, for the benefit of those not astronomically minded, approximately every two weeks there is a period of two or three days when the high tides are higher than usual. These are called spring tides. At such times, the waves come up on the beaches further than they do at most high tides, and reach points on the sand which, after their subsidence, will remain above water until the next spring tides come two weeks later to wash over them again.

The pressure of the life-force against its circumscribing

environment is unceasing. Every last corner in which it can by the most far-fetched means gain a foothold must be utilized. This narrow strip of sand, at the very limit of the tidal zone, is available only at fortnightly intervals, and yet the grunion has arranged its whole life-cycle in such a way as to take advantage of it.

Every two weeks during the spawning season, which lasts from March until July, the grunion mature. Every two weeks their eggs become ripe, and it is with unfailing regularity at the time of a spring tide that their sex products press for release. At night, in great numbers, the fish congregate in the surf. There they wait, rising and falling in the long Pacific roll, until just after high tide. At the proper moment something gives them the signal, and they begin to come in. Like skillful surf-boarders, they ride the crests of the waves, and they bounce and tumble along with the foam until they land high up on the beach. There each female's tail drills a hole in the dripping sand; into it she pours her eggs, which are fertilized by the nearest male; and the fish, except for the unfortunate few who fail to extricate themselves and are found dead the next morning up to their armpits, so to speak, in sand, squirm their way back into the next wave and are sucked out to sea. The mating act, including the selection of partners, the digging of the nest, and the deposition of the sex products, takes no more than sixty seconds, and the whole spawning migration sets what must be an all-time record for speed, for from the moment an individual starts in on the crest of a wave until it is back again in deep water cannot be over three minutes.

The parents, having done what is called their duty, but what in this case must be nothing but a pleasant and exciting excursion, go on their way. The spring tide recedes, next day's sun shines down upon the beach, and there, safely buried three or four inches deep in the warm, moist sand, the eggs develop. Two weeks later the next spring tide scours them from their nest, washes the ready fry out of the egg-membranes, and sweeps them out to sea.

One or two of the subtler points which we have passed over in order not to interrupt our narrative are worth attention. Spawning takes place at night only. The grunion thus escapes many of the dangers which it would run if it spawned in daylight, especially birds of prey. The one bird of prey which it does not fool in this way is man. Formerly the beaches of southern California glittered in the moonlight with great schools of spawning grunion. Motor-cars have brought schools of greedy humans, with shovels and scoops and buckets and barrels, and now the grunion are few. However, the species is not doomed, for a closed season has been put into effect to save it from extinction.

Spawning generally takes place not at the very apex of the spring tide, but one or two nights later, when the waves do not reach quite so high up on the beach. This makes it certain that the next spring tide will reach and release the fry even though through some variation in the conditions it is not quite so high as the one in which the eggs were laid.

The eggs take only nine days to develop, but the fry do not emerge until the waves dig them out of the sand. They are thus ready for the appointment ahead of time, in case winds or other circumstances should bring the releasing tide earlier than usual, but they none the less suspend their progress and wait patiently within the egg until the water comes to set them free. If they did not, they would emerge into the almost dry sand, and would perish.

The whole thing is an equation in timing even more complicated than that of the eel, and, to my mind, prettier. I would rather be a grunion than an eel.

There is one fish which has pushed the matter even further. It apparently appreciates the desirable features of the grunion's system, but being an inhabitant of tropical fresh waters it has no tide to help it, and has to take the parts played by the moon and sun itself. It spawns out of water entirely. Through what feats of acrobatism can only be imagined, the female sticks her eggs to a rock a little above the surface, and the male then goes on duty to keep them wet by splashing water on them until the young hatch. Gilbert and Sullivan could not have thought of anything more nonsensical, nor Alice's White Knight with his

> *. . . plan*
> *To dye one's whiskers green*
> *And always use so large a fan*
> *That they could not be seen.*

The little *Copeina* described above shows a commendable interest in the eggs after they are laid, but there are other fish which go even further. Most touching instance of post-natal care is the so-called "mouth-breeder." Here we have a fish—a cold, dull, selfish animal in the eyes of most people —going without food for weeks for the sake of its children. This occurs not only among the cichlids, which we mentioned in the preceding chapter as outstanding examples of parental solicitude, but also among the catfish. One of the parents—in some species the mother, in some the father— takes the eggs in the mouth after they are fertilized, and not only holds them there throughout development, but also holds a mouthful of squirming fry until the yolk-sac is absorbed. In spite of all temptations, no food is eaten. And in the case of the cichlids the young, even after they are free-swimming, return to the parental mouth each evening and spend the night there until they are literally too big to get in.

The sea-horse is also a good parent but in a different way, and here the father only officiates. For it is the male which has on its abdomen a pouch very much like the marsupial pouch of the female kangaroo. In this pouch the eggs are placed by the mother as she lays them, and here they remain until the young are able to swim. Then, with a series of convulsive movements which make the father look as if he were in great distress, he forces open the pouch, and the little ones are expelled, sometimes one at a time and sometimes in swarms. It looks exactly as if the father were giving birth.

And in a very different species the father, incredible as it may sound, actually does give birth—or, to put it more correctly, the same fish which at one time in its life gives birth later becomes a father. For in one of the live-bearers, *Xyphophorus*, the sword-tail, authentic records are numerous of complete change of sex. An individual starts life as a female, becomes a mother, and gives birth to numerous offspring. After some years of this she gets tired of males, starts taking up with other females, and before long has fathered numerous offspring. As one ichthyologist described it, "A mother becomes the father of her own granddaughter." It seems a happy division of domestic labors, and one which human beings might well envy. After a youthful probationary period during which she underwent the trials, as well as the joys, of womanhood and motherhood, the individual, instead of becoming barren in middle life, would turn into a man, enjoying thenceforth masculine freedom from physical and domestic woes, and assuming masculine responsibilities. What wise old men we should have! For it is difficult for even the most sensitive of us fully to appreciate situations which we have not personally experienced; but an old man who had been in his earlier days maiden, wife, and mother would be capable of a boundless sympathy for and understanding of all mankind.

And now we come to the climax, the ultimate height, the

wildest flight of fancy, exemplified by a certain large and quite ugly deep-sea angler-fish. This animal is a perfect Christmas tree of adaptations. Being an angler, it has the dorsal fin modified into a dangling lure. Being a deep-sea fish, it has, as many deep-sea fish do, phosphorescent organs which light up the darkness in which it lives—whether to signal mates or to lure victims is undetermined. And then it

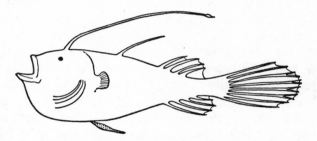

FIGURE 34. FEMALE ANGLER WITH DWARF PARASITIC MALE ATTACHED TO ABDOMEN

goes a step further and stupefies the rest of the animal kingdom by taking unto itself a parasitic mate. Parasitic not in the manner of some human females: here the parasitism is physical, and is practiced by the male. Anyone who does not believe this may go to the American Museum of Natural History in New York City and look at the model in the Hall of Fishes, made from a gruesome couple captured off the coast of England. The female is forty inches long, her devoted husband four inches long—only one one-thousandth of her weight.

This species lives at great depths, in complete blackness. Its numbers are few. The chances of a male finding a female are poor, and of his losing her after he has once found her good. What he does, then, if he has the good luck to find a mate, is to make sure that he will never be separated from her. He takes her by the throat or the back, or some other portion of her anatomy. His jaws sink in. And he never lets go again. By and by his skin grows together with her skin. Her blood-vessels make connection with his blood-vessels. His mouth degenerates and becomes functionless. He becomes literally one with her.

In an earlier chapter it was said that no cases of monogamy in the fish world could be proved; and even here, in spite of first appearances to the contrary, true monogamy does not exist, for the female may attach unto herself several males. But of unswerving masculine devotion to a single spouse this is unquestionably the world's outstanding example. Here is conjugal faithfulness carried to the ultimate degree. Here are no puny words about "till death do us part." Not even death will part this little fish from his mate. If she dies, he at once dies also. Here is marital fidelity beyond the powers of the most virtuous of the human species.

Poor fish, indeed!

Selected References

1946. The early evolution of fishes. Quarterly Review of Biology, vol. XXI, no. 1, pp. 36-39 (March 1946).

Simpson, George Gaylord
1947. The problem of plan and purpose in Nature. The Scientific Monthly, vol. LXIV, no. 6, pp. 481-495 (June 1947).

Smith, J. L. B.
1939. A living fossil. Annual report of the Smithsonian Institution for the year ended June 30, 1940, pp. 321-327 (1941). (Reprinted from the Cape Naturalist, vol. I, no. 6, July 1939.)

Chapman, Wilbert McLeod
1946. Thrice told tales: 1. Concerning the skin and scales of Fish. The Aquarium Journal (San Francisco Aquarium Society), September 1946. (Articles by same author on other phases of fish anatomy appear in succeeding issues.)

Creaser, Charles W.
1926. The structure and growth of the scales of fishes in relation to the interpretation of their life-history, with special reference to the sunfish *Eupomotis gibbosus*. University of Michigan Museum of Zoology, Miscellaneous Publication no. 17, pp. 1-82.

Dahl, Knut
1907. The scales of the herring as a means of determining age, growth and migration. Report on Norwegian Fishery and Marine Investigations, vol. II, pt. II, nr. 6, 36 pp., 3 pls.

Johnston, H. W.
1905. Scales of the Tay salmon as indicative of age, growth and spawning habit. 23rd Annual Report, Fishery Board for Scotland, 1904, pt. II, pp. 63-79 (1905).

Jordan, David Starr
1905. A guide to the study of fishes. (Henry Holt & Company), vol. I, pp. i-xxvi, 1-624; vol. II, pp. i-xxiii, 1-599.

Mast, S. O.
1914. Changes in shade, color and pattern in fishes, and their bearing on the problems of adaptation and behavior, with especial reference to the flounders *Paralichthys* and *Ancylopsetta*. U.S. Bureau of Fisheries Document no. 821, pp. 173-238, pls. XIX-XXXVII (April 10, 1916).

Parker, G. H.
    1943. Animal color changes and their neurohumors. Quarterly Review of Biology, vol. XVIII, no. 1, pp. 205-227 (March 1943).
Sumner, Francis B.
    1911. The adjustment of flatfishes to various backgrounds: a study of adaptive color change. Journal of Experimental Zoology, vol. X, no. 4, pp. 409-505.
    1935. Studies of protective color changes. III. Experiments with fishes both as predators and prey. Proceedings of the National Academy of Sciences, vol. XXI, no. 6, pp. 345-353.
Townsend, Charles Haskins
    1929. Records of changes in color among fishes. Zoologica, vol. IX, no. 9, pp. 321-378, 27 col. pls., 15 figs. (August 31, 1929).
Van Oosten, John
    1929. Life history of the lake herring (*Leucichthys artedi* Le Sueur) of Lake Huron as revealed by its scales, with a critique of the scale method. U.S. Bureau of Fisheries Document no. 1053. (From Bulletin of the Bureau of Fisheries, vol. XLIV, pp. 265-428, 1928.)

CHAPTER IV

Breder, C. M., Jr.
    1926. The locomotion of fishes. Zoologica, vol. IV, no. 5, pp. 157-297.
Gregory, William K.
    1933. Fish skulls: a study of the evolution of natural mechanisms. Transactions of the American Philosophical Society, art. II, vol. XXIII, pt. II, pp. i-vii, 75-481, figs. 1-302.
Gregory, William K., and Raven, Henry C.
    1941. Studies on the origin and early evolution of paired fins and limbs. Annals of New York Academy of Sciences, vol. XLII, art. 3, pp. 273-360.

CHAPTER V

Brown, Frank A., Jr.
    1937. Responses of the large-mouth black bass to colors. State of Illinois, Division of the Natural History Survey, vol. 21, bull. art. 2, pp. 33-55.
Noble, G. K., and Curtis, Brian
    1939. The social behavior of the jewel fish, *Hemichromis bimaculatus* Gill. Bulletin of the American Museum of Natural History, vol. LXXVI, art. 1, pp. 1-46 (issued February 22, 1939).
Parker, G. H.
    1905. The function of the lateral line organs in fishes. Bulletin of the Bureau of Fisheries, vol. XXIV, 1904, pp. 183-207 (issued February 18, 1905).
    1912. The relation of smell, taste and the common chemical sense in vertebrates. Journal of the Academy of Natural Sciences of Philadelphia, vol. XV, 2nd Ser., pp. 221-234.
    1918. A critical survey of the sense of hearing in fishes. Proceedings of the American Philosophical Society, vol. LXVII, pp. 69-98.

Parker, G. H., and Sheldon, R. E.
   1913. The sense of smell in fishes. U.S. Bureau of Fisheries Document
   no. 775, pp. 33-46 (issued March 20, 1913).
von Frisch, K.
   1938. The sense of hearing in fish. Nature, vol. 141, No. 3557, pp.
   8-11 (January 1, 1938).
Walls, Gordon L.
   1942. The vertebrate eye and its adaptive radiation. Cranbrook Institute of Science Bulletin No. 19, pp. i-xiv, 1-785 (August 1942).

CHAPTER VI

Smith, Homer W.
   1932. Kamongo. (The Viking Press, New York), pp. 1-167 (an essay
   on the lung-fish).
Taylor, Harden F.
   1922. Deductions concerning the air bladder and the specific gravity of
   fishes. U.S. Bureau of Fisheries Document no. 921. (From Bulletin
   of the Bureau of Fisheries, vol. XXXVIII, pp. 121-126; issued April
   24, 1922.)
von Frisch, K.
   1938. The sense of hearing in fish. Nature, vol. 141, no. 3557, pp. 8-11
   (January 1, 1938).

CHAPTER VII

Kyle, Harry M.
   1926. The biology of fishes. (The Macmillan Company, New York),
   pp. i-xvi, 1-396.
Smith, Homer W.
   1931. The regulation of the composition of the blood of teleost and
   elasmobranch fishes, and the evolution of the vertebrate kidneys.
   Copeia, no. 4, pp. 147-152 (1931).
   1932. Water regulation and its evolution in the fishes. Quarterly Review of Biology, vol. VII, no. 1, pp. 1-26 (March 1932).

CHAPTER VIII

Innes, William T.
   1947. Exotic aquarium fishes. A work of general reference. (Innes
   Publishing Company, Philadelphia), 8th ed., 507 pp.
Kendall, William Converse
   1921. Peritoneal membranes, ovaries and oviducts of salmonoid fishes
   and their significance in fish-cultural practises. U.S. Bureau of Fisheries Document no. 901. (From Bulletin of the Bureau of Fisheries,
   vol. XXXVII, 1919-20, pp. 183-208, issued March 28, 1921.)

CHAPTER IX

Curtis, Brian
   1934. The golden trout of Cottonwood lakes (*Salmo agua-bonita*

Jordan). Transactions of the American Fisheries Society, vol. 64, pp. 259-265 (1934).

Huntsman, A. G.
1942. Return of a marked salmon from a distant place. Science, vol. 95, no. 2467, pp. 381-382.

Mottley, C. McC.
1934. The effect of temperature during development on the number of scales in the Kamloops trout, *Salmo kamloops* Jordan. Contributions to Canadian Biology and Fisheries, new series, vol. VIII, no. 20, pp. 253-263 (published February 17, 1934).

Needham, P. R., and Taft, A. C.
1934. Observations on the spawning of steelhead trout. Transactions of the American Fisheries Society, vol. 64, pp. 332-338 (1934).

Powers, Edwin B.
1943. Further evidence on chemical factors affecting the migratory movements of fishes, especially the salmon. Ecology, vol. XXIV, no. 1, pp. 109-113 (January 1943).

Pritchard, A. L.
1944. Return of two marked pink salmon (*Oncorhynchus gorbuscha*) to the natal stream from distant places in the sea. Copeia, no. 2, pp. 80-82 (June 30, 1944).

Schultz, Leonard P.
1937. The breeding habits of salmon and trout. Annual report of the Smithsonian Institution, pp. 365-376.

Shapovalov, Leo
1941. The homing instinct in trout and salmon. Proceedings of the Sixth Pacific Science Congress of the Pacific Science Association, vol. III, pp. 317-322 (April 1941).

Smith, Osgood R.
1941. The spawning habits of cutthroat and eastern brook trouts. Journal of Wildlife Management, vol. V, no. 4, pp. 461-471 (October 1941).

Snyder, John O.
1934. A new California trout. California Fish and Game, vol. XX, no. 2, pp. 106-112 (April 1934).

Taft, A. C.
1933. California steelhead trout problems. California Fish and Game, vol. XIX, no. 3, pp. 192-199 (July 1933).

Thorpe, W. H., and Wilkinson, D. H.
1946. Ising's theory of bird orientation. Nature, vol. 58, no. 4025, pp. 903-904.

White, H. C.
1936. The homing of salmon in Apple river, N. S. Journal of the Biological Research Board of Canada, vol. II, no. 4, pp. 391-400 (July-August 1936).

CHAPTER X

Breder, C. M., Jr.
1936. The reproductive habits of North American sunfishes (family Centrarchidae). Zoologica, vol. XXI, no. 1, pp. 1-48.

1942. Social and respiratory behavior of large tarpon. Zoologica, vol. XXVII, pt. 1, pp. 1-4.

1944. Materials for the study of the life history of *Tarpon atlanticus*. Zoologica, vol. XXIX, pt. 4, pp. 217-252.

Calhoun, A. J., and Woodhull, C. A.
  1948. Progress report on studies of striped bass reproduction in relation to the Central Valley Project. California Fish and Game, vol. 34, no. 4, pp. 171-188 (October 1948).

Hubbs, Carl L., and Lagler, Karl F.
  1947. Fishes of the Great Lakes region. Cranbrook Institute of Science Bulletin no. 26, pp. i-xi, 1-186 (October 1947).

Lang, O. W., and Jarvis, N. D.
  1944. Tuna. Fishery Leaflet no. 82, U.S. Fish and Wildlife Service, pp. 175-198.

Merriman, Daniel
  1941. Studies on the striped bass (*Roccus saxatilis*) of the Atlantic coast. Fishery Bulletin 35 from Fishery Bulletin of the U.S. Fish and Wildlife Service, vol. 50, pp. 1-77.

Norman, J. R., and Fraser, J. C.
  1937. Giant fishes, whales and dolphins. (Putnam, London) pp. i-xxvii, 1-361.

Scofield, Eugene C.
  1931. The striped bass of California (*Roccus lineatus*). California Division of Fish and Game, Fish Bulletin no. 29, pp. 1-84. (Note: This is the same fish referred to in the paper by Merriman; the specific name was changed between the date of Scofield's paper and the other from *lineatus* to *saxatilis*.)

Shapovalov, Leo
  1936. Food of the striped bass. California Fish and Game, vol. 22, no. 4, pp. 261-271 (October 1936).

Schlaifer, A.
  1941. Additional social and physiological aspects of respiratory behavior in small tarpon. Zoologica, vol. XXVI, no. 11, pp. 55-60.

Van Oosten, John
  1946. The pikes. Fishery leaflet no. 166. U.S. Fish and Wildlife Service, Washington, D. C.

Woodhull, Chester
  1947. Spawning habits of the striped bass (*Roccus saxatilis*) in California waters. California Fish and Game, vol. 33, no. 2, pp. 97-102 (April 1947).

CHAPTER XI

Bureau of Fisheries (U.S.)
  1915. The tilefish: a new deep sea food fish. Economic Circular no. 19, pp. 1-6 (September 30, 1915).

Eschmeyer, R. W.
  1945. Effects of a year-round open season on fishing in Norris reservoir. Journal of the Tennessee Academy of Sciences, vol. XX, no. 1, pp. 20-34 (January 1945).

Foerster, R. E.
  1946. Restocking depleted sockeye salmon areas by transfer of eggs. Journal of the Fisheries Research Board of Canada, vol. VI, no. 7, pp. 483-490 (October 1946).
Hobbs, Derisley F.
  1937. Natural reproduction of quinnat salmon, brown and rainbow trout in certain New Zealand waters. Fisheries Bulletin no. 6, New Zealand Marine Department, pp. 1-104.
Rich, Willis H.
  1940. The future of the Columbia River salmon fisheries, Stanford Ichthyological Bulletin, vol. 2, no. 2, pp. 37-47 (December 23, 1940).
Russell, E. S.
  1942. The overfishing problem (Cambridge University Press). Pp. i-viii, 1-130.
War Department, Corps of Engineers, U.S. Army
  1947. Power, navigation and fish facilities on the Columbia river at Bonneville dam, Bonneville, Oregon and Washington. Pp. 1-22.

CHAPTER XII
Beebe, William
  1938. *Ceratias*—siren of the deep. Bulletin New York Zoological Society, vol. XLI, no. 2, pp. 50-53 (March-April 1938).
Clark, Frances N.
  1925. The life history of *Leuresthes tenuis*, an atherine fish with tide controlled spawning habits. California Division of Fish and Game, Fish Bulletin no. 10, pp. 1-51.
Coates, Christopher W.
  1947. The kick of an electric eel. The Atlantic Monthly, vol. 180, no. 4, pp. 75-79 (October 1947).
Roule, Louis
  1933. Fishes: their journeys and migrations. (George Rutledge & Sons, Ltd., London), pp. i-x, 1-270. (Translated from the French by Conrad Elphinstone.)
Schmidt, Johannes
  1935. Danish eel investigations during 25 years, 1905-1930. Carlsberg Foundation, Copenhagen, pp. 1-16.
Thévenin, René
  1936. The curious life habits of the sea horse. Natural History, vol. XXXVII, pp. 211-222, with photos by Jean Painlevé (March 1936).

Index

A CATALOGUE OF SELECTED DOVER BOOKS
IN ALL FIELDS OF INTEREST

A CATALOGUE OF SELECTED DOVER
BOOKS IN ALL FIELDS OF INTEREST

CELESTIAL OBJECTS FOR COMMON TELESCOPES, T. W. Webb. The most used book in amateur astronomy: inestimable aid for locating and identifying nearly 4,000 celestial objects. Edited, updated by Margaret W. Mayall. 77 illustrations. Total of 645pp. 5⅜ x 8½.
20917-2, 20918-0 Pa., Two-vol. set $8.00

HISTORICAL STUDIES IN THE LANGUAGE OF CHEMISTRY, M. P. Crosland. The important part language has played in the development of chemistry from the symbolism of alchemy to the adoption of systematic nomenclature in 1892. ". . . wholeheartedly recommended,"—Science. 15 illustrations. 416pp. of text. 5⅝ x 8¼.
63702-6 Pa. $6.00

BURNHAM'S CELESTIAL HANDBOOK, Robert Burnham, Jr. Thorough, readable guide to the stars beyond our solar system. Exhaustive treatment, fully illustrated. Breakdown is alphabetical by constellation: Andromeda to Cetus in Vol. 1; Chamaeleon to Orion in Vol. 2; and Pavo to Vulpecula in Vol. 3. Hundreds of illustrations. Total of about 2000pp. 6⅛ x 9¼.
23567-X, 23568-8, 23673-0 Pa., Three-vol. set $26.85

THEORY OF WING SECTIONS: INCLUDING A SUMMARY OF AIR-FOIL DATA, Ira H. Abbott and A. E. von Doenhoff. Concise compilation of subatomic aerodynamic characteristics of modern NASA wing sections, plus description of theory. 350pp. of tables. 693pp. 5⅜ x 8½.
60586-8 Pa. $6.50

DE RE METALLICA, Georgius Agricola. Translated by Herbert C. Hoover and Lou H. Hoover. The famous Hoover translation of greatest treatise on technological chemistry, engineering, geology, mining of early modern times (1556). All 289 original woodcuts. 638pp. 6¾ x 11.
60006-8 Clothbd. $17.50

THE ORIGIN OF CONTINENTS AND OCEANS, Alfred Wegener. One of the most influential, most controversial books in science, the classic statement for continental drift. Full 1966 translation of Wegener's final (1929) version. 64 illustrations. 246pp. 5⅜ x 8½.
61708-4 Pa. $3.00

THE PRINCIPLES OF PSYCHOLOGY, William James. Famous long course complete, unabridged. Stream of thought, time perception, memory, experimental methods; great work decades ahead of its time. Still valid, useful; read in many classes. 94 figures. Total of 1391pp. 5⅜ x 8½.
20381-6, 20382-4 Pa., Two-vol. set $13.00

THE DEPRESSION YEARS AS PHOTOGRAPHED BY ARTHUR ROTH-STEIN, Arthur Rothstein. First collection devoted entirely to the work of outstanding 1930s photographer: famous dust storm photo, ragged children, unemployed, etc. 120 photographs. Captions. 119pp. 9¼ x 10¾.
23590-4 Pa. $5.00

CAMERA WORK: A PICTORIAL GUIDE, Alfred Stieglitz. All 559 illustrations and plates from the most important periodical in the history of art photography, Camera Work (1903-17). Presented four to a page, reduced in size but still clear, in strict chronological order, with complete captions. Three indexes. Glossary. Bibliography. 176pp. 8⅜ x 11¼.
23591-2 Pa. $6.95

ALVIN LANGDON COBURN, PHOTOGRAPHER, Alvin L. Coburn. Revealing autobiography by one of greatest photographers of 20th century gives insider's version of Photo-Secession, plus comments on his own work. 77 photographs by Coburn. Edited by Helmut and Alison Gernsheim. 160pp. 8⅛ x 11.
23685-4 Pa. $6.00

NEW YORK IN THE FORTIES, Andreas Feininger. 162 brilliant photographs by the well-known photographer, formerly with Life magazine, show commuters, shoppers, Times Square at night, Harlem nightclub, Lower East Side, etc. Introduction and full captions by John von Hartz. 181pp. 9¼ x 10¾.
23585-8 Pa. $6.00

GREAT NEWS PHOTOS AND THE STORIES BEHIND THEM, John Faber. Dramatic volume of 140 great news photos, 1855 through 1976, and revealing stories behind them, with both historical and technical information. Hindenburg disaster, shooting of Oswald, nomination of Jimmy Carter, etc. 160pp. 8¼ x 11.
23667-6 Pa. $5.00

THE ART OF THE CINEMATOGRAPHER, Leonard Maltin. Survey of American cinematography history and anecdotal interviews with 5 masters—Arthur Miller, Hal Mohr, Hal Rosson, Lucien Ballard, and Conrad Hall. Very large selection of behind-the-scenes production photos. 105 photographs. Filmographies. Index. Originally Behind the Camera. 144pp. 8¼ x 11.
23686-2 Pa. $5.00

DESIGNS FOR THE THREE-CORNERED HAT (LE TRICORNE), Pablo Picasso. 32 fabulously rare drawings—including 31 color illustrations of costumes and accessories—for 1919 production of famous ballet. Edited by Parmenia Migel, who has written new introduction. 48pp. 9⅜ x 12¼. (Available in U.S. only)
23709-5 Pa. $5.00

NOTES OF A FILM DIRECTOR, Sergei Eisenstein. Greatest Russian filmmaker explains montage, making of Alexander Nevsky, aesthetics; comments on self, associates, great rivals (Chaplin), similar material. 78 illustrations. 240pp. 5⅜ x 8½.
22392-2 Pa. $4.50

HOLLYWOOD GLAMOUR PORTRAITS, edited by John Kobal. 145 photos capture the stars from 1926-49, the high point in portrait photography. Gable, Harlow, Bogart, Bacall, Hedy Lamarr, Marlene Dietrich, Robert Montgomery, Marlon Brando, Veronica Lake; 94 stars in all. Full background on photographers, technical aspects, much more. Total of 160pp. 8⅜ x 11¼. 23352-9 Pa. $5.00

THE NEW YORK STAGE: FAMOUS PRODUCTIONS IN PHOTO-GRAPHS, edited by Stanley Appelbaum. 148 photographs from Museum of City of New York show 142 plays, 1883-1939. *Peter Pan, The Front Page, Dead End, Our Town*, O'Neill, hundreds of actors and actresses, etc. Full indexes. 154pp. 9½ x 10. 23241-7 Pa. $4.50

MASTERS OF THE DRAMA, John Gassner. Most comprehensive history of the drama, every tradition from Greeks to modern Europe and America, including Orient. Covers 800 dramatists, 2000 plays; biography, plot summaries, criticism, theatre history, etc. 77 illustrations. 890pp. 5⅜ x 8½. 20100-7 Clothbd. $10.00

THE GREAT OPERA STARS IN HISTORIC PHOTOGRAPHS, edited by James Camner. 343 portraits from the 1850s to the 1940s: Tamburini, Mario, Caliapin, Jeritza, Melchior, Melba, Patti, Pinza, Schipa, Caruso, Farrar, Steber, Gobbi, and many more—270 performers in all. Index. 199pp. 8⅜ x 11¼. 23575-0 Pa. $6.50

J. S. BACH, Albert Schweitzer. Great full-length study of Bach, life, background to music, music, by foremost modern scholar. Ernest Newman translation. 650 musical examples. Total of 928pp. 5⅜ x 8½. (Available in U.S. only) 21631-4, 21632-2 Pa., Two-vol. set $9.00

COMPLETE PIANO SONATAS, Ludwig van Beethoven. All sonatas in the fine Schenker edition, with fingering, analytical material. One of best modern editions. Total of 615pp. 9 x 12. (Available in U.S. only) 23134-8, 23135-6 Pa., Two-vol. set $13.00

KEYBOARD MUSIC, J. S. Bach. Bach-Gesellschaft edition. For harpsichord, piano, other keyboard instruments. English Suites, French Suites, Six Partitas, Goldberg Variations, Two-Part Inventions, Three-Part Sinfonias. 312pp. 8⅛ x 11. (Available in U.S. only) 22360-4 Pa. $5.50

FOUR SYMPHONIES IN FULL SCORE, Franz Schubert. Schubert's four most popular symphonies: No. 4 in C Minor ("Tragic"); No. 5 in B-flat Major; No. 8 in B Minor ("Unfinished"); No. 9 in C Major ("Great"). Breitkopf & Hartel edition. Study score. 261pp. 9⅜ x 12¼. 23681-1 Pa. $6.50

THE AUTHENTIC GILBERT & SULLIVAN SONGBOOK, W. S. Gilbert, A. S. Sullivan. Largest selection available; 92 songs, uncut, original keys, in piano rendering approved by Sullivan. Favorites and lesser-known fine numbers. Edited with plot synopses by James Spero. 3 illustrations. 399pp. 9 x 12. 23482-7 Pa. $7.95

YUCATAN BEFORE AND AFTER THE CONQUEST, Diego de Landa. First English translation of basic book in Maya studies, the only significant account of Yucatan written in the early post-Conquest era. Translated by distinguished Maya scholar William Gates. Appendices, introduction, 4 maps and over 120 illustrations added by translator. 162pp. 5⅜ x 8½.
23622-6 Pa. $3.00

THE MALAY ARCHIPELAGO, Alfred R. Wallace. Spirited travel account by one of founders of modern biology. Touches on zoology, botany, ethnography, geography, and geology. 62 illustrations, maps. 515pp. 5⅜ x 8½.
20187-2 Pa. $6.95

THE DISCOVERY OF THE TOMB OF TUTANKHAMEN, Howard Carter, A. C. Mace. Accompany Carter in the thrill of discovery, as ruined passage suddenly reveals unique, untouched, fabulously rich tomb. Fascinating account, with 106 illustrations. New introduction by J. M. White. Total of 382pp. 5⅜ x 8½. (Available in U.S. only)   23500-9 Pa. $4.00

THE WORLD'S GREATEST SPEECHES, edited by Lewis Copeland and Lawrence W. Lamm. Vast collection of 278 speeches from Greeks up to present. Powerful and effective models; unique look at history. Revised to 1970. Indices. 842pp. 5⅜ x 8½.   20468-5 Pa. $6.95

THE 100 GREATEST ADVERTISEMENTS, Julian Watkins. The priceless ingredient; His master's voice; 99 44/100% pure; over 100 others. How they were written, their impact, etc. Remarkable record. 130 illustrations. 233pp. 7⅞ x 10 3/5.   20540-1 Pa. $5.00

CRUICKSHANK PRINTS FOR HAND COLORING, George Cruickshank. 18 illustrations, one side of a page, on fine-quality paper suitable for watercolors. Caricatures of people in society (c. 1820) full of trenchant wit. Very large format. 32pp. 11 x 16.   23684-6 Pa. $4.50

THIRTY-TWO COLOR POSTCARDS OF TWENTIETH-CENTURY AMERICAN ART, Whitney Museum of American Art. Reproduced in full color in postcard form are 31 art works and one shot of the museum. Calder, Hopper, Rauschenberg, others. Detachable. 16pp. 8¼ x 11.
23629-3 Pa. $2.50

MUSIC OF THE SPHERES: THE MATERIAL UNIVERSE FROM ATOM TO QUASAR SIMPLY EXPLAINED, Guy Murchie. Planets, stars, geology, atoms, radiation, relativity, quantum theory, light, antimatter, similar topics. 319 figures. 664pp. 5⅜ x 8½.
21809-0, 21810-4 Pa., Two-vol. set $10.00

EINSTEIN'S THEORY OF RELATIVITY, Max Born. Finest semi-technical account; covers Einstein, Lorentz, Minkowski, and others, with much detail, much explanation of ideas and math not readily available elsewhere on this level. For student, non-specialist. 376pp. 5⅜ x 8½.
60769-0 Pa. $4.00

AMERICAN BIRD ENGRAVINGS, Alexander Wilson et al. All 76 plates. from Wilson's *American Ornithology* (1808-14), most important ornithological work before Audubon, plus 27 plates from the supplement (1825-33) by Charles Bonaparte. Over 250 birds portrayed. 8 plates also reproduced in full color. 111pp. 9⅜ x 12½. 23195-X Pa. $6.00

CRUICKSHANK'S PHOTOGRAPHS OF BIRDS OF AMERICA, Allan D. Cruickshank. Great ornithologist, photographer presents 177 closeups, groupings, panoramas, flightings, etc., of about 150 different birds. Expanded *Wings in the Wilderness*. Introduction by Helen G. Cruickshank. 191pp. 8¼ x 11. 23497-5 Pa. $6.00

AMERICAN WILDLIFE AND PLANTS, A. C. Martin, et al. Describes food habits of more than 1000 species of mammals, birds, fish. Special treatment of important food plants. Over 300 illustrations. 500pp. 5⅜ x 8½. 20793-5 Pa. $4.95

THE PEOPLE CALLED SHAKERS, Edward D. Andrews. Lifetime of research, definitive study of Shakers: origins, beliefs, practices, dances, social organization, furniture and crafts, impact on 19th-century USA, present heritage. Indispensable to student of American history, collector. 33 illustrations. 351pp. 5⅜ x 8½. 21081-2 Pa. $4.00

OLD NEW YORK IN EARLY PHOTOGRAPHS, Mary Black. New York City as it was in 1853-1901, through 196 wonderful photographs from N.-Y. Historical Society. Great Blizzard, Lincoln's funeral procession, great buildings. 228pp. 9 x 12. 22907-6 Pa. $7.95

MR. LINCOLN'S CAMERA MAN: MATHEW BRADY, Roy Meredith. Over 300 Brady photos reproduced directly from original negatives, photos. Jackson, Webster, Grant, Lee, Carnegie, Barnum; Lincoln; Battle Smoke, Death of Rebel Sniper, Atlanta Just After Capture. Lively commentary. 368pp. 8⅜ x 11¼. 23021-X Pa. $6.95

TRAVELS OF WILLIAM BARTRAM, William Bartram. From 1773-8, Bartram explored Northern Florida, Georgia, Carolinas, and reported on wild life, plants, Indians, early settlers. Basic account for period, entertaining reading. Edited by Mark Van Doren. 13 illustrations. 141pp. 5⅜ x 8½. 20013-2 Pa. $4.50

THE GENTLEMAN AND CABINET MAKER'S DIRECTOR, Thomas Chippendale. Full reprint, 1762 style book, most influential of all time; chairs, tables, sofas, mirrors, cabinets, etc. 200 plates, plus 24 photographs of surviving pieces. 249pp. 9⅞ x 12¾. 21601-2 Pa. $6.50

AMERICAN CARRIAGES, SLEIGHS, SULKIES AND CARTS, edited by Don H. Berkebile. 168 Victorian illustrations from catalogues, trade journals, fully captioned. Useful for artists. Author is Assoc. Curator, Div. of Transportation of Smithsonian Institution. 168pp. 8½ x 9½. 23328-6 Pa. $5.00

THE PHILOSOPHY OF HISTORY, Georg W. Hegel. Great classic of Western thought develops concept that history is not chance but a rational process, the evolution of freedom. 457pp. 5⅜ x 8½.   20112-0 Pa. $4.50

LANGUAGE, TRUTH AND LOGIC, Alfred J. Ayer. Famous, clear introduction to Vienna, Cambridge schools of Logical Positivism. Role of philosophy, elimination of metaphysics, nature of analysis, etc. 160pp. 5⅜ x 8½. (Available in U.S. only)   20010-8 Pa. $1.75

A PREFACE TO LOGIC, Morris R. Cohen. Great City College teacher in renowned, easily followed exposition of formal logic, probability, values, logic and world order and similar topics; no previous background needed. 209pp. 5⅜ x 8½.   23517-3 Pa. $3.50

REASON AND NATURE, Morris R. Cohen. Brilliant analysis of reason and its multitudinous ramifications by charismatic teacher. Interdisciplinary, synthesizing work widely praised when it first appeared in 1931. Second (1953) edition. Indexes. 496pp. 5⅜ x 8½.   23633-1 Pa. $6.00

AN ESSAY CONCERNING HUMAN UNDERSTANDING, John Locke. The only complete edition of enormously important classic, with authoritative editorial material by A. C. Fraser. Total of 1176pp. 5⅜ x 8½.
20530-4, 20531-2 Pa., Two-vol. set $14.00

HANDBOOK OF MATHEMATICAL FUNCTIONS WITH FORMULAS, GRAPHS, AND MATHEMATICAL TABLES, edited by Milton Abramowitz and Irene A. Stegun. Vast compendium: 29 sets of tables, some to as high as 20 places. 1,046pp. 8 x 10½.   61272-4 Pa. $12.50

MATHEMATICS FOR THE PHYSICAL SCIENCES, Herbert S. Wilf. Highly acclaimed work offers clear presentations of vector spaces and matrices, orthogonal functions, roots of polynomial equations, conformal mapping, calculus of variations, etc. Knowledge of theory of functions of real and complex variables is assumed. Exercises and solutions. Index. 284pp. 5⅝ x 8¼.   63635-6 Pa. $4.50

THE PRINCIPLE OF RELATIVITY, Albert Einstein et al. Eleven most important original papers on special and general theories. Seven by Einstein, two by Lorentz, one each by Minkowski and Weyl. All translated, unabridged. 216pp. 5⅜ x 8½.   60081-5 Pa. $3.00

THERMODYNAMICS, Enrico Fermi. A classic of modern science. Clear, organized treatment of systems, first and second laws, entropy, thermodynamic potentials, gaseous reactions, dilute solutions, entropy constant. No math beyond calculus required. Problems. 160pp. 5⅜ x 8½.
60361-X Pa. $2.75

ELEMENTARY MECHANICS OF FLUIDS, Hunter Rouse. Classic undergraduate text widely considered to be far better than many later books. Ranges from fluid velocity and acceleration to role of compressibility in fluid motion. Numerous examples, questions, problems. 224 illustrations. 376pp. 5⅝ x 8¼.   63699-2 Pa. $5.00

THE COMPLETE BOOK OF DOLL MAKING AND COLLECTING, Catherine Christopher. Instructions, patterns for dozens of dolls, from rag doll on up to elaborate, historically accurate figures. Mould faces, sew clothing, make doll houses, etc. Also collecting information. Many illustrations. 288pp. 6 x 9. 22066-4 Pa. $4.00

THE DAGUERREOTYPE IN AMERICA, Beaumont Newhall. Wonderful portraits, 1850's townscapes, landscapes; full text plus 104 photographs. The basic book. Enlarged 1976 edition. 272pp. 8¼ x 11¼. 23322-7 Pa. $6.00

CRAFTSMAN HOMES, Gustav Stickley. 296 architectural drawings, floor plans, and photographs illustrate 40 different kinds of "Mission-style" homes from The Craftsman (1901-16), voice of American style of simplicity and organic harmony. Thorough coverage of Craftsman idea in text and picture, now collector's item. 224pp. 8⅛ x 11. 23791-5 Pa. $6.00

PEWTER-WORKING: INSTRUCTIONS AND PROJECTS, Burl N. Osborn. & Gordon O. Wilber. Introduction to pewter-working for amateur craftsman. History and characteristics of pewter; tools, materials, step-by-step instructions. Photos, line drawings, diagrams. Total of 160pp. 7⅞ x 10¾. 23786-9 Pa. $3.50

THE GREAT CHICAGO FIRE, edited by David Lowe. 10 dramatic, eyewitness accounts of the 1871 disaster, including one of the aftermath and rebuilding, plus 70 contemporary photographs and illustrations of the ruins—courthouse, Palmer House, Great Central Depot, etc. Introduction by David Lowe. 87pp. 8¼ x 11. 23771-0 Pa. $4.00

SILHOUETTES: A PICTORIAL ARCHIVE OF VARIED ILLUSTRATIONS, edited by Carol Belanger Grafton. Over 600 silhouettes from the 18th to 20th centuries include profiles and full figures of men and women, children, birds and animals, groups and scenes, nature, ships, an alphabet. Dozens of uses for commercial artists and craftspeople. 144pp. 8⅜ x 11¼. 23781-8 Pa. $4.00

ANIMALS: 1,419 COPYRIGHT-FREE ILLUSTRATIONS OF MAMMALS, BIRDS, FISH, INSECTS, ETC., edited by Jim Harter. Clear wood engravings present, in extremely lifelike poses, over 1,000 species of animals. One of the most extensive copyright-free pictorial sourcebooks of its kind. Captions. Index. 284pp. 9 x 12. 23766-4 Pa. $7.50

INDIAN DESIGNS FROM ANCIENT ECUADOR, Frederick W. Shaffer. 282 original designs by pre-Columbian Indians of Ecuador (500-1500 A.D.). Designs include people, mammals, birds, reptiles, fish, plants, heads, geometric designs. Use as is or alter for advertising, textiles, leathercraft, etc. Introduction. 95pp. 8¾ x 11¼. 23764-8 Pa. $3.50

SZIGETI ON THE VIOLIN, Joseph Szigeti. Genial, loosely structured tour by premier violinist, featuring a pleasant mixture of reminiscenes, insights into great music and musicians, innumerable tips for practicing violinists. 385 musical passages. 256pp. 5⅝ x 8¼. 23763-X Pa. $3.50

TONE POEMS, SERIES II: TILL EULENSPIEGELS LUSTIGE STREICHE, ALSO SPRACH ZARATHUSTRA, AND EIN HELDEN-LEBEN, Richard Strauss. Three important orchestral works, including very popular *Till Eulenspiegel's Marry Pranks*, reproduced in full score from original editions. Study score. 315pp. 9⅜ x 12¼. (Available in U.S. only)
23755-9 Pa. $7.50

TONE POEMS, SERIES I: DON JUAN, TOD UND VERKLARUNG AND DON QUIXOTE, Richard Strauss. Three of the most often performed and recorded works in entire orchestral repertoire, reproduced in full score from original editions. Study score. 286pp. 9⅜ x 12¼. (Available in U.S. only)
23754-0 Pa. $7.50

11 LATE STRING QUARTETS, Franz Joseph Haydn. The form which Haydn defined and "brought to perfection." (*Grove's*). 11 string quartets in complete score, his last and his best. The first in a projected series of the complete Haydn string quartets. Reliable modern Eulenberg edition, otherwise difficult to obtain. 320pp. 8⅜ x 11¼. (Available in U.S. only)
23753-2 Pa. $6.95

FOURTH, FIFTH AND SIXTH SYMPHONIES IN FULL SCORE, Peter Ilyitch Tchaikovsky. Complete orchestral scores of Symphony No. 4 in F Minor, Op. 36; Symphony No. 5 in E Minor, Op. 64; Symphony No. 6 in B Minor, "Pathetique," Op. 74. Bretikopf & Hartel eds. Study score. 480pp. 9⅜ x 12¼.
23861-X Pa. $10.95

THE MARRIAGE OF FIGARO: COMPLETE SCORE, Wolfgang A. Mozart. Finest comic opera ever written. Full score, not to be confused with piano renderings. Peters edition. Study score. 448pp. 9⅜ x 12¼. (Available in U.S. only)
23751-6 Pa. $11.95

"IMAGE" ON THE ART AND EVOLUTION OF THE FILM, edited by Marshall Deutelbaum. Pioneering book brings together for first time 38 groundbreaking articles on early silent films from *Image* and 263 illustrations newly shot from rare prints in the collection of the International Museum of Photography. A landmark work. Index. 256pp. 8¼ x 11.
23777-X Pa. $8.95

AROUND-THE-WORLD COOKY BOOK, Lois Lintner Sumption and Marguerite Lintner Ashbrook. 373 cooky and frosting recipes from 28 countries (America, Austria, China, Russia, Italy, etc.) include Viennese kisses, rice wafers, London strips, lady fingers, hony, sugar spice, maple cookies, etc. Clear instructions. All tested. 38 drawings. 182pp. 5⅜ x 8.
23802-4 Pa. $2.50

THE ART NOUVEAU STYLE, edited by Roberta Waddell. 579 rare photographs, not available elsewhere, of works in jewelry, metalwork, glass, ceramics, textiles, architecture and furniture by 175 artists—Mucha, Seguy, Lalique, Tiffany, Gaudin, Hohlwein, Saarinen, and many others. 288pp. 8⅜ x 11¼.
23515-7 Pa. $6.95

THE AMERICAN SENATOR, Anthony Trollope. Little known, long unavailable Trollope novel on a grand scale. Here are humorous comment on American vs. English culture, and stunning portrayal of a heroine/villainess. Superb evocation of Victorian village life. 561pp. 5⅜ x 8½.
23801-6 Pa. $6.00

WAS IT MURDER? James Hilton. The author of *Lost Horizon* and *Goodbye, Mr. Chips* wrote one detective novel (under a pen-name) which was quickly forgotten and virtually lost, even at the height of Hilton's fame. This edition brings it back—a finely crafted public school puzzle resplendent with Hilton's stylish atmosphere. A thoroughly English thriller by the creator of Shangri-la. 252pp. 5⅜ x 8. (Available in U.S. only)
23774-5 Pa. $3.00

CENTRAL PARK: A PHOTOGRAPHIC GUIDE, Victor Laredo and Henry Hope Reed. 121 superb photographs show dramatic views of Central Park: Bethesda Fountain, Cleopatra's Needle, Sheep Meadow, the Blockhouse, plus people engaged in many park activities: ice skating, bike riding, etc. Captions by former Curator of Central Park, Henry Hope Reed, provide historical view, changes, etc. Also photos of N.Y. landmarks on park's periphery. 96pp. 8½ x 11.
23750-8 Pa. $4.50

NANTUCKET IN THE NINETEENTH CENTURY, Clay Lancaster. 180 rare photographs, stereographs, maps, drawings and floor plans recreate unique American island society. Authentic scenes of shipwreck, lighthouses, streets, homes are arranged in geographic sequence to provide walking-tour guide to old Nantucket existing today. Introduction, captions. 160pp. 8⅞ x 11¾.
23747-8 Pa. $6.95

STONE AND MAN: A PHOTOGRAPHIC EXPLORATION, Andreas Feininger. 106 photographs by *Life* photographer Feininger portray man's deep passion for stone through the ages. Stonehenge-like megaliths, fortified towns, sculpted marble and crumbling tenements show textures, beauties, fascination. 128pp. 9¼ x 10¾.
23756-7 Pa. $5.95

CIRCLES, A MATHEMATICAL VIEW, D. Pedoe. Fundamental aspects of college geometry, non-Euclidean geometry, and other branches of mathematics: representing circle by point. Poincare model, isoperimetric property, etc. Stimulating recreational reading. 66 figures. 96pp. 5⅝ x 8¼.
63698-4 Pa. $2.75

THE DISCOVERY OF NEPTUNE, Morton Grosser. Dramatic scientific history of the investigations leading up to the actual discovery of the eighth planet of our solar system. Lucid, well-researched book by well-known historian of science. 172pp. 5⅜ x 8½.
23726-5 Pa. $3.00

THE DEVIL'S DICTIONARY. Ambrose Bierce. Barbed, bitter, brilliant witticisms in the form of a dictionary. Best, most ferocious satire America has produced. 145pp. 5⅜ x 8½.
20487-1 Pa. $1.75

MUSHROOMS, EDIBLE AND OTHERWISE, Miron E. Hard. Profusely illustrated, very useful guide to over 500 species of mushrooms growing in the Midwest and East. Nomenclature updated to 1976. 505 illustrations. 628pp. 6½ x 9¼.   23309-X Pa. $7.95

AN ILLUSTRATED FLORA OF THE NORTHERN UNITED STATES AND CANADA, Nathaniel L. Britton, Addison Brown. Encyclopedic work covers 4666 species, ferns on up. Everything. Full botanical information, illustration for each. This earlier edition is preferred by many to more recent revisions. 1913 edition. Over 4000 illustrations, total of 2087pp. 6⅛ x 9¼.   22642-5, 22643-3, 22644-1 Pa., Three-vol. set $24.00

MANUAL OF THE GRASSES OF THE UNITED STATES, A. S. Hitchcock, U.S. Dept. of Agriculture. The basic study of American grasses, both indigenous and escapes, cultivated and wild. Over 1400 species. Full descriptions, information. Over 1100 maps, illustrations. Total of 1051pp. 5⅜ x 8½.   22717-0, 22718-9 Pa., Two-vol. set $12.00

THE CACTACEAE,, Nathaniel L. Britton, John N. Rose. Exhaustive, definitive. Every cactus in the world. Full botanical descriptions. Thorough statement of nomenclatures, habitat, detailed finding keys. The one book needed by every cactus enthusiast. Over 1275 illustrations. Total of 1080pp. 8 x 10¼.   21191-6, 21192-4 Clothbd., Two-vol. set $35.00

AMERICAN MEDICINAL PLANTS, Charles F. Millspaugh. Full descriptions, 180 plants covered: history; physical description; methods of preparation with all chemical constituents extracted; all claimed curative or adverse effects. 180 full-page plates. Classification table. 804pp. 6½ x 9¼.
                    23034-1 Pa. $10.00

A MODERN HERBAL, Margaret Grieve. Much the fullest, most exact, most useful compilation of herbal material. Gigantic alphabetical encyclopedia, from aconite to zedoary, gives botanical information, medical properties, folklore, economic uses, and much else. Indispensable to serious reader. 161 illustrations. 888pp. 6½ x 9¼. (Available in U.S. only)
                    22798-7, 22799-5 Pa., Two-vol. set $11.00

THE HERBAL or GENERAL HISTORY OF PLANTS, John Gerard. The 1633 edition revised and enlarged by Thomas Johnson. Containing almost 2850 plant descriptions and 2705 superb illustrations, Gerard's *Herbal* is a monumental work, the book all modern English herbals are derived from, the one herbal every serious enthusiast should have in its entirety. Original editions are worth perhaps $750. 1678pp. 8½ x 12¼.
                    23147-X Clothbd. $50.00

MANUAL OF THE TREES OF NORTH AMERICA, Charles S. Sargent. The basic survey of every native tree and tree-like shrub, 717 species in all. Extremely full descriptions, information on habitat, growth, locales, economics, etc. Necessary to every serious tree lover. Over 100 finding keys. 783 illustrations. Total of 986pp. 5⅜ x 8½.
                    20277-1, 20278-X Pa., Two-vol. set $10.00

"OSCAR" OF THE WALDORF'S COOKBOOK, Oscar Tschirky. Famous American chef reveals 3455 recipes that made Waldorf great; cream of French, German, American cooking, in all categories. Full instructions, easy home use. 1896 edition. 907pp. 6⅝ x 9⅜.   20790-0 Clothbd. $15.00

COOKING WITH BEER, Carole Fahy. Beer has as superb an effect on food as wine, and at fraction of cost. Over 250 recipes for appetizers, soups, main dishes, desserts, breads, etc. Index. 144pp. 5⅜ x 8½. (Available in U.S. only)   23661-7 Pa. $2.50

STEWS AND RAGOUTS, Kay Shaw Nelson. This international cookbook offers wide range of 108 recipes perfect for everyday, special occasions, meals-in-themselves, main dishes. Economical, nutritious, easy-to-prepare: goulash, Irish stew, boeuf bourguignon, etc. Index. 134pp. 5⅜ x 8½.
23662-5 Pa. $2.50

DELICIOUS MAIN COURSE DISHES, Marian Tracy. Main courses are the most important part of any meal. These 200 nutritious, economical recipes from around the world make every meal a delight. "I . . . have found it so useful in my own household,"—N.Y. Times. Index. 219pp. 5⅜ x 8½.   23664-1 Pa. $3.00

FIVE ACRES AND INDEPENDENCE, Maurice G. Kains. Great back-to-the-land classic explains basics of self-sufficient farming: economics, plants, crops, animals, orchards, soils, land selection, host of other necessary things. Do not confuse with skimpy faddist literature; Kains was one of America's greatest agriculturalists. 95 illustrations. 397pp. 5⅜ x 8½.
20974-1 Pa. $3.50

A PRACTICAL GUIDE FOR THE BEGINNING FARMER, Herbert Jacobs. Basic, extremely useful first book for anyone thinking about moving to the country and starting a farm. Simpler than Kains, with greater emphasis on country living in general. 246pp. 5⅜ x 8½.
23675-7 Pa. $3.50

HARDY BULBS, Louise Beebe Wilder. Fullest, most thorough book on plants grown from bulbs, corms, rhizomes and tubers. 40 genera and 335 species covered: selecting, cultivating, naturalizing; name, origins, blooming season, when to plant, special requirements. 127 illustrations. 432pp. 5⅜ x 8½.   23102-X Pa. $4.50

A GARDEN OF PLEASANT FLOWERS (PARADISI IN SOLE: PARADISUS TERRESTRIS), John Parkinson. Complete, unabridged reprint of first (1629) edition of earliest great English book on gardens and gardening. More than 1000 plants & flowers of Elizabethan, Jacobean garden fully described, most with woodcut illustrations. Botanically very reliable, a "speaking garden" of exceeding charm. 812 illustrations. 628pp. 8½ x 12¼.   23392-8 Clothbd. $25.00

SECOND PIATIGORSKY CUP, edited by Isaac Kashdan. One of the greatest tournament books ever produced in the English language. All 90 games of the 1966 tournament, annotated by players, most annotated by both players. Features Petrosian, Spassky, Fischer, Larsen, six others. 228pp. 5⅜ x 8½.   23572-6 Pa. $3.50

ENCYCLOPEDIA OF CARD TRICKS, revised and edited by Jean Hugard. How to perform over 600 card tricks, devised by the world's greatest magicians: impromptus, spelling tricks, key cards, using special packs, much, much more. Additional chapter on card technique. 66 illustrations. 402pp. 5⅜ x 8½. (Available in U.S. only)   21252-1 Pa. $3.95

MAGIC: STAGE ILLUSIONS, SPECIAL EFFECTS AND TRICK PHOTOGRAPHY, Albert A. Hopkins, Henry R. Evans. One of the great classics; fullest, most authoritative explanation of vanishing lady, levitations, scores of other great stage effects. Also small magic, automata, stunts. 446 illustrations. 556pp. 5⅜ x 8½.   23344-8 Pa. $5.00

THE SECRETS OF HOUDINI, J. C. Cannell. Classic study of Houdini's incredible magic, exposing closely-kept professional secrets and revealing, in general terms, the whole art of stage magic. 67 illustrations. 279pp. 5⅜ x 8½.   22913-0 Pa. $3.00

HOFFMANN'S MODERN MAGIC, Professor Hoffmann. One of the best, and best-known, magicians' manuals of the past century. Hundreds of tricks from card tricks and simple sleight of hand to elaborate illusions involving construction of complicated machinery. 332 illustrations. 563pp. 5⅜ x 8½.   23623-4 Pa. $6.00

MADAME PRUNIER'S FISH COOKERY BOOK, Mme. S. B. Prunier. More than 1000 recipes from world famous Prunier's of Paris and London, specially adapted here for American kitchen. Grilled tournedos with anchovy butter, Lobster a la Bordelaise, Prunier's prized desserts, more. Glossary. 340pp. 5⅜ x 8½. (Available in U.S. only)   22679-4 Pa. $3.00

FRENCH COUNTRY COOKING FOR AMERICANS, Louis Diat. 500 easy-to-make, authentic provincial recipes compiled by former head chef at New York's Fitz-Carlton Hotel: onion soup, lamb stew, potato pie, more. 309pp. 5⅜ x 8½.   23665-X Pa. $3.95

SAUCES, FRENCH AND FAMOUS, Louis Diat. Complete book gives over 200 specific recipes: bechamel, Bordelaise, hollandaise, Cumberland, apricot, etc. Author was one of this century's finest chefs, originator of vichyssoise and many other dishes. Index. 156pp. 5⅜ x 8.
23663-3 Pa. $2.50

TOLL HOUSE TRIED AND TRUE RECIPES, Ruth Graves Wakefield. Authentic recipes from the famous Mass. restaurant: popovers, veal and ham loaf, Toll House baked beans, chocolate cake crumb pudding, much more. Many helpful hints. Nearly 700 recipes. Index. 376pp. 5⅜ x 8½.
23560-2 Pa. $4.0

HISTORY OF BACTERIOLOGY, William Bulloch. The only comprehensive history of bacteriology from the beginnings through the 19th century. Special emphasis is given to biography-Leeuwenhoek, etc. Brief accounts of 350 bacteriologists form a separate section. No clearer, fuller study, suitable to scientists and general readers, has yet been written. 52 illustrations. 448pp. 5⅝ x 8¼.   23761-3 Pa. $6.50

THE COMPLETE NONSENSE OF EDWARD LEAR, Edward Lear. All nonsense limericks, zany alphabets, Owl and Pussycat, songs, nonsense botany, etc., illustrated by Lear. Total of 321pp. 5⅜ x 8½. (Available in U.S. only)
                                                            20167-8 Pa. $3.00

INGENIOUS MATHEMATICAL PROBLEMS AND METHODS, Louis A. Graham. Sophisticated material from Graham Dial, applied and pure; stresses solution methods. Logic, number theory, networks, inversions, etc. 237pp. 5⅜ x 8½.   20545-2 Pa. $3.50

BEST MATHEMATICAL PUZZLES OF SAM LOYD, edited by Martin Gardner. Bizarre, original, whimsical puzzles by America's greatest puzzler. From fabulously rare Cyclopedia, including famous 14-15 puzzles, the Horse of a Different Color, 115 more. Elementary math. 150 illustrations. 167pp. 5⅜ x 8½.   20498-7 Pa. $2.50

THE BASIS OF COMBINATION IN CHESS, J. du Mont. Easy-to-follow, instructive book on elements of combination play, with chapters on each piece and every powerful combination team—two knights, bishop and knight, rook and bishop, etc. 250 diagrams. 218pp. 5⅜ x 8½. (Available in U.S. only)
                                                            23644-7 Pa. $3.50

MODERN CHESS STRATEGY, Ludek Pachman. The use of the queen, the active king, exchanges, pawn play, the center, weak squares, etc. Section on rook alone worth price of the book. Stress on the moderns. Often considered the most important book on strategy. 314pp. 5⅜ x 8½.
                                                            20290-9 Pa. $3.50

LASKER'S MANUAL OF CHESS, Dr. Emanuel Lasker. Great world champion offers very thorough coverage of all aspects of chess. Combinations, position play, openings, end game, aesthetics of chess, philosophy of struggle, much more. Filled with analyzed games. 390pp. 5⅜ x 8½.
                                                            20640-8 Pa. $4.00

'00 MASTER GAMES OF CHESS, S. Tartakower, J. du Mont. Vast 'ection of great chess games from 1798-1938, with much material no- else readily available. Fully annotated, arranged by opening for 'tudy. 664pp. 5⅜ x 8½.   23208-5 Pa. $6.00

' TO CHESS ENDINGS, Dr. Max Euwe, David Hooper. One ' modern works on chess endings. Thorough analysis of the 'ly encountered endings by former world champion. 331 'vith diagram. 248pp. 5⅜ x 8½.   23332-4 Pa. $3.50

GEOMETRY, RELATIVITY AND THE FOURTH DIMENSION, Rudolf Rucker. Exposition of fourth dimension, means of visualization, concepts of relativity as Flatland characters continue adventures. Popular, easily followed yet accurate, profound. 141 illustrations. 133pp. 5⅜ x 8½.
23400-2 Pa. $2.75

THE ORIGIN OF LIFE, A. I. Oparin. Modern classic in biochemistry, the first rigorous examination of possible evolution of life from nitrocarbon compounds. Non-technical, easily followed. Total of 295pp. 5⅜ x 8½.
60213-3 Pa. $4.00

THE CURVES OF LIFE, Theodore A. Cook. Examination of shells, leaves, horns, human body, art, etc., in *"the* classic reference on how the golden ratio applies to spirals and helices in nature . . . ."—Martin Gardner. 426 illustrations. Total of 512pp. 5⅜ x 8½.   23701-X Pa. $5.95

PLANETS, STARS AND GALAXIES, A. E. Fanning. Comprehensive introductory survey: the sun, solar system, stars, galaxies, universe, cosmology; quasars, radio stars, etc. 24pp. of photographs. 189pp. 5⅜ x 8½. (Available in U.S. only)   21680-2 Pa. $3.00

THE THIRTEEN BOOKS OF EUCLID'S ELEMENTS, translated with introduction and commentary by Sir Thomas L. Heath. Definitive edition. Textual and linguistic notes, mathematical analysis, 2500 years of critical commentary. Do not confuse with abridged school editions. Total of 1414pp. 5⅜ x 8½.   60088-2, 60089-0, 60090-4 Pa., Three-vol. set $18.00

DIALOGUES CONCERNING TWO NEW SCIENCES, Galileo Galilei. Encompassing 30 years of experiment and thought, these dialogues deal with geometric demonstrations of fracture of solid bodies, cohesion, leverage, speed of light and sound, pendulums, falling bodies, accelerated motion, etc. 300pp. 5⅜ x 8½.   60099-8 Pa. $4.00

Prices subject to change without notice.

Available at your book dealer or write for free catalogue to Dept. GI, Dover Publications, Inc., 180 Varick St., N.Y., N.Y. 10014. Dover publishes mor than 175 books each year on science, elementary and advanced mathematic biology, music, art, literary history, social sciences and other areas.